BRIEF AND EXTENDED CASEWORK

BRIEF AND EXTENDED CASEWORK

*William J. Reid and
Ann W. Shyne*

WITH A FOREWORD BY
Helen Harris Perlman

Columbia University Press

NEW YORK LONDON

WILLIAM J. REID *is Associate Professor in the School of Social Service Administration at the University of Chicago.*

ANN W. SHYNE *is Director of Research in the Child Welfare League of America.*

This is a project of the Community Service Society of New York funded in part by Grant 185 from the Welfare Administration of the U. S. Department of Health, Education and Welfare.

The authors wish to give special acknowledgment to Sophie Silverstein and Theodore Hackman for their contribution to the conduct of the project.

FOREWORD

IT IS ALWAYS a special delight to discover that what plain common sense has long suggested proves out, indeed, to be true. When a careful piece of research gives the stamp of affirmation to ideas and beliefs and clinically observed facts which were subject to repeated doubt and question there results (at least for this practitioner and ponderer) a suffusing sense of pleasure. This book proffers such pleasure.

William Reid and Ann Shyne, both of whom know casework from inside as well as out, set out to compare the outcomes and relative effectiveness of two major modes of casework for interpersonal problems: one, planned short-term treatment; the other, continued service, open-ended as to time. Their research sample consisted of middle-income families, voluntarily seeking agency help with clearly perceived problems in marital or parent-child transactions—in brief, the "ideal" clients of caseworkers. And their major finding was that short-term treatment yielded more progress than long-continued service; furthermore, this progress was judged to be equally durable.

This has been claimed before, by occasional practitioners, by a few theoreticians, by several researchers in psychotherapy. Yet, interestingly, there has remained among most caseworkers and their agencies some unyielding belief that only long-term treatment is legitimate or lasting or prestigious. The reasons for this fixed idea deserve thoughtful professional self-search and analysis. They are a complex of wistful wish and cognitive confusion.

v

Among the factors that have reinforced the caseworker's espousal of long-term treatment are the failure to differentiate between the psychoanalytic model for treatment and that of casework; between what the caseworker, who himself may have been a user of psychotherapy, wanted and used from that experience and what the applicant to a social agency is seeking. Added to this has been the caseworker's aspiration (rarely his client's) to goals that are illusory: achieving "cure," for instance, rather than the more realistic goal of achieving some restored or new equilibrium; that of bringing the client to some problem-free state rather than exercising and enhancing his problem-solving powers upon his designated problems; that of personality change rather than of attitude and behavioral change in relation to a defined problem area. And there have long been misreadings of psychodynamic theory in its implications for casework practice—the assumption for instance, that "depth" help depended on historical explorations and leafing through the layers of personality development, and the accompanying blindness to those crucial experiences of the immediate present which may strike into the depths of a person's being and force his change for better or for worse.

Now comes this study, done within an agency that for many years has given leadership in casework, designed by researchers with casework sophistication, participated in by caseworker judges, to test the long-held hypothesis that open-ended treatment is likely to yield greater client satisfaction and better outcome than short-term treatment. The hypothesis has been disproved. The reasons are worth thinking about.

Of course time-span itself—"long" or "short," "brief" or "extended"—is not the phenomenon that turns the screw. The discussion of the findings makes this plain, but it deserves being said again in the face of today's fad for all manner of short-order, sweep-the-dust-under-the-rug forms of quick help that are gaining momentum and favor under the short-term crisis-action banner. The dynamic for change lies (as the Rankians proposed long ago) not simply in that life-measure we call "time" but in its psychological effects upon both client and caseworker and the uses to which it is put.

Time limits force mobilization of both client and caseworker. Both must do what must be done within a stipulated span of days or weeks. (And, of course, if it turns out that the task takes longer, there is nothing to prevent a second measure-out of time.) Time limits force partialization both of the problem to be worked and of the goal to be reached. So there is likely to be some small change accomplished and this accomplishment may feel rewarding and therefore further motivating to the client. Time limits force focus and selective attention on the part of both caseworker and client. That focus is likely to be upon today's difficulties and upon those behavioral readjustments that are sustained by a vital relationship and propelled by conscious motivations and uses of self. So anxiety is bounded, and "how I got this way," sometimes a painful or sometimes a siren song, lulling client and caseworker into inaction, must give way to "what I can do *now*."

The point is that short-term treatment is not just a small sample of what the client might be lucky to get more of. It is a different experience, as this study shows. It requires that the caseworker understand not only the dynamics inherent in limits but also, turned about, the limits within the dynamic forces and focus he undertakes to deal with when he chooses the short-term mode.

A second focus of the Reid-Shyne research is upon differentiated methods, an examination of the comparative values in "supportive" versus "modifying" patterns of treatment. The finding that in practice these are inextricably interlocked techniques will surprise no practitioner and perhaps only a few theoreticians. True, the caseworker's *intent* may be to "support" at one time and in one place and to "modify" in another. But the *consequence* may be that one client's support is another client's modification. (And so, when we try to classify treatment modes do we classify by the caseworker's intention or by the client's response?) Such findings open to plain view some of the beloved ambiguities that have long veiled casework practice. These and other findings offer to caseworkers, supervisors, agency administrators, and teachers a host of interesting and change-provoking facts and ideas.

Not the least of this study's merit is that it is readable. Even the caseworker who runs may catch its gist. For him who reads with care this research offers a kind of vicarious pleasure in exploring long-familiar territory in the company of two knowledgeable people who know their facts, who point to fresh perspectives, who confirm or shake-up but surely light up and aerate one's long-held perceptions and beliefs. Now this familiar territory begins to look somewhat different and to suggest to caseworkers and their agencies and to those who organize and transmit the profession's knowledge that some new maps may need to be drawn, some new paths taken.

Helen Harris Perlman

August 1968

PREFACE

THIS BOOK IS the report of a rather unusual experiment in social work, which we believe will be of interest and practical use to practitioners and administrators, to faculty and students in schools of social work, and to researchers. We have therefore tried to write with this diversified audience in mind. Some non-researchers may find the going a little heavy at points, but we trust that they will not find it too rough. Some researchers, on the other hand, may feel that we have slighted their interests in detail of design and procedure, but we hope that they will find reasonably adequate documentation. If we have not communicated our message effectively, we have done a disservice to the field and to the many persons who have made this experiment possible.

The research was carried out at the Community Service Society of New York, a voluntary nonsectarian agency whose activities are directed toward betterment of family and community life. Its program comprises direct service to families and individuals, community action, and research. Through its Institute of Welfare Research, it has pioneered in the application of research methods in social work, introducing over the years many approaches that have subsequently come into common usage. In this instance the agency administration and the casework leaders gave their blessing to an experimental design that called for random assignment of cases to different patterns of service, without regard to individual case diagnosis. Obviously, without such administrative support, the whole endeavor would have been impossible.

This investigation was supported in part by a grant from the Welfare Administration (now the Social and Rehabilitation Service) of the United States Department of Health, Education, and Welfare, Washington, D.C. We are deeply grateful to the Society and to HEW for giving us the opportunity to carry out this project.

The project was carried out within the Department of Family Services, in cooperation with the Institute of Welfare Research. It would be impractical to try to name all of the individuals who contributed directly to the experiment. We do wish, however, to express our appreciation to the major staff participants. Else Siegle and Gertrude Leyendecker of the Department of Family Services were key members of a staff committee that helped plan the project. Sophie Silverstein has described herself as a "conveyor belt." Associated with the project throughout most of its four years, she was responsible for planning work assignments and for all phases of data control.

Theodore Hackman carried very ably the crucial and difficult responsibility of supervising the caseworkers assigned to the project to help them carry out the patterns of service prescribed. The caseworkers who had the demanding role of offering eight different patterns of service to the families in the experiment were Donald Brown, Roberta Copenhaver, Helen Kinslow, Maria Modica, Helen North, and Lucille Wolfe.* They were extremely cooperative and participated in the experiment with a high degree of commitment to its objectives.

To a large extent, our findings rest on the judgments of the research interviewers: Thelma Caplan, Terry Smolar, Mary Wat-

---

* Ada Mere and Mary Weidenborner also participated in the early months of the project.

kins, and Max Weisser. It took patience and persistence as well as a high degree of skill to engage the clients in the interviews needed for assessment of service.

Several agency field instructors gave time to listening to interminable tape recordings and analyzing the content of the casework service. The staff of the Data Analysis Unit as well as research aides on the project staff contributed to analysis of the mountains of data accumulated.

We were fortunate to have expert statistical consultation from Dr. Leonard S. Kogan, formerly director of the Institute of Welfare Research and presently director of the Center for Social Research of the City University of New York.

Of the secretarial staff we should like to give a special word of thanks to Helen Larmore and Edith Oxley, who coped with the manuscript at all phases of legibility.

Finally, we should like to clarify our own roles. The second author designed the experiment and directed it during its first year of operation. At the end of that time, the first author joined the staff as co-director of the project and subsequently carried major responsibility for directing it and bringing it to completion.

William J. Reid
Ann W. Shyne

June 1968

CONTENTS

BRIEF AND EXTENDED CASEWORK

ONE · TWO FORMS OF TREATMENT

IN NINETEEN HUNDRED and sixty-four the Community Service Society of New York undertook a four-year field experiment to test the relative effectiveness of contrasting patterns of casework treatment of problems in family relations. The findings of major interest stemmed from one phase of this experiment: a test comparing a brief service of fixed duration and an open-ended service that could be, and frequently was, of extended duration. Through random procedures, sixty families were assigned to each service. There were no appreciable differences between the two groups of families before service began. But by the end of service one group of families had made significantly more progress than the other toward the solution of the problems for which help was sought.

The finding that one of these contrasting patterns of treatment yielded distinctly better outcomes is of particular interest at the present time. Casework practitioners are currently engaged in an unprecedented search for faster and more economical treatment methods. While caseworkers continue to be in short supply, the clienteles of casework continue to grow. The search for briefer methods has resulted in considerable controversy, much of it over the question of how much treatment is desirable or necessary. One position holds that long-term treatment is usually necessary to effect changes in the complex and deeply entrenched psychological and social problems dealt with in casework practice. According to the proponents of this position, brief service has its place, as a means of affording symptom relief or dealing with minor problems, but should be seen as a type of first aid rather than a major treatment modality. Shortages of practitioners should not impel us to attempt "patch-work" treatment with excessive numbers of clients or patients. Critics of this position contend, on the other hand, that the values of long-term treatment have never been demonstrated and have, in fact, been oversold. Short-term casework, particularly if given at the opportune time, such as during a period of crisis, can often accomplish as much, if not more, than treatment of longer duration. Given our limited resources, it is the only practical means of providing necessary help to growing numbers of needful people. The findings of the present experiment should prove highly relevant to this controversy.

In order to set the stage for the presentation of the study and its results, let us consider the issue of brief versus extended treatment in broader context and in greater depth. Casework practiced in the project was a form of *interpersonal treatment of psychosocial problems of individuals and families,* that is, treatment in which the active ingredients are found within the communications that occur between its practitioners and recipients. When it takes this form casework resembles, in objectives and techniques, psychotherapy and counseling of families and individuals carried on in a wide variety of settings by practitioners from diverse disciplines. Just as the findings of the experiment are relevant to the field of interpersonal treatment, developments in this broader field form the context of the experiment. Within this context it may be fruitful to consider more closely the forms brief and extended treatment may take, the comparison at issue in the present experiment, and some of the questions that need to be answered in finding appropriate roles for services of different durations.

FORMS OF BRIEF AND
EXTENDED TREATMENT

Notions of what may be "brief" treatment and what may be "extended" are of course entirely relative to one another. Since the most prestigious models of interpersonal treatment in recent decades have been provided by psychoanalysis and psycho-analytically oriented psychotherapy and since these forms of treatment are generally thought of as lasting from one to several years, brief treatment has come to mean treatment whose dura-tion is measured in months rather than years.

Three rather distinct kinds of treatment have been called "short-term." First, the label has been applied to cases terminat-ing early in a projected course of long-term treatment; they may be thought of as receiving unplanned short-term or abortive long-term treatment. In such cases the client or patient usually leaves against the advice of the practitioner, who is apt to regard the client's termination as "premature," even though the client may have received some benefit or may feel that there is nothing more to be gained from continuing. Second, treatment may be short because of the limited nature of the problem or treatment objectives, with the type of setting frequently playing a role. For example, casework with transients in Traveler's Aid Societies is necessarily short-term, as is much casework in hospitals, par-ticularly when treatment objectives are limited to such areas as discharge planning and the like. A third category is the type tested in the experiment, treatment that is short *by design*. The course of treatment is normally defined in advance as compris-ing so many interviews in so many months.

Unlike the first type, unplanned brief treatment, planned short-term service is conducted under the assumption that the contact will be limited. Unlike treatment that is short because of the nature of the problem or treatment objective, planned brief treat-ment by its design forces limitations on the problems to be dealt with and on the scope of the objectives. If the problem dealt with is in itself highly circumscribed and if treatment would normally be short, there is no particular need for planned limits, even though there may be such. The prearranged limits restrict treatment that could otherwise be extended indefinitely. For this reason it is applicable in treatment of individuals or families who are potential candidates for extended treatment. Thus, planned brief treatment bears a certain resemblance to formal learning experiences which normally have fixed durations, even though (or perhaps because) the amount that could be learned in almost any area is virtually limitless.

Extended treatment also assumes a variety of forms. It may be of long duration but of low intensity (occasional interviews over a period of years); it may be (though seldom is) set up to last a specified but relatively long time (a year or two); it may be a part of a program of long-term care, such as institutionalization, public assistance, foster home placement, and the like. The dominant form is what might be called "open-ended" treatment, the type contrasted with planned short-term service in our comparative test. Theoretically open-ended treatment continues until there is no further need for it, though its practitioners and recipients may not necessarily agree when that point has been reached. While it may turn out to be short, often because of the recipient's unwillingness to continue, its practitioners expect it to be of long duration and in fact usually regard a certain amount of contact (four interviews is a conventional number[1]) as necessary before the recipient can begin to make meaningful use of treatment.

1. See for example Lilian Ripple, *Motivation, Capacity and Opportunity: Studies in Casework Theory and Practice.*

THE COMPARISON AT ISSUE

The comparison of primary concern in this book relates to two kinds of *structures* of interpersonal treatment of complex psychosocial problems. In one structure treatment is limited in advance as to input and duration. This therapeutic structure is referred to variously as "brief limited treatment," "planned short-term service" (as in the experiment), or more simply on occasion as "brief treatment" or "short-term service."

In the opposing structure neither the recipient nor the practitioner is given any predetermined limits as to amount of input or duration. We are concerned generally with treatment that is expected by its practitioners to be of relatively long duration (at least longer than the limits given for short-term service), even though the projected length of treatment is not made explicit or may not be achieved. It will be variously referred to as "continued service" (as in the present experiment), "open-ended," or "conventional" treatment, or when it is in fact of long duration as "extended" treatment.

The comparison would have been purer, of course, if the input, or amount of service, in the two contrasting patterns could have been confined to specified levels, for example, brief treatment consisting of one interview a week for a given number of weeks, versus extended treatment, consisting of weekly interviews over a much longer period. But it was not feasible to do so in a field experiment with voluntary clients. It is not possible to hold clients assigned to either extended or brief service for stipulated periods. This problem becomes particularly serious in an extended service trial. The early drop-outs from a projected course of extended service cannot be counted as having received *planned* brief treatment nor can they be discarded from the group actually receiving extended treatment, since to do so would obviously violate the experimental design. The best we could have done was to have compared services undertaken as brief and extended treatment, and this kind of design comes very close to the actual design of the experiment. In summary, then, the comparison is not simply between services of different lengths. It is rather a comparison between services with a number of structural differences, one of which is length, projected and actual.

SOME QUESTIONS

The objectives and findings of the experiment are relevant to a number of general questions concerning the use of short-term and conventional treatment of psychosocial problems. Some of these questions will now be considered. The questions will focus on the capabilities and characteristics of short-term treatment, the lesser tried and lesser known of the two.

When is the use of planned brief treatment appropriate? Perhaps this question first needs to be placed in its historical context. Most forms of modern interpersonal treatment had their origins in the psychoanalytic movement or have been at least strongly influenced by it. As Malan has suggested, treatment carried out in the early days of psychoanalysis tended to be short by today's standards.[2] Freud's celebrated case of "Dora," for example, was completed within three months. Certainly one reason psychoanalysis began as a relatively brief treatment was its initial emphasis upon resolution of relatively specific disabilities. As psychoanalysis and its off-shoots, analytically oriented casework and psychotherapy, began to be applied to more diffuse problems in psychosocial adaptation, such as character neuroses or chronic difficulties in interpersonal relations, treatment began to consume greater blocks of time. By the same token, its application to general problems of living enormously increased its potential beneficiaries. Increasing time requirements per case

2. D. H. Malan, *A Study of Brief Psychotherapy*, p. 9.

thus coincided with increasing demands for therapeutic services. These trends in combination led to a severe overburdening of treatment resources. Planned brief treatment was developed in part as a solution to this problem. If treatment, which otherwise might be interminable, could be arbitrarily limited in duration, larger numbers of people could be helped. Moreover, it became increasingly apparent that sizable proportions of clients and patients either did not need or were unable to profit from continued long-term treatment. For these individuals short-term treatment was seen as a form of modest help that could be given in lieu of longer treatment.

The origins of these conceptions of short-term treatment were essentially pragmatic, whether such treatment was viewed as a second-best offering for the many or the best offering for the few. In this view short-term treatment rests on no special theories of personality, of change, or of intervention. Its theoretical base is essentially that of conventional treatment, with whatever ad hoc modifications may be necessary to accommodate to its shortness. It is cast basically as an abbreviated version of long-term treatment.

Some forms of planned brief treatment, however, have been fostered more by theory than necessity, even though their development was in some cases furthered by practical considerations. For example, the functional school of casework, following the teachings of Otto Rank and Jessie Taft, held that a fixed limit on the duration of treatment was an essential part of the helping process.[3] A quite different rationale for short-term treatment was introduced by the crisis theorists, who proposed that the time-limited nature of certain crises demanded immediate, brief intervention, if help was to be optimally effective.[4]

3. Jessie Taft, *The Dynamics of Therapy in a Controlled Relationship.*
4. Lydia Rapoport, "The State of Crisis: Some Theoretical Considerations," *Social Service Review*, XXXVI (June 1962), 211-17.

The question of when short-term service might be indicated would thus be answered differently according to one's conception of this model of treatment and of treatment in general. A conventional practitioner might advocate its use with cases meeting certain criteria. A community psychiatrist might suggest it be used as the basic pattern of service to meet emergency mental health needs in a high density area. A functional caseworker might use only short-term service, out of conviction about the benefits a client receives from experiencing a time-limited relationship. A crisis theorist might see brief intervention as the only sensible means of helping people cope with crisis situations.

In the dominant view, which appears to be essentially pragmatic in origin, planned brief treatment has been assigned a rather limited role, a treatment for use only when certain conditions are met. In general it has been confined to special projects or programs in facilities whose standard offering is open-ended treatment. Thus, in their survey of 457 child guidance clinics and family agencies (virtually the total membership of the American Association of Psychiatric Clinics for Children and the Family Service Association of America) the Parads found that only a minority of these facilities (31 per cent of the clinics and 17 per cent of the agencies) reported the existence of planned short-term treatment programs.[5] Moreover, the number of cases carried in such programs tended to be quite small on the average. In the 98 programs studied in detail, the median number of cases assigned to short-term treatment during a 3-month period was 8 for clinics and 18 for agencies.

When brief treatment is viewed as an adjunct to conventional treatment, logic demands the development of criteria by which cases suitable for the briefer treatment can be selected. Judging

5. Howard J. Parad and Libbie G. Parad, "A Study of Crisis-Oriented Planned Short-Term Treatment, Part I," *Social Casework*, XLIX (June 1968), 346-55.

from the literature, such criteria have either concerned the characteristics of the treatment candidate or the projected goals of treatment, or both client characteristics and treatment goals.

Two diagnostic categories suitable for short-term treatment are frequently mentioned. One category consists of a configuration of indicators that usually adds up to a relatively healthy, well-motivated recipient, with acute problems of fairly recent origin and with capacity to develop an early, positive relationship with the practitioner. Visher, for example, cites as favorable indicators for brief therapy[6] "readiness for change," "acute problems" with "definite precipitating factors," "environmental stability," "some evidence of an adequate, previous adjustment to the life situation," and initial "ability to use suggestions and interpretations." Respondents to the Parads' survey ranked "relatively healthy ego-functioning" and "clients in crisis situations" as the two most important criteria for a choice of planned short-term treatment.[7] Candidates in this category are obviously those who may not need more extended help. In most respects they could be expected to do well in any form of interpersonal treatment.

A second category, less frequently mentioned, describes patients or clients whose prognosis for conventional treatment is dim, because of the degree of disturbance, lack of capacity for relationship, and so on.[8] Their characteristics, when cited, tend to be the polar opposite of the characteristics of those in the first group. For these individuals the limited help that short-term treatment can provide may be all that is possible or advisable. The function of both sets of criteria seems to be, as

6. John S. Visher, "Brief Psychotherapy in a Mental Hygiene Clinic," *American Journal of Psychotherapy,* XIII (1959), 336.

7. Howard J. Parad, "Time and Crisis: A Survey of 98 Planned Short-Term Treatment Programs," p. 126.

8. See, for example, Visher, *American Journal of Psychotherapy,* XIII (1959), p. 337

implied earlier, to select out applicants who either do not need or cannot use conventional treatment.

Such criteria have dubious value. Like most diagnostic indicators they are essentially vague. If interpreted strictly, few candidates would fall in either category; if interpreted broadly, few would be excluded. Even more troublesome is the lack of clear differentiation between the ideal candidates for short-term treatment (the first group) and ideal candidates for continued treatment. Practitioners with a bias toward conventional treatment, who are certainly in the majority, could easily see excellent potential for open-ended treatment in the kind of well-motivated, not-too-disturbed individual who theoretically should also be a prime candidate for short-term treatment.

A second and less common approach to developing criteria for short-term service has centered on the projected goals of treatment. Usually some combination of treatment goals and diagnostic characteristics are used. For example, among Wolberg's "conditions for short-term treatment," one finds situations "where the goal is rapid restoration of homeostasis in an acute neurotic disorder," and "where the goal is a resolution of an acute upset in a chronic personality disorder."[9] This formulation suggests that patients with acute disturbance could be treated through brief methods if the goal was alleviation of the presenting problem or through long-term methods if the objective were more ambitious. If this logic is followed, short-term treatment would be a possibility for the very large number of applicants who come for help with acute problems. In general, the use of goals as criteria for selection of the appropriate form of treatment would considerably broaden the potential relevance of short-term approaches, since limited objectives are possible for most cases.

Although consideration of treatment objectives is probably essential in reaching meaningful decisions about use of short-

9. Lewis R. Wolberg, *Short Term Psychotherapy*, p. 141.

term treatment, we need to know far more than we do about the relative effectiveness of short-term and long-term methods, that is, what each can be expected to accomplish. Since the clinician's goal-setting would be based in part on what he could expect to accomplish with a particular kind of client or patient, it would still be necessary to take diagnostic criteria into account.

Finally discussions of criteria seem to assume that short-term treatment comes in one standard package. When we consider, as does Sifneos, for example, that brief methods may assume a variety of forms, the criteria issue becomes much more complicated.[10] It may be, as he suggests, that different diagnoses demand different kinds of brief treatment. To extend this logic, decisions about whether to use brief or extended treatment would depend on the types of brief treatment available.

What has been lacking is a general framework for decision-making about the uses of short-term and continued treatment. Such a framework would take into account not only diagnostic criteria, treatment objectives and expected results, and differences in types of brief and continued treatment, but also the availability of treatment resources and the extent of needs for treatment in populations of concern. The applicability of short-term service obviously involves issues that cannot be settled in the practitioner's office. Clinical decisions about its use must be related to administrative decisions and ultimately to community decisions.

What can be accomplished in planned brief treatment? There seems to be general agreement that brief treatment is capable of achieving limited objectives in the treatment of psychosocial problems. These objectives are apt to be defined either as alleviation of specific problems or of some specific aspects of

10. Peter E. Sifneos, "Two Different Kinds of Psychotherapy of Short Duration," *American Journal of Psychiatry*, 123 (1967), 1069-74.

larger problem configurations. A husband and wife can be helped to reach a particular decision, parents may be able to gain a little better understanding of their children, a school phobic child may be relieved of his symptoms and returned to school. More far-reaching objectives, such as change in character traits or substantial alleviation of deeply rooted interpersonal problems, are usually not seen as attainable through brief methods.

This formulation does not prove very helpful, however, in an attempt to state the capabilities of brief treatment in precise terms. How limited must the objectives be? What kinds of problems specifically are likely to respond to brief treatment and to what degree? Do different types of brief treatment differ in effectiveness, and so on? The considerable range of accomplishments credited to short-term treatment would make one cautious about placing an arbitrary ceiling upon its potentials.[11] Perhaps closer to the heart of the matter, at least as far as the present study is concerned, is the relative effectiveness of brief and continued treatment. If we say that short-term treatment cannot be expected to make much headway with deeply rooted family problems and is therefore not the treatment of choice when the goal is the resolution of such problems, then the obvious implication is that longer treatment would result in significantly greater progress toward this goal. This kind of assumption, however, has never been adequately tested. Quite possibly short-term treatment would prove to be of quite limited effectiveness; quite possibly extended treatment would prove no more effective. The limitations of short-term treatment must be seen then in relation to the limitations of treatment of longer duration.

We must recognize from the outset the problems inherent in comparing results of these two forms of service. First, they

11. A number of studies of short-term treatment outcome are reviewed in Chapter Eight.

cannot be readily compared on any single variable. Though the difference of greatest interest may be duration, it is practically impossible, as noted, to test the effects of this variable in a definitive way with voluntary recipients. One must settle, as we did, for a test of differences between projected patterns of brief and extended service. In so doing one automatically introduces other variables, such as the effects of *proposed plans* of service on the practitioner's and recipient's expectations. Treatment drop-outs form ambiguous groups. Effects associated with the simple passage of time, particularly in extended service, are difficult to extract from effects associated with treatment itself. Measures of improvement, crude at best, in this kind of research, may be difficult to equate in assessing outcomes of the two patterns of service. Although these and other limitations are dealt with more fully as we proceed, it should be apparent that the comparative assessment of these forms of treatment is fraught with uncertainties.

An assessment of the differences in effectiveness between these two services may reasonably include consideration of the cost differences. The cost of treatment may be seen not only in monetary terms, such as the unit cost of an interview, but also as expenditures of practitioner and client time. If the two forms of treatment are equally effective, then one could argue for expanded use of the less costly briefer service. Should the longer service prove clearly more effective, one would need to weigh its greater margin of effectiveness against the cost difference. The cost-effectiveness of treatment is, of course, impossible to determine with any precision. Progress toward the solution of human problems simply cannot be "priced" in absolute terms. Yet comparisons between alternative services in respect to results achieved at given costs can be made, in fact must be, if our allocation of treatment resources is to have a rational foundation.

How durable are its results? According to some, gains resulting from brief treatment may be limited not only in degree but also in duration. Brief treatment may be able to resolve minor problems or the surface manifestations of major problems, but such progress is apt to be short-lived. At the cessation of treatment, or shortly thereafter, one can anticipate a recurrence of the original difficulties or the appearance of new problems as substitutes for those apparently alleviated.

This view assumes that the client's presenting problems are expressions or symptoms of underlying disorders that should be the primary target of treatment. If the underlying problems are resolved, then specific or surface manifestations will take care of themselves, and normally an extended period of treatment is needed for this purpose.

Others have questioned this application of the "disease model" to human problems, pointing to evidence indicating that behavioral "symptoms" can be permanently removed without treatment of underlying causes. Whatever model we use, we need to know more about the interdependence of psychosocial problems. For example, if we grant that a child with adjustment difficulties is expressing certain basic family conflicts, does it necessarily follow that these conflicts need to be modified before any lasting improvement in the child's difficulties can be realized? It would depend among other things on the degree of dependence between the difficulties of child and family. The family conflicts could be one of several contributory causes. The removal of other, more immediate causes, perhaps generated by the school situation, might be sufficient to alleviate the problem permanently without altering family conflicts. Or, to raise a quite different question, is it not possible that a small amount of improvement in a specific problem can set in motion a cycle of positive change that may substantially ameliorate an underlying disorder?

The durability of outcomes of brief service must be seen, of course, in relation to extended treatment. Although it is usually assumed that progress resulting from long-term treatment has a more substantial basis and will be longer lasting, the relation between duration of gains and the duration of treatment has yet to be demonstrated. It is possible that certain kinds of clients backslide quickly whenever treatment is withdrawn, regardless of its length. A given relapse rate for brief treatment would be viewed much differently, and probably with less concern, if it proved to be no greater than the rate for extended treatment.

What are the special characteristics of brief treatment and their relation to outcome? Consideration of the appropriateness or effects of any kind of treatment becomes rather futile unless one can specify of what the treatment consists. Although we may have some general notions of the characteristics of interpersonal treatment, systematic knowledge of its specific ingredients, especially the characteristics of brief service, is sorely lacking.

Although brief treatment may come in a variety of forms, we are mainly concerned with special features of treatment method that result when conventional treatment is confined to a fixed limited period, in particular with features that distinguish brief from open-ended treatment, apart from the obvious ones relating to duration of service and planning of termination. It has been assumed that in short-term treatment the practitioner's goals are more limited and his role more active.[12] Do these assumptions have any validity? If so, to what extent do conditions of short-term service limit his goals or increase his activity? How else may his communications with the client be affected? How is the client's participation in treatment influenced by limits on its duration?

Of greater importance, how are differences in inputs between

12. See, for example, Wolberg, *Short Term Psychotherapy,* pp. 129-35.

two forms of treatment related to differences in outcome? For example, if continued treatment does in fact yield better results, to what input factors are these better results attributable? It could be that repetitive and progressive interpretations of central conflicts, not possible in briefer treatment, might contribute to the advantage of the extended service. Or the crucial difference might lie in the greater depth of the practitioner-client relationship in the longer service. The relation between specific characteristics of intervention and outcome in short-term treatment would also be of interest. For example, how do clients react to the brevity and fixed limits of brief treatment? Linking possible causes with possible effects can help tell us what kinds of interventions may be the effective ones. Such knowledge is essential to the improvement of both brief and extended methods.

These then are the questions to which this book is addressed. Although the experiment to be reported, which is the core of the volume, began with a broader focus, its major findings pertain largely to these questions. The findings provide no definitive answers; indeed there are none for such questions. However, the results of the study, in combination with the results of other research, do offer a base for certain conclusions about the positions of brief and extended casework in the spectrum of treatment services.

TWO · AN EXPERIMENT WITH CONTRASTING MODES OF SERVICE

THE COMPARATIVE STUDY of short-term and continued service was carried out as part of an experiment in which several alternative patterns of casework treatment were tested. As the contrast between short-term and continued service produced the findings of principal interest, we were tempted to confine the report to this comparison. We decided not to for two reasons. First, the test of short-term and continued service can be best understood in the context of the total experiment. Second, the other comparisons are of some interest in their own right and their results add to our knowledge of the relative characteristics and effectiveness of short-term and continued service.

Accordingly, the design of the project is presented as it was originally conceived.[1] The comparison of major concern, short-term and continued service, can then be placed in appropriate perspective with the other variables of the experiment.

OBJECTIVES OF THE EXPERIMENT

The major objectives of the project were threefold:

1. To assess the relative effectiveness of different patterns of casework service in alleviating family problems;

---

1. Certain portions of this chapter have been adapted from Ann W. Shyne, "An Experimental Study of Casework Methods," *Social Casework,* XLVI (November 1965), 535-41.

2. To develop diagnostic criteria for treatment planning by identifying the characteristics of clients who respond most favorably to the different patterns of service examined;

3. To study the treatment process and its relation to client change.

These objectives were applied to three sets of practice alternatives: (1) short-term versus continued service; (2) supportive versus modifying methods of treatment; and (3) use of individual interviews only versus use of a combination of individual and joint interviews. Within the limits of these alternatives, we were interested in determining what kind of treatment achieved what kind of results with what kind of family, and, further, what special features of the treatment might account for the results achieved.

The only hypothesis of the experiment was that variation in treatment approach would be associated with at least some variation in results; in other words, that the type of service received would make a difference. Although we had our private expectations, we did not think we had sufficient basis for predicting how results might differ among the patterns. Since most of our hunches turned out to be wrong, it is perhaps just as well we did not add to our embarrassment by converting them into formal predictions.

THE EXPERIMENTAL SERVICE PATTERNS

General questions relating to the short-term and continued service alternatives have already been discussed. Some attention should be given, however, to the use of these patterns in agency practice at the time of the study and to our initial view of their investigation.

Three years before the study was conceived the Community Service Society had introduced planned short-term service (PSTS) defined as a service to be rendered within not more than eight in-person client interviews to be conducted within three months after the completion of intake. It was this service that was tested in the experiment. Such service was considered appropriate only if exploration (within a maximum of three interviews) was sufficient to evaluate the situation and establish treatment objectives and plans likely to be accomplished within the time and interview limits. Other cases received "continued" or open-ended service (CS), which had no limits as to number of interviews or duration. For purposes of this experiment, we set a limit of eighteen months of service for CS. At Community Service Society, as in most agencies and clinics, only a small proportion of the cases that continued beyond intake were assigned to PSTS. This disposition was rarely made if the focal problems appeared to be difficulty on the client's part in interpersonal relations.[2] By design, the caseworker in usual Society practice did not use insight-oriented techniques in cases assigned to planned short-term service.

When the project was designed, it was assumed that CS was a more effective service than PSTS but the possibility was entertained that the difference in effectiveness might be less than usually thought. PSTS was seen as a modality of limited and specialized usefulness, an auxiliary of open-ended service, which at the Community Service Society, as elsewhere, has been the accepted model of interpersonal treatment for family problems. Besides, the PSTS-CS test seemed unfair since CS could provide a much longer period of service. And it was anticipated that lengthy treatment would be needed if any appreciable dent was to be made in the difficult family problems that we would have to deal with. In fact the project design was criticized by some

2. Ann W. Shyne and Patricia Coursey, *A Search for Criteria for Planned Short-Term Service.*

practitioners on grounds that eighteen months of continued service was really not enough. There was perhaps more interest in testing the feasibility of PSTS as a medium for treatment of complex family problems than in comparing its effectiveness with that of a service whose greater potency few questioned. It was thought that results of this test would have practical value, perhaps by identifying certain kinds of problem situations that could be dealt with through the more economical PSTS. The test was not seen as contributing substantially to casework theory.

The treatment comparison of primary interest at the inception of the project concerned the modifying and supportive methods of casework. The division of casework into these two modalities had been suggested in a document prepared by a staff group at the Community Service Society in 1958,[3] and by the time of the study had become the agency's "official" formulation of casework practice.

Both supportive and modifying methods were to be directed toward improvement in the client's social functioning and his ability to cope with problems. The supportive method was to attain this end through use of reassurance, advice, and logical discussion of problems in the client's current life situation, without a deliberate aim of increasing his self-understanding or of effecting other internal change. The modifying method, on the other hand, was to utilize techniques that encouraged self-examination by the client so that he might be helped to achieve better social functioning through increased understanding of himself and the dynamics and origin of his behavior.

In practice most cases turned out to be supportive under this system, according to informal reports of caseworkers and super-

3. *Method and Process in Social Casework, Report of a Staff Committee of the Community Service Society of New York*, pp. 13-22.

visors, since the modifying method was considered appropriate only if a number of conditions were met. It was to be used only if greater self-understanding was deemed essential to effect a change in the client's social functioning, only if his ego was sufficiently intact that self-scrutiny could be used without possible psychological damage, and only if he was not subject to excessive external stress. Furthermore, the modifying method was to be applied only after an extended period of psychosocial study and usually consultation with a psychiatrist.

This view of treatment was of more than local interest. The document setting it forth was (and still is) widely used in social work education and practice. Moreover, this dichotomy is but one of several derivatives of a common formulation of psychotherapy.[4] This type of formulation conceives of the therapist's efforts to develop the patient's insight or self-awareness as a distinct treatment modality. This modality has usually been seen as the therapist's most powerful means of effecting deep and lasting change. Because of the commanding importance given insight development there has been a tendency in these formulations to lump together other, and presumably less significant, activities of the therapist into a residual category. The insight development category generally gets a label indicating that the therapist really means business ("reconstructive," "uncovering," or, as in the present case, "modifying") whereas the remaining category or categories are described in more flaccid terms ("supportive" is as good example as any). Thus, the modifying-supportive typology reflects some basic issues in interpersonal treatment, relating to how treatment is defined, and to the kind of treatment that is most effective in producing change.

The validity of this typology has been questioned within and

4. See, for example, Lewis R. Wolberg, *The Technique of Psychotherapy,* p. 8.

outside the Community Service Society. Can casework be practiced as two distinctive methods or does it fundamentally consist of some core of techniques used in different combinations, according to the needs of the client or the style of the caseworker? If modifying and supportive treatment *are* distinguishable in practice, how do they compare in effectiveness in contributing to improvement in the client's social and psychosocial functioning? Should wider use be made of the modifying method, and if so, what criteria should guide the caseworker in selecting it?

The third pair of alternatives comprised individual-client interviews and a combination of individual and joint interviews with the marital partners. In recent years, caseworkers and other practitioners of interpersonal treatment have made increasing use of multiple-client interviewing because of the advantages it affords them in observing and dealing directly with family interactions. They usually use this type of interviewing in conjunction with individual interviews, since the latter are believed more useful in exploring the history of an individual client and in dealing with his intrapsychic problems. Although considerable literature had accumulated on multiple-client interviewing,[5] the circumstances that favor its use had not been tested under controlled conditions. In this study, therefore, possible differences were to be examined in the objectives, techniques, and outcomes of service when the caseworker confined his treatment to individual-client interviewing and when he used one type of multiple-client interviews (that is, joint interviews with the marital partners) as well as individual client interviews.

Each pair of alternatives contained a "conventional" and an "innovative" pattern, at least in terms of usual casework practice at the Community Service Society. On the conventional

5. See, for example, *Casework Treatment of the Family Unit.*

side was the supportive method, continued service, and treatment through the medium of individual interviews. The innovative components comprised the modifying method, short-term service, and treatment using a combination of individual and joint interviews. (Use of the modifying method within short-term service had not been attempted at all within the agency.) There was little question about the *feasibility* of the conventional approaches. Their use in regular agency practice proved at least that they could be carried out. It was less certain that the more innovative methods could be as easily implemented. Moreover, there was question about how much of an innovative burden the caseworkers could bear, since each was being asked to carry cases simultaneously in all the patterns. For these reasons it seemed sound, if not essential, to give the caseworkers a certain amount of latitude in carrying out the innovative services. Still, we needed to achieve adequate differentiation between the innovative and conventional approaches. Otherwise the comparative tests would be meaningless.

In order to accomplish these different purposes we tried to exclude innovative features from the conventional patterns but, at the same time, to build certain "escape hatches" into the innovative patterns. Thus, assignment to the supportive method limited the caseworker to use the supportive techniques; assignment to the modifying method directed the caseworker to *attempt* to engage at least one of the marital partners in self-examination. Similarly, the caseworkers were not to use preplanned time or service limits in CS, but rather to allow the case to run its course; in PSTS, on the other hand, time and interview limits were to be set up with the client, with the provision that these limits could be extended if there were urgent need for additional service *at* the prearranged closing time. Although clients in all patterns were to be advised to wait six months, until completion of the follow-up interviews, before returning for further service, it was recognized that clients receiving a brief service might need help at an earlier date. Such help was to be given at any point *after* closing, if it was decided that the client required immediate attention. Finally, in cases for which individual interviewers were prescribed, the caseworker was not permitted to use joint interviews; where a combination of individual and joint interviews was prescribed, the caseworker was instructed to try to arrange joint interviews with family members, with the understanding that she might not succeed in all cases.

Implementation of treatment alternatives depended in part on practical considerations of the degree of control that can be exercised on the client. In the case of the PSTS-CS patterns, it might be possible for the caseworker to adhere to the limits of the less conventional PSTS, but it would not be feasible, even if desirable, to hold the client in CS beyond the amount of service he was willing to accept. With respect to the supportive-modifying alternatives, the caseworker could presumably confine his approach to supportive techniques, but could not utilize the modifying method unless the client were responsive to efforts to engage him in self-examination. Similarly, the caseworker could refrain from holding joint interviews, but there was no guarantee that both spouses would make themselves available for joint interviews just because the caseworker tried to arrange them.

Obviously the treatment alternatives to be examined are not cleancut, mutually exclusive, discrete types, such as might be achieved in a laboratory experiment. They represented instead the closest approach to such a model that appeared practical in a casework field experiment.

The three pairs of treatment alternatives produce eight different patterns of service or "prescriptions" as shown in the diagram below.

PSTS				CS			
Modifying		*Supportive*		*Modifying*		*Supportive*	
Indi-vidual	Combina-tion	Indi-vidual	Combina-tion	Indi-vidual	Combina-tion	Indi-vidual	Combina-tion
1	2	3	4	5	6	7	8

Thus, each service pattern involved three elements. A case assigned to pattern 1, for example, was to receive PSTS, carried out with modifying methods and individual interviews. One-eighth of the cases were assigned to each of the eight patterns. However, at the same time, *half* the cases were assigned to either member of each pair of treatment patterns; for example, all cases in patterns 1, 2, 3, and 4 were assigned to PSTS, and all in patterns 5, 6, 7, and 8 to CS, while all cases in patterns 1, 2, 5, and 6 were assigned to modifying treatment and all in the remaining patterns to supportive treatment.

This design made it possible to study simultaneously three different dimensions of treatment with a relatively small number of cases.[6] In addition the design also presented the opportunity to compare the relative effectiveness of different configurations of approaches. Thus, the eight specific patterns could be compared with one another.

For purposes of this book the modifying-supportive and individual-combination contrasts can best be seen as elaborations of the study of short-term and continued service. For example, are differences in outcome between short-term and continued

6. For discussion of this type of design, technically known as a 2x2x2 factorial, see Allan L. Edwards, *Experimental Design in Psychological Research*, pp. 175-200.

service affected by whether modifying or supportive methods were attempted? Within short-term service or within continued service, are better results achieved through use of a mixture of joint and individual interviews or through individual interviews only? This view of the design is more reflective of the service patterns as they were implemented in practice than the original conception in which the various partners were given more or less equal weight. As will be indicated subsequently, the basic design, as it emerged in practice, was a division of the 120 participating families into groups receiving either continued or short-term service. The other service variables became secondary themes in the comparison of these two groups.

A NOTE ON THE LACK OF A CONTROL GROUP

Increasingly, research on interpersonal treatment is making use of experimental designs in systematic testing of the effects of different treatment approaches against one another, or against rates of "spontaneous" improvement achieved by individuals. Experimental designs, like the present one, that test the relative effectiveness of alternate treatment approaches are in the ascendancy at present. Although they lack comparisons of treated with untreated groups, and as a result cannot produce hard findings on the effects of treatment *per se,* they have the advantage of indicating whether one approach yields apparently better results than another. Such information is more immediately useful to clinicians than knowledge of the effectiveness of their efforts in general. In order to function with any sense of adequacy, clinicians must assume that their efforts have some positive effects. Studies that assess the general effectiveness of their practice against groups receiving no treatment may reassure or depress them, depending on the results, but have little impact on the decisions that guide their efforts. Given no tested alternatives, the clinician can only continue along the same path. However, he can put to immediate use findings that suggest a certain approach may be more efficacious or more economical than another. He can then be guided by research evidence in a choice between viable alternatives. The kind of research that pits treatment against no-treatment is certainly needed to tell us, if nothing else, whether the whole structure of treatment services has a rational foundation. Meanwhile, experiments comparing different approaches must provide the basis for deciding on the best among an ever expanding number of dark horses.

THE PROJECT CASEWORKERS, SUPERVISOR, AND PSYCHIATRIC CONSULTANTS

The service patterns have been described as they came off the drawing board. It was up to the caseworkers to put them into practice as best they could. Altogether eight caseworkers carried project cases, although only six were employed at any one time.[7] All were well qualified, experienced practitioners. Each had received a master's degree from a school of social work. Half the group had had at least six years of casework practice following the professional degree, and all had at least three years; all but one were women.[8] They were especially recruited for the project both from inside and outside the agency. It was thought preferable to secure practitioners who were willing from the start to accept the research requirements of the project, rather than attempt to force these requirements upon a group of draftees.

7. Two of the original six left the agency during the early part of the service phase. Their active caseloads, which were still quite small, were transferred to their replacements. There was no other turnover among caseworker staff during the service phase.
8. The female pronoun will be used in reference to all project caseworkers.

The caseworkers represented a rather diverse range of professional orientations and points of view about practice. Like most caseworkers they were inclined to see short-term service as a modality of limited usefulness in treatment of family problems, although they were willing to "give it a try." Most had not used PSTS in the treatment of family problems. All had some experience with the kind of insight-oriented treatment outlined under the modifying method although they lacked experience, as did most caseworkers in the agency, in working with this method as a primary mode of practice. Only two had had substantial experience in the use of joint interviews, although all had at least some familiarity with this type of interview.

The caseworkers were supervised by a full-time member of the research team, a person with considerable experience in both casework practice and supervision. One of his major responsibilities was to give direction to the caseworkers in their carrying out of the service patterns of the experiment. It soon became apparent that there were few points of certainty in translating the abstract service designs into practice realities. It was the supervisor who bore the brunt of questions raised by the caseworkers in their efforts to fit their practice to the research design. "What do I do with Mrs. A, who was assigned to supportive treatment but wants me to help her find out why she's so neurotic?" "How can I develop a modifying insight-oriented approach with Mr. B—it would normally take a year or so—in the five interviews that I have left in this case?" "Just about every relationship in this large, complicated family is presenting a problem; why on earth did this case have to be assigned to planned short-term service?" "How can I hold joint interviews with this couple if the husband doesn't want to be seen at all?"

The supervisor was in turn responsible to the project co-directors (Reid and Shyne). This administrative structure enabled the researchers to exercise a greater degree of control over all aspects of the service phase of the experiment than is usually the case in a field experiment.[9]

The project caseworkers made substantial use of psychiatric consultation, provided by four psychiatric consultants. Consultations were obtained on 42 per cent of the project cases. Although the numbers of PSTS cases (22) and CS cases (28) receiving consultations did not differ greatly, most of the PSTS consultations (18 of the 22) were on cases assigned to modifying prescriptions. This imbalanced use of the consultants within the PSTS caseload resulted largely from the caseworkers' own wishes to obtain consultation before attempting to use insight-oriented techniques in brief treatment. For example, there was often question about the capacity of the client to tolerate self-examination that necessarily would need to begin with little preparation or testing out. Since psychiatric consultation in such cases might provide some safeguards for the client, we decided not to restrict its use. Although we recognized that the disproportionate use of consultation with PSTS modifying cases might affect outcome comparisons within PSTS, we assumed it would not make a difference in comparisons of outcomes between PSTS and CS cases.

SELECTION OF CASES

Several criteria were followed in selection of cases for the project. Some of these were set to insure a degree of homogeneity. The spouses were to be between 21 and 50 years of age and were not to have received casework service from the agency

9. For further discussion of the administrative structure of the project see William J. Reid, "The Center for Social Casework Research: Its Potential for Social Work Education," *Social Work Education Reporter,* 15 (December 1967), pp. 20-21.

previously. The presenting problems were to include difficulties in marital or parent-child relationships, whether deriving from medical, social, economic, or psychological roots and whether expressed directly by the applicant or inferred from his statement of the problem. For practical reasons, families were excluded if the clients did not have sufficient facility in speaking English for interviews to be conducted without an interpreter.

Another group of criteria was dictated by the nature of the project. The family had to comprise a couple living together, or, if temporarily separated, interested in reconciliation, since use of joint interviews with the spouses would obviously be impossible if the family unit did not include both marital partners. Neither spouse could be so seriously disturbed psychologically that use of the modifying method of treatment might jeopardize his balance. Since independent research interviews were to be a major source of data, as will be indicated later, at least one of the spouses had to participate in an initial research interview. Finally, if the treatment patterns were to be compared, the family had to receive at least one casework interview after the treatment pattern was prescribed.

Beginning in January 1965, all families applying to the Community Service Society for help and who were identified at application as potentially meeting project criteria were given intake appointments with one of six project caseworkers.[10] Since applications to the agency were averaging about 900 a month at the time of the project and since we planned on only 160 cases, we confidently expected to complete our sample within a reasonably short period—six months, according to our calculations. Our confidence proved ill-founded and our calculations erroneous, however. It actually took a year and a half to com-

10. Families applied directly to a CSS Family Service Center. Two of these Centers are located in mid-town Manhattan, one is in Queens, and the other in the Bronx. Each Center had at least one project caseworker.

plete our sample, and at that we had to settle for only 120 cases in order to avoid an undue extension of the service phase of the experiment. In retrospect, we had overestimated the rate of eligible applications for two of the Service Centers (where half our caseworkers were placed). In a third Center there were often more applications meeting our criteria than our project caseworkers could handle at one time.

In addition, most of the 625 applicants deemed eligible and referred for intake appointments did not materialize as project cases. The details of this attrition may be instructive. The first point of loss occurred in the 200 applicant families who failed to appear for an initial intake interview. The waiting period between application and the first intake appointment (discussed below) was doubtless one factor in the losses at this point. In 188 instances service was completed or the clients decided not to continue in the course of intake, which could comprise one, two, or three interviews. A smaller number, 86, failed to meet one or more criteria and were assigned for service to a caseworker not participating in the project. The remaining 151 cases completed intake and were tentatively screened into the project, but in 13 instances it was not possible to obtain a research interview, and in 18 others the family discontinued after the initial research interview and assignment to a service pattern but before a single interview occurred within the prescribed treatment pattern. The 120 cases that were finally funneled into the project and are the subject of this report are described in the next chapter.

The losses following acceptance at application were fairly typical of patterns of attrition found in family agencies generally.[11] The idea of participating in a research project seemed to be a deterrent for only a few clients.

11. For example, member agencies of the Family Service Association of America reported that, on the average, only 28 per cent of families receiv-

There was a median interval of three months between the point of application and the first service interview. When the intake and research interviews were completed without delay, the length of time between these points was confined to two or three weeks. For most project families, however, there was a waiting period of several weeks before an intake interview could be held and in some instances there were delays in scheduling or completing the research interviews. While the period between application and assignment to ongoing service was not excessive by usual standards, it needs to be taken into account in a project involving planned short-term service. Some models of brief treatment, particularly those addressed to resolution of crises and emergencies, predicate *immediate* intervention at the point help is sought. Obviously PSTS in the project was not of this type.

ASSIGNMENT PROCEDURES

Crucial to the experiment was random assignment of cases to service patterns since the intent was to compare use of different methods with similar clients. The idea that service methods should be determined arbitrarily is difficult for the practitioner to accept, since it contravenes usual professional practice of selecting service methods on the basis of assessment of the case. It can be justified professionally and was accepted by the participating caseworkers, because no client was denied a treatment known to be more effective than the type offered nor exposed to a treatment considered potentially harmful.

For each caseworker a sheet was prepared in which the eight service prescriptions were listed in random order, that is, in an order determined entirely by chance. For example, caseworker

---

ing one interview went on to receive more than five. The comparable figure for our sample (taking into account early dropouts in the service phase) was 29 per cent. See *Family Service Statistics,* Part III, p. 2.

A's list began with patterns 1, 5, 8, 2. Her first case was thus assigned to a pattern in which short-term service was to be conducted through modifying methods and individual interviews.

If pure random ordering had been adhered to, it would have been possible, through chance alone, for certain workers to wind up with disproportionate shares of certain patterns. The caseloads of the workers were not large enough to insure that the frequency of various prescriptions would be balanced out in a simple random assignment. Accordingly, ceilings were placed on the proportion of cases that could be assigned in any pattern for any caseworker. Once a caseworker had achieved her quota of cases in a given pattern, she received no further assignments in that pattern. This procedure, which actually resulted in only minor adjustments in the original random orderings, resulted in better control over possible differences in caseworker effectiveness.[12]

The caseworkers had no knowledge of the order of assignment in store for them or that their caseloads were being balanced. During the intake phase of the case, that is prior to the final acceptance of the case into the project and assignment to a service pattern, the caseworker could only guess what the eventual assignment would be. After a caseworker decided that a case was eligible for the project and this decision was approved by the supervisor, the case was then sent to a research technician who automatically made the assignment to pattern from the next number on the worker's list. The caseworker was then informed what the pattern would be.

These procedures were used to assign the 120 project cases to the 8 patterns, with each pattern receiving 15 cases. Each major service pattern (for example, PSTS and CS) received 60

12. It should also be noted that this procedure was carried out according to a fixed formula, routinely applied.

cases each. The size and characteristics of the caseloads of each worker were determined largely by the service center to which she was assigned. All but two workers were assigned at least 10 project cases; no worker was assigned more than 25. As it turned out, the most experienced half of our practitioners carried about two-thirds of the cases. Since the clienteles of the four service centers at CSS have somewhat different characteristics, the caseloads of the project caseworkers were not comparable. This fact was of no particular consequence in comparing service patterns but needs to be kept in mind in comparisons among caseworkers.

DATA ON CLIENT CHARACTERISTICS AND SERVICE OUTCOMES

To answer the questions posed, clearly a good deal of information was needed about the clients, the service, and the outcome, and a good deal of information was gathered from a variety of sources. The primary method for obtaining data on the clients and the outcome of service was research interviewing conducted usually in the home, with at least one spouse and usually with both, at three points of time: (1) at completion of intake; (2) at termination of casework service; and (3) six months after service termination. These interviews were conducted by four highly experienced caseworkers who had no responsibility for service and had initially only minimal identifying information on each case. The interviewers were assigned cases in an unselected fashion, except that each interviewer was given a proportionate share of cases in each major service pattern. The same interviewer conducted the research interviews at intake and closing and, in most cases, the follow-up interviews with a particular family, although he did not have access in subsequent interviews to material he had obtained earlier. This plan was devised to minimize possible discomfort to the client in having to see a different interviewer each time. It probably resulted in fewer refusals at closing and follow-up than would otherwise have occurred. These advantages were thought to offset the disadvantage of having the interviewer influenced in later interviews by his memory of early interviews. The research interviewers were of course not informed of the service pattern to which the case was assigned, although they could often guess from clues provided by the client's comments, the time span of service, and so forth.

The research interviews had two purposes. The first was to elicit material to serve as a basis for subsequent judgments about individual and family functioning and change. In pursuing this objective, the interviewer had considerable latitude in his method of eliciting the information needed for him to make the judgments called for on the interview schedule. Thus he might probe for underlying feelings, challenge a statement that seemed specious, or concentrate on areas in which change had occurred. The second purpose was to educe the client's opinions and attitudes with respect to his problems, his functioning, and service. This portion of the interview consisted of specific questions to the client, usually requiring the client to choose among several possible responses. The interviewer was required to record the responses as given, without bringing his own judgment to bear.

The content of the research schedule varied somewhat for the three research interviews at intake, case closing, and follow-up. Each called for judgments on client and family functioning and on the client's and the interviewer's perception of the problem. The initial interview included, in addition, information on the social characteristics of the family and considerable detail related to client motivation for problem resolution and his expectations of service, while the closing and follow-up research interview schedules called for information on change in problem and in functioning and on the client's perception of the service. The follow-up interview also inquired into events subsequent to termination of service, especially other services utilized and still needed. The bulk of the interview schedules and instructions for their use preclude their inclusion in this volume. Their general content is, we believe, apparent from the data reported in subsequent chapters, where specific items are discussed as findings are reported. The interviewers participated in developing the schedules and instructions, and numerous training sessions were held to help them reach a common understanding of their use.

Two aspects of the research interviews deserve comment here; our success in obtaining them and their use as a basis for an additional set of judgments. No case was admitted to the project unless an initial research interview was obtained with at least one of the spouses, and in all but 5 cases interviews were obtained with both spouses. In the absence of an interview with one of the marital partners, certain items could not be completed, but the bulk of the schedule was filled out on the basis of the one interview obtained. At closing, interviews were held with both spouses in 88 cases and with at least one spouse, usually the wife, in 28 others. In the remaining 4 cases independence of judgment was sacrificed in the interests of getting some "after" data in all cases and partial information was obtained from the caseworker's dictated and taped recordings of her service interviews. Our data on outcome of service at point of case closing are therefore reasonably complete. Six months later when follow-up interviews were sought there were some losses, as anticipated, despite use of long distance telephone calls to reach former clients living at some distance from New York or unwilling to give a face-to-face interview. Follow-up interviews were completed with both spouses in 73 cases and with one spouse in 36 cases, but interviews could not be secured in 11 cases. Thus, complete or partial follow-up data were obtained for 91 per cent of the cases. On the whole then, we were reasonably successful in obtaining at least one interview per family at each of the three points of time. Where interviews were not obtained the reason generally appeared to be the client's refusal to be interviewed. In many cases clients seemed reluctant to be interviewed for the second or third time, particularly if their feelings about the services they received were less positive.[13]

Research interviews were tape recorded in order to permit another interviewer, or review judge, to complete an identical schedule based on information obtained in the interview.[14] Whereas the same interviewer normally conducted the intake, closing, and follow-up interviews with a family, different review judges were generally used for the three sets of interviews in a given case. With some exceptions, a judge did not review a case in which he had conducted an interview.[15]

By this means it was possible to obtain a complete check on the judgments of the interviewers and to increase the precision of measurement by averaging the ratings of the interviewers and judges. While the review judges were handicapped by the poor sound quality of some of the tapes and the lack of visual clues, their judgments were free of biases that could result from face-to-face encounters with the clients or from recall of earlier interviews.

Caseworkers completed schedules at intake and at case closing

13. The problem of "missing data" is discussed in Appendix II, pp. 227–28.
14. Eleven interviews were not judged because tapes could not be obtained or were too poor in sound quality to be understood.
15. In sixteen cases the research interviewer who had conducted initial and closing interviews served as the review judge for the follow-up interviews.

identical with those used by the research interviewers and review judges. Caseworkers did not, however, participate in the follow-up phase of the experiment. The caseworker's estimations of client characteristics and service outcomes were to be given secondary emphasis. Presumably the ratings of the research observers (the research interviews and review judges) would be more objective than those of the caseworkers who might be biased by involvement in the case and by knowledge of the pattern. Nonetheless, the caseworker's schedule provided a useful supplement to and check on the information from the research observers. Finally, certain outcome findings prompted inquiry into the caseworkers' perception of the service patterns and led to use of tapes of casework interviews as a basis for a measure of client progress in CS cases. The nature of these investigations will be described within the context of the findings that gave rise to them (Chapter Five). Thus, from client, research interviewer, review judge, and caseworker, extensive data were obtained about the client family, changes in individual and family functioning, changes in problem situation, apparent effects of service, and client perception of what the service comprised and what it accomplished. Analysis of the characteristics of the actual service input required other data-gathering procedures.

ANALYSIS OF SERVICE

In order to get the caseworker's perception of his service input, she was asked to submit a schedule for each service interview (Caseworker's Interview Schedule) on which she checked off the objectives to which the particular interview had been directed and the techniques utilized. It was recognized that the caseworker is hardly an unbiased observer of her own action, and that independent judgment of the techniques used would be desirable. Therefore, tape recordings were made of all service interviews on a substantial proportion (60 per cent) of cases assigned to the various patterns. Interview analysts, experienced caseworkers whose usual role in the agency was that of student field instructor, listened to a selected sample of interviews and classified each caseworker response according to technique. For this purpose, a much more detailed and explicit scheme for identifying techniques had to be developed than was provided by the general description of methods and techniques within which the caseworkers were to operate.[16] Our own efforts at precise description of casework intervention through analysis of interview tapes were supplemented by several student projects that made use of either our data or instruments. These endeavors will be presented in the course of analyzing the service characteristics (Chapter Four).

A further source of data on service was the Caseworker's Diagnostic Schedule, completed by the caseworker early in her service contact on each case. We anticipated that case outcome might be affected by whether the caseworker was following the pattern of service she would have selected or whether she was forced by the pattern to operate in a way that seemed inappropriate to her. On the Diagnostic Schedule, she was therefore asked to describe briefly her assessment of the problem, the objectives of service, the prognosis, and the service pattern of her choice. If her choice differed from the prescribed pattern, she indicated what her objectives and prognosis would have been if she had been able to follow the pattern she preferred.

Finally, use was made of the caseworkers' narrative recording to provide gross estimates of certain characteristics of service. Caseworkers recorded one to two page summaries of each interview and, at the end of service, summaries of the case as a

16. *Method and Process in Social Casework*, pp. 20-22.

whole. Although this material was too subjective and voluminous to warrant formal analysis, its review did yield impressions about aspects of service on which more systematic data were lacking.

INSTRUMENT RELIABILITY

Considerable information was obtained on the extent of agreement between different observers in the use of the project instruments. In fact, all observations that purported to be objective appraisals of the client, the casework process, or service outcomes, were repeated in whole or in part, as will be explained in presenting the data. A reasonable level of agreement between judges is normally required if a measurement is to be regarded as reliable. One type of measurement that had been intended as a major method of assessing outcomes was not used because it proved grossly unreliable. This was an attempt to measure change in client functioning through determining the differences between ratings made at opening and closing, rather than through obtaining retrospective judgments of change. All measures upon which the reported findings of the project are based proved generally reliable by conventional standards.[17]

17. Data pertaining to reliability of project instruments are presented and discussed in Appendix II, pp. 236–45.

THREE · CHARACTERISTICS OF
CLIENTS PRIOR TO SERVICE

THE CHARACTERISTICS of the 120 families on which this research is focused were shaped by two factors: the project selection criteria and the families' own self-selection into the project. As a result, the families were intact and first-time applicants for service at the agency. The spouses were English speaking, relatively young, and generally free of gross psychopathology. Since the families not only came voluntarily to a social agency for help, but remained through the intake process and accepted an offer of further service, certain other characteristics of the families and their members may be assumed: for example, the presence and persistence of felt needs for help with family problems, motivation for service, and some degree of hope that service would be beneficial.

Selected characteristics of families assigned to PSTS and CS are summarized in Table 1 of Appendix I. These and other characteristics of our sample are the focus of discussion in this chapter.

SOCIO-ECONOMIC CHARACTERISTICS

Two-thirds of the 120 families had gross incomes falling between $5,000 and $10,000 per year, with roughly equal proportions falling on either side of that range. The median gross weekly income was $140, appreciably higher than the comparable figure of $118 for New York City families as a whole at the time the study began.[1] The adequacy of the family's income was assessed through a scale that took into account income, rent, the size of the family, and the number of wage-earners.[2] Only 2 families were found to have incomes at or below the "public assistance" level, one criterion of a poverty-level income in New York City. All told, 23 per cent of the families fell below a "modest but adequate" standard of living as defined by this scale, 20 per cent were at this level, and the remaining 57 per cent had incomes above it. This distribution differs markedly from that of the general caseload of the agency; only 25 per cent of agency families had incomes above a "modest but adequate" standard in 1964.

The occupations of the husbands were classified on a 7-point scale developed by Hollingshead, in which an occupation is rated from a high of 1 to a low of 7, according to the amount of social status it reflects.[3] The majority of our husbands (58 per cent) held positions in the middle to lower portion of this scale, categories 4-6, which comprise clerical and sales workers, technicians, skilled and semi-skilled manual employers. Twenty-nine per cent held higher status occupations (for example, as professionals, administrators, owners of small businesses); only 13 per cent fell in the bottom category of this scale(for example, unskilled laborers). In terms of this scale, the mid-point of our sample was the occupational category "skilled manual employee," which was also the most common, accounting for 28 per cent of the husbands.

In respect to education, just about all of our clients, 91 per cent, had attended high school and 35 per cent were either

1. *Population Characteristics 1964.*
2. This scale is described in Patricia Coursey et al., "A Socio-Economic Study of Agency Clients," *Social Casework,* XLVI (June 1965), 331-38.
3. August B. Hollingshead, *Two Factor Index of Social Position.*

college graduates or had at least some college training (the comparable per cents for the agency caseload in 1964 were 40 and 14). The median educational level for both husbands and wives was high school graduation, that is twelve years of schooling. On the whole, project clients were better educated than the average New Yorker. In 1960, only 15 per cent of New York City adults over 25 years of age had any college training; the median for school years completed was ten.[4]

In order to obtain a more precise and summarized picture of the social status of the families, each family was classified according to the Hollingshead Two Factor Index of Social Position.[5] This system generates five classes of social status based upon the occupation of the head of the household and his level of education. Class I is the top and Class V the bottom position. The largest group of families (43 per cent) fell into Class IV, with the next largest groups falling on either side (23 per cent, Class V and 15 per cent, Class III). Class II accounted for 13 per cent and Class I, for only 6 per cent.

That the families were intact, with incomes generally above the poverty line, and with spouses of better than average education must be taken into account in evaluating their social class distributions, particularly at the lower levels. Thus, even the Class V families, almost a quarter of the sample, were obviously not the extremely impoverished, female-headed families that that category would also include. For example, in the Class V families the median gross income was $115 a week; the husband had ten years of schooling on the average, and the wife, twelve.

Perhaps the terms "working class" and "lower-middle class" come closest to describing the socio-economic status of the great majority of our families. In respect to income and educational

4. *Statistical Guide for New York City 1964*, p. 21.
5. Hollingshead, *Two Factor Index*.

levels the families in these classes were probably toward the top of their strata.

The majority of the clients (58 per cent) were white, with a substantial proportion Negro (36 per cent), and the remaining (6 per cent) mostly Puerto Rican, a distribution almost identical with that of the 1964 agency caseload. Negroes made up a considerably higher proportion of our clientele than would be expected from the proportion of Negroes in New York City, approximately 14 per cent of the population in the 21 to 50 year age range in 1960.[6] While families headed by Negroes tended to be significantly lower in social position, only about one-third of such families (16 out of 44) were in Class V.

Project criteria limited the age range of the spouse to 21 to 50 years. The median age of the husbands was 36 years and of the wives, 32 years. The age of the families was measured from the date of marriage. The majority (57 per cent) had been established within the last ten years; only 6 per cent had been in existence longer than twenty years. Ninety per cent of the families had one or more children.

PROBLEM TYPES

To be eligible for the project a family had to be seeking help for a problem in family relations. This criterion was interpreted to include families whose presenting problem consisted primarily of a child's difficulties at school or in the community, on grounds that the parents' request for help with such difficulties signified that a problem existed between parents and children. Also, families were accepted if their request for help for some other type of problem was thought to *imply* clearly a request for help with a problem in family relations even though the latter was not stated explicitly at application.

In almost all cases either the husband or the wife, generally

6. *Statistical Guide*, p. 17.

both, indicated to the interviewer during the initial research interview that their major problems included marital or child-related[7] difficulties. In almost half of the 120 cases (45 per cent) only marital problems were mentioned by the couple.[8] In about a third of the cases (35 per cent) only child-related problems were mentioned as a major source of difficulty in family relations. About a sixth of the couples (16 per cent) cited both marital and child-related problems. For the most part, this last group comprised cases in which there was some disagreement between husband and wife on the nature of the major problems. In some instances one partner would mention both kinds of problems, the other partner only one, and in other cases one partner would see only a marital problem and the other only a child-related problem. In the remaining 5 cases (4 per cent) neither spouse perceived a problem in family relations.

The only other kind of major problem mentioned with any frequency was "emotional distress in self or family member," cited by husband or wife in about a third of the cases, almost always in conjunction with a problem in family relations. Only rarely did a client cite "emotional distress" in itself as the primary reason for seeking help. The clients were asked about other kinds of problems that sometimes bring families to family agencies, such as problems pertaining to employment, housing, financial need and management, and social relations outside the family. Of these, problems of financial management were the most frequently cited, but such problems were mentioned as major problems by the husband or wife in only 6 cases.

A similar picture emerged from the research observers' and

7. This term will be used to describe problems confined to the parent-child relationship as well as problems involving the relations of parents, child, and the school or community.

8. If a client mentioned three or more problems he was asked to designate the two problems he regarded as major. These data pertain to major problems only.

caseworkers' appraisals of the major problems for which help was indicated. In order to gain a better rounded picture of the major problems in family relations in each case, the judgments of all observers (clients, research interviewers, review judges, and caseworkers) were taken into account. A family was regarded as having a particular problem if at least *two* of these observers reported it as a major difficulty. This method of classification produced about the same proportions of families with marital, child-related, and both marital and child-related problems, as were obtained using only the client's judgments. There was a shift in only 7 cases, in 3 of which neither partner acknowledged a problem in family relations but such a problem was perceived by at least two of the three professional observers.[9]

Thus most project families tended to fall into either the marital or the child-related problem group, whether families were classified according to the clients' own estimates of their problems or according to the combined judgments of all observers. It is fair to say that the families tended to present their problems in this way and the professional observers generally agreed with the clients' view. This is not to suggest that families classified as having a marital problem primarily were experiencing no child-related difficulties, or vice versa, but only to suggest that for most families one or the other problem area tended to be predominant in their initial request for help.

It is also clear that marital problems were more prevalent. Sixty-four per cent of all families were classified as having a major marital problem, including cases in which both marital and child-related problems were considered important, as opposed to 51 per cent of families categorized as presenting child-

9. The distribution of families by problems given in Table 1 in Appendix I was based on the second or final method of classification. This method is used in subsequent data analysis concerned with family problems at intake.

related problems, either exclusively or in combination with marital difficulties.

The vignettes below will serve to illustrate the range of problems brought to us. These brief descriptions were prepared by the caseworker shortly after the beginning of service (Caseworker's Diagnostic Schedule). They were to be rough-and-ready statements of the heart of the problem for which the caseworker felt service was needed. The final problem classification given each case follows each description, although the descriptions themselves were not used as a basis for problem classification.

Long-standing marital problem in middle-aged couple exacerbated by wife's anxiety over her heart condition and impending loss of eldest son who plans to leave home to attend college. (primarily marital)

Husband and wife involved in a sado-masochistic marriage. She struggles to continue a very close relationship with her mother; as a result he feels inadequate and secondary, and abuses her physically; he fears she may be trying to poison him through witchcraft. (primarily marital)

An eight-year old boy who is a behavior problem at home and school; mother becoming increasingly frustrated over how to control him; father, a salesman, away a good deal, ineffectual when at home (primarily child-related)

Both children emotionally disturbed and presenting problems in school; inadequate care by parents, both of whom drink excessively. (primarily child-related)

Over-protective parents with a need to infantilize their adolescent son; their depression over his immaturity and dependency prevent them from meeting each other's needs. (both marital and child-related)

Chronic marital difficulties brought to a head by nine-year old son's disturbed behavior; intense conflicts between them over how boy should be handled; their request for help precipitated by their failure to work out a separation; now want to resolve difficulties. (both marital and child-related).

RECENCY OF ORIGIN OF PROBLEM

The various observers were asked to estimate the recency and nature of origin of the current problem situation presented by the family. Did the family's difficulties develop recently (within the past six months) in previously trouble-free relationships? Was the problem chronic in nature, with little recent change? Or did the problem represent a recent intensification of a long-standing difficulty? Clients, caseworkers, and research observers agreed that most problem situations (about two-thirds of the cases, in the judgment of the research interviewer) fell into the last category.[10] In 23 per cent of the cases the interviewers regarded the family's problems as chronic, with little evidence of recent change; only rarely was a problem situation judged to have been of purely recent origin.

The problems of our families then were problems of long-standing, in most cases recently aggravated. The intensification of the problem doubtless precipitated the decision of these families to seek help. In some cases customary ways of managing problems seemed to have been upset by a specific event, such as the son's leaving home, as in one of the illustrations just given. In other cases problems were aggravated by the spiraling of vicious cycles; for example, in another of the cases mentioned above, the wife's dependence on her mother provoked her husband to "act-out" in ways that could only further intensify the dependence, which in turn caused further acting out on the husband's part, and so on.

10. In general, research interviewers' assessments only will be reported where they are typical of the judgments of other observers and where the nature of the item does not readily permit combining ratings of different observers. The reliability of research interviewer ratings is dealt with in Appendix II, pp. 236–41.

CLIENT'S PERCEPTION OF CAUSE
OF PROBLEM

The research observers generally, and predictably, saw the major cause of the families' problem as lying within the interaction of family members, particularly the spouses. However, the client generally (perhaps also predictably) saw the behavior and attitudes of other family members as the major cause of the problem. Thus only 13 per cent of the husbands and wives thought that their own behavior and attitudes were primarily responsible for the family's problems; 51 per cent of the husbands and wives attributed primary responsibility to their spouses; 28 per cent saw the behavior and attitudes of their children as the major cause. The remaining clients (7 per cent) thought their difficulties resulted largely from factors outside the home, such as current social or economic conditions. Still, clients did show some acknowledgement of their role in the problem. Forty-nine per cent indicated that their own behavior and attitudes constituted at least one cause of the difficulty.

It was not surprising that clients with problems in family relations tended to see other family members as primarily responsible for them. This kind of "cross-blaming" is well-known to clinicians. The defensive posture assumed by most of our clients must be taken into account, however, in assessing such client characteristics as motivation for help. That the clients agreed to accept an offer of service is in itself testimony to their motivation to find solutions for their problems. But since our clients usually thought the behavior and attitudes of some other family members were the major cause of the problem, it is likely that they also saw the other members as primarily responsible for the solution. Thus the clients' motivation in seeking help may have largely been in the direction of getting other family members to change.

When we think of the "motivated client" we are apt to think of a client who will make good use of service. But we need to ask "motivated for *what*?" If the client's push in treatment is to get another family member to change, his own use of treatment may be limited. The effectiveness of casework depends in large measure on the willingness of the client to modify his own functioning. A family whose members see change in one another as the way forward presents a formidable challenge to the clinician.

THE CLIENTS' REACTION TO THE PROBLEM

Various dimensions of the clients' reactions to the family's problem situation were rated by the research observers (research interviewers and review judges).[11] The findings of principal interest concerned differences in the reactions of husbands and wives.

Although both husbands and wives were rated as reacting to the problem with noticeable discomfort, the wives were seen as experiencing greater discomfort than their husbands. Thus 66 per cent of the wives were judged to be reacting with "severe" discomfort, as opposed to 35 per cent of the husbands. By contrast only 3 per cent of the wives were rated as experiencing "mild" discomfort, as opposed to 19 per cent of the husbands. To put it another way, the wife's discomfort exceeded her husband's in 51 per cent of the 120 cases, whereas the reverse was true for only 5 per cent of the cases.[12] Wives and husbands also differed in their handling of the discomfort, according to

11. Here and elsewhere "research observers' ratings" will refer to the means of the research interviewer and review judge ratings.

12. This difference was statistically significant $p < .01$ (Sign Test). That is, we can be reasonably certain the difference was not the result of chance variation. For a fuller explanation of the concept of statistical significance as used in this study, see Appendix II, pp. 249–50.

both the research interviewers and review judges. Husbands were more likely to be seen as running away from the problem (35 per cent) than wives (10 per cent) although wives were judged to be more likely to rebel or lash out at people or circumstances (38 per cent) than husbands (23 per cent). Wives (49 per cent) more often than husbands (39 per cent) were judged to be attempting to cope with the problem (other than by seeking professional help).[13] Finally, wives were rated by the research observers as having a greater intensity of desire to resolve the problem. In 58 per cent of the cases the intensity of the wife's desire for problem resolution was rated higher than her husband's; in only 24 per cent was the husband's rating higher than his wife's in this respect.

In sum, wives were judged to be in greater distress, less inclined to retreat from the problem, and more anxious to resolve it. These findings accord with the generally held notion that wives are usually more concerned with problems of the family and more affected by them, than their husbands.

Wives were also rated as showing greater potential than their husbands for using casework service. When members of individual couples were compared, wives were about twice as likely as their husbands to receive a more positive rating in respect to willingness to consider one's own role in the problem, motivation to use caseworker help, and feeling toward the caseworker.[14] Wives appeared then not only to have a greater investment in the problem but also in casework as a means of solving it. These

13. Per cents are based on judgments of the research interviewers only. The differences between husbands and wives are statistically significant $p < .05$, (Chi square, 1 d.f.). The remaining category "client immobilized" which accounted for only 3 per cent of husbands and wives, was not included in the analysis.

14. Wife-husband differences $p < .01$ or .05, depending on the item (Sign Test).

differences should not be interpreted to mean that husbands were rated low on any of these variables. In fact ratings for most husbands and wives tended to fall in the middle range of scales to assess willingness to consider their own roles and their motivation to use casework, and toward the positive end of the scale that measured feeling toward the caseworker. It was just that, when differences in ratings occurred, it was the wife's rating that tended to be higher.

FAMILY AND INDIVIDUAL FUNCTIONING

A vast amount of data was collected on various aspects of family and individual functioning. These data proved useful in comparison of specific groups, as in tests to determine if clients assigned to different service patterns were comparable in these characteristics. They are not of great value, however, in describing the characteristics of the sample as a whole. The reason lies in the highly relative nature of most of the data. For example, the quality or level of functioning of families and individuals was rated by the research observers on 11-point scales. For the most part these ratings were concentrated in the middle of the scale (the "fair" range), a fairly typical result when such scales are used; very few families or individuals were rated either "very poor" or "very good" on any aspect of functioning. The fact that all families were seeking help for problems in these areas of functioning constrained research observers from rating functioning at a high level, and the fact that all families were intact, operating units with members generally free of gross psychopathology limited the frequency of low ratings. Although research observers were to base their judgments on "societal norms," these norms were not articulated with enough precision to permit meaningful description of "good" or "poor" functioning in any area. Moreover, in practice the research observers tended to anchor their ratings in the actual norms of the sample. Thus a marriage rated as "good" in quality would probably have more positive features than a marriage rated as "fair," but we would be hard put to say just what these features might be or to justify the ratings of "good" or "fair" in any absolute sense.

An attempt to classify clients according to clinical diagnostic categories did not prove sufficiently reliable to warrant detailed analysis of the results. Suffice it to say that the great majority of clients were classified as "deviating in the direction of character disorder," and most of the others as "deviating in the direction of neurosis." Few clients were judged to be "deviating in the direction of psychosis"; in fact in only five cases did the research observers agree that a husband or wife had psychotic tendencies.

THE LIMITS OF THE SAMPLE

The characteristics of the project clientele obviously limit the relevance of the experiment. Most notable in their absence are poverty-level, "hard-to-reach," and broken families. Still, the study sample seems somewhat representative of a fairly large group of clients who receive ongoing service at family agencies and similar facilities. Although the families ultimately served in the project represented a highly selected sample of a much larger group, so too does any group of clients who go through customary application and intake processes to the point of participation in ongoing service.

Because of their motivation for service, their youthfulness, better-than-average level of education, and lack of gross psychopathology, these families constitute a group of potentially "good continued treatment cases" by the standards of most practitioners. In fact, our clients were rather enviously regarded by non-project agency caseworkers as representing the "cream of the crop." Despite its limitations this kind of sample has at least one advantage. In some ways it offers an ideal testing ground for certain hypotheses about casework practice. For example, if extended treatment aimed at modifying patterns of behavior through insight-oriented techniques constitutes an especially effective mode of casework, as has been widely thought, then its effectiveness should be demonstrable in treatment of a group of clients such as those in the project, who appear particularly well suited for it. If such a treatment approach does not prove to be clearly more effective with this group, then its usefulness with less suitable groups can be seriously challenged. Similarly if PSTS works well with families who are usually considered prime candidates for "standard," that is open-ended treatment, then our conception of what should constitute standard treatment may need some more thinking.

COMPARABILITY OF CLIENT GROUPS

The random assignment of clients yielded essentially similar groups of families and individuals across the various prescriptions. Whatever differences occurred were within the limits one might expect from sampling variation and showed no particular pattern.[15] The groups of major interest, those assigned to planned short-term service (PSTS) and continued service (CS), were comparable in respect to all measurements.[16] Thus it was assumed that differences in outcome among service patterns, and in particular, outcome differences between PSTS and CS, could not be attributed to differences in the initial characteristics of clients assigned to these patterns.

15. Analysis of variance tests on ratings of clients assigned to the eight prescriptions showed no systematic differences at the .05 level of confidence. Chi-square tests between major patterns for nominal items likewise revealed no pattern of statistically significant differences.
16. See Appendix I, Table I, p. 219.

FOUR · CHARACTERISTICS OF
THE SERVICE PATTERNS

ANALYSIS OF SERVICE characteristics was undertaken for two reasons. First, any test of the results of different services must take into account the characteristics of those services, not as they appeared on paper but as they worked out in practice. It does little good to state that treatment x had better results than treatment y, if we cannot say of what the treatments consisted. Second, a specification of the characteristics of the various service approaches has value in itself, regardless of outcomes. Information about distinctive features of the service patterns or about features common to all the patterns may contribute to general knowledge of the characteristics of casework.

Primary attention in this analysis will be given to the characteristics of PSTS and CS, since most findings of interest pertain to these patterns. Because PSTS was the innovative service, a particular effort will be made to delineate its special features.

INITIAL STRUCTURING OF THE DURATION
OF SERVICE

In CS cases, consideration of the duration of service was customarily not introduced by the caseworker at the outset. Caseworkers usually conveyed the impression that service would continue as long as the family was in need of it. The eighteen-month cut-off was too far in the future to be presented as a

55

limit, and the chances were that the majority of CS cases would close of their own accord before this point had been reached. In most cases the question of termination was first raised by the client, at a point when he began to think of quitting or had decided to quit. In this respect, as in most others, CS was carried out along conventional lines, with the caseworkers following practices generally accepted in the conduct of open-ended interpersonal treatment.

In PSTS, on the other hand, the caseworker necessarily had to face the client with the limits of service at the beginning. This was normally done in the first interview after intake. Caseworkers generally informed their clients that treatment would consist of eight interviews within a three-month period. The family was not led to believe that its problems would be solved within this period but was given the impression that meaningful changes for the better could be achieved. The end of service was presented as the beginning of an opportunity for family members to try out possible solutions developed during treatment.

Regardless of the actual length of treatment in PSTS and CS, the two services were begun and carried out under quite different sets of expectations about the duration of service. These differing expectations may well have led to quite different orientations on the part of the caseworker and the client toward the problems at issue, toward treatment, and toward each other. Unfortunately, we lack systematic data to test out such possibilities, although various kinds of evidence presented suggest ways in which both the conduct and the outcomes of service may have been affected by differing expectations of their duration.

NUMBER OF INTERVIEWS AND
DURATION OF SERVICE

The number of service interviews[1] with clients was to be one of the major points of difference between PSTS and CS. PSTS was to be limited to eight in-person interviews per family. The number of interviews in CS was to be limited only by the requirement that no case in this pattern remain open longer than eighteen months. While there was no lower limit on the number of interviews for either pattern, it was expected that most families in PSTS would receive close to the maximum of eight interviews and that most CS families would receive considerably more than this number. Table 4.1 presents data on the number of interviews actually conducted with families during the service period.

The two services were well differentiated in respect to the number of interviews received by families. About two-thirds of the PSTS families (41) were given exactly eight interviews; only three families exceeded the maximum and then by only one interview. A majority of CS families (38 or 63 per cent) received at least ten interviews, or more than the maximum received by any PSTS family. About a third of the CS families received more than 30 interviews. The median number of interviews for CS families (19) was over twice the median for PSTS families (8).[2] The gap between PSTS and CS in mean

1. Service interviews, or hereafter simply "interviews," will refer to in-person interviews with the client occurring after assignment to a service pattern. Intake interviews, conducted prior to assignment (usually two to three per case), are not included in subsequent tabulations, nor are interviews with collaterals.

2. The median length of service for CS cases was eight months; 22 per cent remained in treatment a year or longer. The median duration of PSTS cases was three months. Clients were customarily seen at weekly intervals.

Table 4.1. Families by number of interviews received, PSTS and CS

Interviews per family	Number of families	
	PSTS	CS
1 only	1	7
2-3	7	3
4-5	2	4
6-7	6	4
8-9	44	4
10-29		17
30-49		9
50-69		8
70 or more*		4
Total	60	60
Median number of interviews	8.0	19.0
Mean number of interviews	7.0	26.0
Total number of interviews	422	1562

* The maximum number of interviews received by any CS case was 100.

number of interviews per family is even greater since the mean for CS cases was elevated by cases receiving a large number of interviews.

Another way of viewing the input differences in PSTS and CS is to consider the total number of interviews expended for each pattern. As may be seen, almost four times as many interviews took place in CS (1562) as in PSTS (422). This difference becomes important when the costs of the two services are taken into account. It is in no way diminished by the fact that a small number of CS cases contributed a highly disproportionate share of the interviews in that pattern. One of the cost risks of CS is that a very large number of interviews may be expended on a very few cases. Although no attempt was made in this study to determine precise interview costs, it is quite apparent that whatever the unit costs were, CS was by far the more expensive of the two services.

An interesting difference between PSTS and CS emerged in relation to families who dropped out of treatment after the first interview. Only one PSTS family failed to return for a second interview, whereas 7 CS families failed to do so. Although the numbers are too small to be decisive, the difference suggests that presentation to clients of a plan for limited service, as was done in the first interview in PSTS, may have provided an inducement for them to return that was not offered in CS.[3]

In general, it is difficult to compare the two patterns in respect to discontinuance, that is, premature withdrawal from treatment. Four interviews in PSTS represent half the projected course of treatment, whereas this number is usually seen as the beginning of CS. On the other hand, CS was defined as an open-ended, rather than as an extended service, with no requirement that a CS case be carried for any specified number of interviews. Thus, theoretically, a CS case could be successfully completed within the span of interviews allotted to PSTS.

It was expected, however, that the caseworkers would perceive few CS cases terminating within the PSTS service span as having received sufficient treatment. This proved to be the case. In fact, in not one of the 22 CS cases that terminated with less than ten interviews did the caseworkers at closing give "need met" as the reason for termination. (By contrast this reason was given in 14 of the 38 CS cases that received more than this number of interviews.) The great majority of these 22 cases were closed "not according to plan," that is the clients withdrew

3. Similarly, the Parads found that clients receiving short-term treatment were more likely to return if informed of the limits of service than if not. Libbie G. Parad and Howard J. Parad, "A Study of Crisis-Oriented Planned Short-Term Treatment, Part II," *Social Casework,* XLIX (July 1968), 424.

despite the caseworker's plan for further treatment. Of the 5 cases in this group that were closed "according to plan," in all but one, the reason for termination given by the caseworker was "inability to use casework services." Thus there was little doubt that the caseworkers expected CS to provide more extensive service than PSTS; CS cases of "PSTS length" were viewed either as closing prematurely or as treatment failures.

These observations also remind us of the well-known gap in CS between the amount of service practitioners feel is indicated and the amount clients are willing to accept. The select nature of the project cases, however, adds a certain emphasis. With a group of families meeting all the usual criteria for "good" long-term treatment cases, continued service still proved to be a service with a highly variable duration.

The duration of CS was affected in some measure by project requirements. Five cases had to be closed because of the 18-month limit. The closing of an additional 4 cases at the end of one year's service was necessary in order to avoid undue delay in completing the service phase of the project. Each of these cases, however, had received considerably more service than any PSTS case in the project.

Finally, there is some evidence to suggest that the duration of service was affected differently in PSTS and CS by the type of problem for which the family sought help. In CS, 9 families with primarily marital problems terminated service prior to the fifth interview, whereas only one family with primarily parent-child problems did so. In PSTS the opposite tendency occurred: only 2 families with primarily marital problems dropped out prior to the fifth interview as opposed to 5 with primarily parent-child problems. While the significance of these opposing tendencies is limited by the small number of cases, one obvious consequence was to create a somewhat different distribution of problems in surviving CS cases than in surviving PSTS cases.

Let us now turn to the number of interviews with individual clients in PSTS and CS. For this purpose, each time the client was seen was counted as an interview with that client. Thus a joint interview with husband and wife was counted as one interview for the husband and one for the wife. The findings of principal interest concern the differences between husbands and wives in the number of interviews within PSTS and CS. Overall, husbands had fewer interviews than wives, a finding in accord with the well-documented tendency for women to be the principal recipients of service in family agencies.[4] Thus, the median number of interviews for wives in CS cases was 12, for husbands, 6.5; in PSTS cases wives had a median of 5 interviews, husbands 3.5.

As may be surmised from the above, interviews were more evenly divided between husbands and wives in PSTS than in CS. In 35 PSTS cases but only 15 CS cases husbands and wives were not more than one interview apart in the total each received. This difference seemed due in part to the greater use of joint interviews in PSTS (see page 95) and in part to the greater ease in balancing input between husbands and wives in a brief, planned series of interviews. Obviously the longer service extends, the greater the likelihood of one partner's dropping out or behind. In the longer CS cases wives tended to remain as clients, while their husbands either left treatment altogether or were seen less frequently. Thus, there were 12 CS cases in which wives received at least ten more interviews than their husbands, but only one CS case in which a husband received as many as ten more interviews than his wife.

The tendency of husbands to fade out of CS cases after a certain point resulted in a relatively narrow spread between the median number of interviews received by PSTS and CS hus-

4. Dorothy Fahs Beck, *Patterns in Use of Family Agency Service*, p. 6, and Ripple, *Motivation, Capacity, and Opportunity*, p. 70.

bands (3.5 as opposed to 6.5). In fact, just about half the CS husbands (29) had no more than four interviews.

Interviews with children were used sparingly in the project, and in no project case was a child the principal interviewee. Children, if interviewed at all, were usually seen in individual sessions, but in some instances they were seen with one or both parents. Interviews were more likely to be conducted with children in CS than in PSTS cases. Thus, in only 11 PSTS cases were children interviewed, and in none of these cases were there more than four interviews involving a child. Children were seen in 23 CS cases, and in about half these cases a child was involved in at least five interviews.

The greater use of interviews with children in CS is easily explained. Because of the limit on the number of interviews in PSTS, it was usually decided to concentrate on the parents. Also, the better implementation in PSTS of the joint-interview prescription resulted in fewer direct interviews with children, since by design the joint interviews were to be conducted with husband and wife. There may be some question as to why interviews with children were not used even more in CS. The reason seems to lie as much in the orientation of the caseworkers and the agency, as in the project requirements. Treatment of child-related problems at Community Service Society was generally conducted through work with the parents, a fairly typical approach in the family agency field at the time of the study.

TREATMENT STRATEGY IN PSTS

Within the limits of pattern requirements, caseworkers were free to conduct treatment pretty much as they saw fit. An attempt was made, however, to develop some guidelines for treatment in PSTS. Because treatment of complex family problems in a brief, limited period of time was a new experience for most of our practitioners, they felt the need of some general formulations of treatment strategy. Moreover, because of its brevity and limits, PSTS, in particular, lent itself to the development of such formulations. That is, it is much easier to generate some general notions about how treatment can be carried out, if treatment is limited in advance to eight interviews, than if it is to be of lengthy and variable duration. Accordingly certain common treatment strategies for PSTS were worked out with the caseworkers through individual and group conferences. It seems appropriate to discuss these guidelines in relation to characteristics of service, since they doubtless shaped the nature of service within PSTS.

Perhaps the essential feature of PSTS treatment strategy was the attempt of the caseworkers to restrict the focus of treatment, if possible, to a key aspect of the problem for which help was being sought. With time at a premium, it seemed sounder to work intensively on a limited area than to attempt to relate to all facets of the family's problems. It was assumed that the problems given primary attention would be representative of the larger problems of the family. If the key area to be dealt with could provide a fulcrum, treatment then might be able to serve as a lever to promote changes in the family's problems as a whole.

The treatment focus was to be shaped through collaboration with the client, leading hopefully to the development of shared, explicit treatment objectives. Presumably these objectives would center on alleviation of the presenting problem and its precipitating causes, though what aspects of the problem or its causes were to be dealt with would depend on the caseworker's diagnostic assessment and the client's motivation and capacity. To the extent possible the focus agreed upon was to be adhered to. Caseworkers were encouraged to be open and direct, particularly in expressing expectation for change, and to risk communication in emotionally charged areas. Toward the end of service there was to be a recapitulation of the client's treatment experience, including a review of the understanding gained, and an assessment of the extent to which the initially established goals had been realized. Finally, attention was to be given to ways in which the family could continue to work on its problems following termination of contact.

We cannot be at all sure how well the actual conduct of treatment in PSTS followed this general plan. Abstract directives, such as those outlined, are likely to be implemented in a wide variety of forms.

Our most comprehensive picture of how treatment was carried out was provided by the caseworker's own recording. Although the records were not systematically analyzed for reasons given earlier and although they provided, at best, the caseworker's *perception* of treatment, they were examined for whatever insights they might afford. A review of the caseworker's closing summaries did yield the impression that some effort was made to organize short-term treatment around some particular aspect of the family's problems, the heart of the treatment strategy envisioned for PSTS. In fact most PSTS closing summaries contained expressions of such focal treatment themes. Some examples, drawn from the summaries of seven of the eight project caseworkers, are presented below:

The oedipal struggle which was being fostered by Mr. C. and which Mrs. C. was unable to understand or deal with initially, was the focus of casework activity. This was handled with Mr. C., by direct interpretation of the struggle going on between him and his daughter, which he was able to carry further by defining in his own words that he was treating Nancy as an adult rather than a child.

The problem in toilet training Robert was a primary focus in treatment, although this was certainly not representative of the larger problems which can be seen in both Mr. and Mrs. R. individually and as a couple.

An effort was made to engage Mr. D. around marital counseling but he did not accept this. Casework activity was then directed at helping Mrs. D. with her wish to evaluate the status of her marriage, the question of separation, her investment in the relationship with husband, and her need for help to try to cope with the problems attendant to husband's deterioration which was seen primarily in his spotty working.

Casework was directed toward enabling Mrs. F. to make some shift from her rigid withholding from her husband and children.

Casework activity was directed toward looking at what in Mr. and Mrs. A's handling had contributed to Harold's problems and what they needed to do differently.

I attempted to help Mrs. Y. alter her expectations of her husband in respect to his job planning and to help her to be more accepting of her own need for achievement.

Casework activity was directed towards helping Mrs. F. to accept her need to be dependent on her husband and her right to be dependent on him.

Emphasis was placed primarily on helping Mr. R. to return to gainful employment as soon as possible under the circumstances, as well as supporting his masculine image at home. Work with Mrs. R. centered around helping her accept her husband's limitations.

Emphasis was placed on helping Mr. and Mrs. E. relate more effectively with one another. Mrs. E. was helped to express her complaints more directly to her husband and to see what it is that she is doing to push him away. Mr. E. was encouraged to see the situation more realistically and to take a more active part in family affairs.

These excerpts from the closing summaries illustrate the kind of treatment foci that seemed to be characteristic of PSTS. As can be seen, the scope of the caseworkers' interventions was not always narrowly defined or representative of larger family problems. Nevertheless it seemed specific enough in most cases to permit one to obtain a ready grasp of the main concerns of treatment.

It was assumed that treatment in CS cases, particularly the longer ones, was addressed to a wider range of client problems or to major problems more or less in their entirety rather than to aspects of them. Although this point may seem self-evident, there is still need to know just how CS differed from PSTS in this respect. Again we must settle for the clues provided by an impressionistic review of the caseworkers' closing summaries.

In general, there were relatively few CS summaries in which the focus of treatment was expressed in capsule form, as in the PSTS cases. Such brief descriptions were more likely to occur in cases with few interviews. When an attempt was made in the long-term cases to wrap up the major concerns of treatment in a sentence or two, the result was often a statement at a fairly high level of generality, for example:

Casework activity was directed toward problem areas in the parent-child relationships, in the marital relationship, and in the individual personality functioning of both Mr. and Mrs. Y.

Usually in the longer cases the scope of casework intervention was described as it evolved or shifted over the life of the case. For example:

In the early part of casework contact we worked to improve communication between the marital partners. . . . After their separation casework was directed towards clarifying their expectations of the marriage. . . .

On the whole a focusing of treatment on a central aspect of the family's problem seemed to be a distinctive practice of PSTS. Given the lack of systematic objective data we cannot be either certain or precise about this point, nor can we say how often features of treatment strategy projected for PSTS were carried out. Data to be presented on the caseworkers' goals and techniques will hopefully shed further light on these matters.

THE CASEWORKER'S GOALS

Shortly after assignment of a case to a service pattern, caseworkers were asked to write out statements of their actual and hypothetical goals (Caseworker's Diagnostic Schedule). The hypothetical goals were those the caseworker would have attempted to achieve had she been free of pattern requirements. Although the caseworker's actual goals do not in themselves constitute a characteristic of service, they suggest the path she followed in treatment. Since these goals were formulated after treatment had begun, there was strong reason to suppose that they would reflect the actual direction of service. Goals were not recorded for cases dropping out of treatment prior to the third interview in PSTS or the fifth interview in CS. As families with marital problems tended to drop out in the early phase of CS and families with parent-child problems were more likely to be early terminators in PSTS, it was not surprising that the caseworkers' goals were more often concerned with alleviation of marital problems in PSTS than in CS cases (62 per cent versus 49 per cent) or that in a higher proportion of CS than PSTS cases (49 per cent versus 38 per cent) the caseworkers' goals related to alleviation of difficulties in parent-child problems.[5] In effect, the caseworkers' goals in the continuing PSTS caseload tended to be skewed somewhat toward marital problems and in the continuing CS caseload somewhat toward parent-child problems.

It had been expected that the caseworker's goals in PSTS

5. Goals in each case were coded according to the type of problem toward which directed.

would be less general and more circumscribed than in CS, that her objectives would necessarily be more limited, given the shorter span of service. As noted, caseworkers were encouraged to concentrate in PSTS on some particular family problem or some segment of a problem. To test this hypothesis of greater specificity of goal in PSTS, the degree of specificity of each goal was rated on a 5-point scale. Rated as general (scale points 1 and 2) were such goals as "to facilitate deeper satisfactions in all family relationships," or "to increase wife's image of self as woman." Goals judged to be "mid-range" in specificity usually turned out to contain both general and specific elements, such as "to gratify the client's narcissistic needs so she can separate from her son." At the specific end of the scale (points 4 and 5) were more highly structured and limited goals, such as "to relieve guilt over having had a defective daughter" (specific), or "to help family move to more adequate quarters" (very specific). Goals for each case were rated independently by two judges operating in ignorance of the pattern for the case. Disagreements were reconciled through the conference method. If a case had multiple goals, each goal was rated separately and the ratings averaged.

On the whole, the caseworker's goals were more specific in PSTS.[6] The difference between the two services was greatest in respect to cases in which goals were defined as general (23 per cent in PSTS, 41 per cent in CS). Differences were not marked in respect to cases in which goals were defined as specific (28 per cent in PSTS as opposed to 21 per cent in CS). Very few goals in either pattern were rated as very specific. It is not known whether these distributions were affected by missing cases or by differences between PSTS and CS in the timing of goal formulations. In both services goals tended to be fairly broad in

6. The differences were statistically significant, $p < .05$, Mann-Whitney U.

definition. Assignment to PSTS seemed to place a kind of ceiling on the generality of the caseworker's goals. It did not appear, however, to produce any strong tendency for goals to be cast in specific or very specific terms.

Further insight into PSTS-CS differences in the caseworkers' treatment goals was gleaned from their statement of hypothetical goals. In brief, hypothetical goals were stated in a higher proportion of PSTS cases (61 per cent) than CS cases (33 per cent).[7] It seemed as if caseworkers in PSTS had goals they felt could not be attained, presumably because of the limited nature of the service. Hence, they were likely to take advantage of the opportunity to say what they would try to do if they could proceed as they wished. Apparently caseworkers felt they could accomplish more in the less restricted CS, since they less often formulated hypothetical goals.

THE CASEWORKER'S INTERVENTIONS

The caseworker's interventions or techniques, terms that we use interchangeably, consisted of specific efforts to help clients resolve their problems and improve their functioning. Since treatment in the project was almost exclusively interpersonal, these efforts can be defined as various kinds of caseworker-to-client communication in face-to-face interviews.

Although caseworkers were not required to use different types of interventions in PSTS as opposed to CS, it was expected that the contrasting structures of the two services would lend themselves to somewhat different types of treatment approaches. The caseworker's interventions in PSTS and CS were classified according to a treatment classification system derived from the system developed by the Community Service Society.[8] To trans-

7. PSTS-CS differences $p < .05$, Chi Square, 1 d.f.
8. *Method and Process in Social Casework*, pp. 20-21.

late this rather broad system into a form suitable for a "fine-grained" analysis of casework techniques, it was necessary to omit certain categories, add others, and to redefine the rest in more specific terms. The categories in the resulting scheme for classifying *the caseworker's interventions in verbal communication with the client* are presented in condensed form and illustrated below.[9]

1. *Exploration concerning the client's milieu and his relation to it*

   Inquiries about external circumstances, characteristics of others, interactions with others, et cetera.

   "How does your husband react to your anger?"

2. *Exploration concerning the client's own behavior*

   Inquiries about the client's own feeling states, personality characteristics, patterns of functioning, childhood, et cetera.

   "How do you really feel about the marriage?"

3. *Structuring the treatment relationship or communication within it*

   Explanation of treatment, explicit suggestions of topics for discussion, consideration of fees, et cetera.

   "I think it best if I could work with both you and your husband."

   "Let's go back to the point you made about John."

4. *Reassurance*

   Overt expressions of understanding, sympathy, concern, general encouragement, and appreciation of the client's abilities or qualities.

   "Your anger is quite understandable."

9. These categories were more fully explained in an 18-page manual of definitions and coding instructions. The specification of these categories was influenced by the work of Florence Hollis. See Florence Hollis, "Explorations in the Development of a Typology of Casework Treatment," *Social Casework*, XLVIII (June 1967), 338-39. The authors' debt is acknowledged.

5. *Advice*

Recommendations designed to influence the client's decisions and behavior in specific directions.

"Perhaps you need to talk these plans over with your husband."

6. *Logical discussion*

A. Formulations designed to enhance the client's understanding of his situation and other persons.

"Do you thing this might be his way of expressing affection?"

B. Formulations designed to enhance the client's understanding of logical connections between his recognized or hypothetical behavior and the behavior of others or situational events.

"It seems when you get angry at Johnny he turns to his father for support."

7. *Identifying specific reactions*

Formulations designed to help the client become aware of the nature or meaning of specific incidents in his behavior or feelings.

"Do you think you might have over-reacted here?"

8. *Confrontation*

Formulations designed to help the client become aware of the nature or meaning of patterns of response in his behavior, attitudes, or feelings in respect to:

A. His functioning in the treatment situation

"Whenever I bring this subject up in the interview, you seem to get anxious."

B. His functioning in family roles

"Aren't you provoking your husband with this behavior?"

C. His functioning in other roles or situations

"Perhaps you are too perfectionistic about your work."

D. His personality functioning in general

"Isn't this another example of your tendency to get involved with people who hurt you?"

9. *Clarifying current intrapsychic causation*

Formulations designed to enhance the client's understanding of the current intrapsychic causes of his patterns of response. Subcategories A-D, as in Confrontation.

"Perhaps you provoke your husband because you feel it's better to quarrel than not communicate at all." (B)

10. *Clarifying developmental causation*

Formulations designed to enhance the client's understanding of developmental origins of patterns of response.

"The fact that your mother never appreciated you when you were a child makes you particularly sensitive to your wife's lack of appreciation."

This revised system rests on certain assumptions. The "exploration" and "structuring" techniques (categories 1 through 3) are viewed as laying the groundwork for techniques more directly concerned with changing the client's functioning. In exploration, the caseworker simultaneously obtains information to increase his own understanding of the client's problems and implicitly directs communication into presumably productive channels. In structuring the treatment relationship, the caseworker's objective is to create an optimal medium for work on the client's problems. Although use of these techniques may lead to change in the client's functioning (for example, exploration in itself may help clarify the client's thoughts and feelings), in neither technique does the caseworker convey specific information or feedback about the kind of change intended.

In the remaining techniques, however, the caseworker conveys a message designed to affect the client's perceptions, attitudes, feelings, or behavior, as these may operate in his life situation. These messages may convey the caseworker's advice or reassurance (categories 4. and 5.) or they may consist of the caseworker's formulations, that is, his hypotheses or evaluations, concerning the client's milieu, his behavior, or their interrelation (categories 6. through 10.). Such messages may be presented explicitly, as in explanations or interpretations of the behavior of the client or others. They may also be conveyed implicitly in the form of leading or challenging questions, for example, in questions containing hypotheses ("Aren't you really saying that you can't stand him?").

This classification scheme was used to analyze differences between PSTS and CS in caseworker intervention. Thirty cases, 15 each from PSTS and CS, were drawn from a large number that had been randomly selected for taping.[10] Cases with fewer than three interviews with a given client were not selected. Only individual interviews were chosen, in part because of the paucity of joint interviews in CS and in part because of difficulties in applying the classification system to worker intervention in this type of interview. Each project caseworker was represented by at least one case in each pattern.[11]

From each case the first four individual interviews with the client receiving the most service were selected for analysis. In most PSTS cases this set of interviews constituted the whole of direct service for the chosen client. For most CS cases these interviews constituted only the initial phase of treatment. In all, 121 interviews were analyzed.

Four of the agency's field work instructors, all experienced caseworkers themselves, served as interview analysts. Two

10. The PSTS and CS subsamples each contained 8 modifying and 7 supportive cases.
11. Two caseworkers were not included because of a lack of a sufficient number of usable tapes.

analysts listened independently to each taped interview, and placed each caseworker response into one of the categories of the classification scheme presented above. A caseworker response was defined as everything the caseworker said between two distinct client communications. As most caseworker responses were brief, usually a single question or comment, most could be classified into one of the several categories without undue difficulty. In the case of long or complex responses, which sometimes incorporated elements of several techniques, analysts were asked to record the dominant technique in the response. Profiles for each interview were determined by computing the frequencies of responses in the various categories. The double judging produced two profiles for each interview, which were combined by averaging the frequencies. Thus, if one judge classified 4 responses in a particular interview as advice and the second judge listening to the same interview classified 6 responses in that category, the final profile for that interview would show an average of five uses of advice. To facilitate comparison of interviews, the average frequencies of use of various techniques were then converted into percentages of total responses. Since the average number of caseworker responses per interview was 104, the percentage for any technique is roughly equivalent to the average number of times that technique occurred per interview.[12]

To investigate differences in intervention between PSTS and CS cases we used a method of analysis that took into account the caseworker and the location of the interview in the sequence of service. Thus caseworker A's average use of exploration in her first service interviews in short-term cases was compared with her average use of that technique in first service interviews in continued service cases, and so on, for each worker and tech-

12. These percentages were treated as scores in further analyses— that is, mean percentages across interviews were unweighted by the number of responses per interview.

nique through the first four client interviews in each pattern. The comparison was then essentially between short-term service, pretty much in its entirety for the clients sampled, and the beginning interviews in continued service.

Table 4.2 presents the results for one type of intervention, advice. In addition to illustrating the method of analysis used, it demonstrates the importance of the caseworkers' individual styles, a factor that must be kept constantly in mind in any consideration of differences in intervention among prescriptions.

Table 4.2. Mean percentages of responses classified as advice, caseworkers' first four interviews with selected PSTS and CS clients

Interview and prescription	Caseworker						Mean percentage (interviews)
	A	*B*	*C*	*D*	*E*	*F*	
First							
PSTS	6	2	3	11	4	2	5
CS	3	1	0	2	3	1	2
Second							
PSTS	6	6	6	9	2	1	5
CS	13	1	1	4	3	1	4
Third							
PSTS	10	2	1	4	13	3	6
CS	6	1	6	1	8	2	4
Fourth							
PSTS	8	6	9	7	8	3	7
CS	9	4	1	2	2	1	3
Mean percentage (caseworkers)	8	3	3	5	5	2	

It is apparent from Table 4.2 that caseworkers' use of advice increased as they moved from CS to PSTS. Although this pattern can be seen in the differences between the interview means for PSTS and CS, it emerges more clearly when the services are compared caseworker by caseworker. Thus, for the first interview, each caseworker had a higher percentage of advice responses in PSTS than CS. In all, out of 24 comparisons (six caseworkers x four interviews), 19 conform to the pattern of greater use of advice in PSTS.[13]

Differences in caseworker levels in use of advice (caseworker means) must be taken into account. For example, worker E makes generally greater use of advice (mean, 5) than worker F (mean, 2). In fact, on an interview-by-interview comparison, worker E's level for CS clients is usually higher than worker F's for PSTS clients, although both workers make greater use of advice with PSTS than CS clients. We also note that the spread of six points between the highest (worker A) and lowest (worker F) users of advice is greater than any observed between PSTS and CS interview means.[14]

The possible effect of the PSTS prescription on the caseworker's use of advice must be seen then in relation to the levels or styles of individual caseworkers. In general, workers who persistently made less use of advice used it more in work with PSTS than CS clients. The same can be said for workers whose use of advice tended to be characteristically high. If one were to generalize from the findings, one might say that for a given set of caseworkers, advice tends to be used more frequently in PSTS interviews than in beginning CS interviews. To say that clients assigned to PSTS would tend to receive more advice per interview than clients assigned to CS, regardless of the caseworker, would of course be an error. If the PSTS clients in this

13. If each of the 24 comparisons can be assumed to be independent, then PSTS-CS differences are statistically significant (Wilcoxon Sign Ranks Test, $p < .01$).

14. Differences in use of advice among caseworkers was statistically significant; $p < .01$ (Kruskal-Wallis, One Way Analysis of Variance).

project had been seen by workers characteristically low on advice and CS clients by caseworkers characteristically high on advice, the results could well have been reversed.

For this category of intervention, as well as most others, differences in caseworker style were a dominant factor.[15] Granted this, one can still ask how these styles are affected by different modes of service. Having seen that advice giving by our caseworkers systematically differed between CS and PSTS, we may now turn our attention to other types of intervention.

The same method of analysis revealed that caseworkers also made significantly *less* use of exploration, and significantly *greater* use of logical discussion in PSTS interviews than in matched CS interviews.[16] There were no consistent differences in the remaining categories of intervention across the set of four interviews, although caseworkers tended to make somewhat greater use of techniques to enhance the client's self-understanding in the first two PSTS interviews than in the first two CS interviews. Thus, within the limits of their style differences, caseworkers tended in PSTS interviews to make consistently greater use of types of intervention (advice and logical discussion) explicitly directed toward promoting change in the client's perceptions, attitudes, or functioning. They made consistently less use of exploration, an operation whose function is less clear. In the PSTS interviews, then, caseworkers made greater use of *active* interventions, if an active intervention can be thought of as a suggestion or formulation designed to stimulate specific kinds of change.

Of the four interviews, the first differed most between the

15. For a fuller discussion of these differences see William J. Reid, "Characteristics of Casework Intervention," *Welfare in Review,* V (October 1967), 15-18. Certain sections of that paper have been incorporated in the present chapter.
16. $p < .05$, Wilcoxon Signed Ranks Test.

short-term and the continued service patterns. For the first service interviews in CS, 61 per cent of responses on the average were classified as exploration as opposed to 46 per cent for the first interviews in PSTS. By contrast, advice, logical discussion, and confrontation accounted for 42 per cent of responses in the first service interviews in short-term service as opposed to only 28 per cent in the first interviews in continued service.

Finally, the lack of difference between PSTS and CS interviews in respect to one technique, structuring the treatment relationship, merits some comment. The expectation that this technique would receive relatively greater uses in PSTS because of the emphasis placed on structuring treatment in that pattern was not borne out. Approximately 7 per cent of caseworker responses fell into this category in both PSTS and CS interviews. Whatever structural differences there may have been between the two services were apparently not brought about by differential use of structuring techniques. Possibly no more explicit interventions were needed to keep clients focused on specific problems in PSTS than were needed to guide client communications in CS. Also this category of technique included a rather disparate variety of caseworker responses, some of which, such as discussion of fees, might not be expected to vary between the two services.

Thus far casework intervention in PSTS has been compared to the initial phase of treatment in CS. In comparing intervention in PSTS and CS as a whole, at least two problems are encountered. First, the results of such comparisons are difficult to interpret because of differences in the amounts of service given. For example, it has been seen that caseworkers devoted a greater proportion of their interviews in PSTS to advising the client. On the other hand, as there were many more CS than PSTS interviews, the average CS client may have received more advice in the long run, although in a less concentrated dose. The best solution for this problem seemed to be to compare the relative use of intervention in the two services; for example, was advice used in a higher proportion of PSTS than CS interviews? Such comparison sheds light on differences in patterns of intervention between the two services, but not on absolute difference in quantity. The former question is really the more interesting; it can be safely assumed that CS clients on the average received a greater quantity of all types of intervention that did PSTS clients.

Second, it did not prove feasible to carry out detailed content analysis of tape recordings (a very costly procedure) for a comprehensive sample of CS interviews. Therefore, our appraisal of differences in intervention between PSTS and CS involves use of less precise data, for example, the caseworkers' own estimates of their interventions. With these limitations in mind, we shall consider, in summary fashion, evidence from the caseworkers that bears upon the question of general differences in intervention between PSTS and CS.

Following each interview the caseworker completed a check list (the Caseworker's Interview Schedule) on which she estimated the amount of use made of various types of intervention, that is, major use, minor use, or no use. The check list, which included a set of categories of intervention similar to the set used for the content analysis of the tapes presented earlier, was filled out for virtually all PSTS and CS interviews, including joint interviews.

Certain of the results were consistent with those found when PSTS was compared with the initial phase of CS. Major use of interventions of an exploratory type were reported in a significantly higher proportion of CS than PSTS interviews (45 to 39 per cent). Major use of advice, on the other hand, was reported in a significantly higher proportion of PSTS interviews (27 per cent) than CS interviews (21 per cent). However, the greatest difference reported by caseworkers, and it was quite large, not only did not conform with the earlier results, but was completely contrary to theoretical expectations. Insight-oriented interventions (those comparable to confrontation and clarification of intrapsychic and developmental causation) were reported used to a major extent in a significantly higher proportion of PSTS interviews. Thus, major use of clarification of intrapsychic and developmental causation was reported for only 11 per cent of CS interviews but 29 per cent of PSTS interviews. Although it is customarily thought that caseworkers cannot make much use of these techniques until well along in treatment, our caseworkers reported far greater use of these techniques in brief service than in extended service. Even if the caseworkers over-estimated their use of these interventions in PSTS (as subsequent findings show, p. 87), nevertheless, it is of interest that they were more likely to perceive PSTS than CS as the medium for insight-oriented interventions. Thus the caseworkers perceived themselves as making greater use of more active techniques in PSTS (advice, confrontation, and so on) and less use of more passive exploratory operations. These findings support the conclusion from data presented earlier that the caseworkers were generally more active in PSTS than in CS.[17]

The greater caseworker activity in PSTS would seem to be a

17. A related study provided further support for this conclusion. Thirty-three interviews drawn from the last half of eleven arbitrarily selected PSTS cases were compared with sixty interviews drawn from the latter phase of treatment of thirteen CS cases similarly selected. Caseworker interventions from taped segments of these interviews were scaled according to the level of activity they exhibited. Interventions lacking an explicit change goal, such as exploration, were rated low in activity, whereas high ratings were given to interventions, such as advice or interpretations, in which the explicit goal was stimulating change in the client's thinking, feelings or actions. Findings based on content analysis carried out by judges uninformed of service pattern, revealed that caseworkers were significantly more active in the later PSTS interviews than in the later

logical consequence of the brief, time-limited nature of the service. With treatment confined to a small number of interviews, the caseworker was perhaps more inclined to be immediate and direct in her efforts to bring about change. There was no time to carry out the more extensive diagnostic exploration of the client's problem that was at least possible in CS. Nor perhaps was there time to use exploration as an indirect method to stimulate change. As Wolberg has said, "Anathema to short-term therapy is passivity in the therapist. Where time is of no object, the therapist can settle back comfortably and let the patient pick his way through the lush jungles of his psyche."[18] In other words, when time is short you get to the point faster.

That these differences in intervention were particularly marked in the first interview merits some comment. In the initial interview in PSTS the caseworker activity was predominantly change-oriented; in the initial CS interview it was predominantly exploratory. It is possible that these initial differences in approach may have given clients in PSTS and CS somewhat different images of treatment to come. With treatment, as with people, the importance of first impressions cannot be dismissed. The possibility that PSTS clients were more favorably impressed is at least consistent with the fact that only one family in this pattern failed to return for a second interview as opposed to seven CS families.

In an extensive review of the literature on short-term therapy Parad observed: "In general, the treatment techniques used in short-term therapy have been considered substantially the same as those used in long-term therapy but with certain modifications and adaptions. A primary change in technique is the more active

---

CS interviews. The study is reported in full in Ruth Yamner and Judith Jaffe, "The Relations Between Characteristics of the Casework Interview and Changes in the Client's Functioning."

18. Wolberg, *Short Term Psychotherapy,* p. 135.

role of the therapist."[19] The findings of this study essentially support these statements. Most clinicians would agree with Parad's observations, even without the benefit of our results. They would be hard put, however, to define what they might mean by "activity" or to specify how much more active practitioners might be in brief as opposed to extended treatment. The present study makes some contributions in these respects. Since an active intervention was defined in a certain way, it is possible to state in what way caseworkers in PSTS were more active. It also becomes possible to make some beginning judgments about the size of the increase in activity in PSTS, in relation to such factors as caseworker style and the general range of activity within which caseworkers may operate. At this point, however, the question of "How active is active?" in PSTS can perhaps best be approached through consideration of the use of specific techniques. Let us take one of the more active interventions, advice, as an example. One can say that in PSTS caseworkers made greater use of advice. We must keep in mind, however, greater use meant only that an average of 6 per cent of caseworkers' responses were classified as advice in PSTS as opposed to an average of 3 per cent in CS. And we must keep in mind that other techniques, including exploration, were used far more frequently in PSTS than was advice. Although such statements still leave much unsaid, they offer a way toward more accurate specifications of casework intervention.

MODIFYING VERSUS SUPPORTIVE TREATMENT

In cases assigned to the modifying pattern, caseworkers were instructed to stress, as much as possible, interventions to enhance

19. Howard J. Parad, "Time and Crisis: A Survey of 98 Planned Short-Term Treatment Programs," p. 40.

the client's self-understanding (categories 7–10). Techniques 9 and 10, which concerned the development of insight into intrapsychic and developmental causation of the client's behavior, were to be given particular emphasis. In supportive cases, they were to refrain as much as possible from the use of these interventions and to emphasize instead the remaining categories within the system. Several types of evidence were used to determine how well these prescriptions were implemented.

First, caseworker interventions in PSTS supportive and modifying cases were compared as part of the content analysis of interview tapes previously described. As will be shown subsequently, modifying and supportive patterns, according to the caseworker's own estimates, were better differentiated within PSTS than CS. So there was more reason to expect differences in techniques in PSTS interviews than CS interviews.

Six project caseworkers had taped both supportive and modifying PSTS cases. One case per worker was arbitrarily selected from each of these two prescriptions, and the first four interviews with the spouse receiving the most service were analyzed.[20] The patterns of intervention for the modifying and supportive PSTS cases were generally similar. No significant differences were found between modifying and supportive cases for any category of intervention, although there was a slight tendency, on the whole, for modifying techniques to be used more in modifying cases.

The techniques that were to constitute the core of the modifying method (9 and 10) turned out to be used very little. Only 2 per cent of the responses in modifying cases and 1 per cent in supportive cases fell into these categories. Although theoretically these two techniques were to complement each

20. The method of analysis and tests of significance used in comparing intervention between PSTS and CS cases was applied here (see pp. 74–76).

other as steps in effecting modification in the client's behavior, use of one was not strongly associated with use of the other. In fact, greater-than-average use of clarifying intrapsychic causation (technique 9) tended to occur with less-than-average use of clarifying developmental causation (technique 10), and vice versa. In other words, the correlation was in a negative direction.

Confrontation, the most heavily used modifying technique, likewise showed only slightly greater use in modifying cases (11 per cent) than in supportive cases (9 per cent). The greatest difference occurred in respect to exploration concerning the client's own behavior (13 per cent in modifying cases, 8 per cent in supportive cases). Although this difference was not significant and did not apply to a modifying technique as such, it may suggest the prescription of modifying or supportive treatment had its greatest effect, if it had any at all, on the caseworker's use of *exploration* concerning the client's feeling states, personality characteristics, patterns of functioning, and the like. To complicate matters further the caseworkers tended toward greater use of logical discussion, a supportive technique, in modifying cases (29 per cent) than in supportive cases (26 per cent).

Two workers (*B* and *F*), who together carried a third of the project caseload, accounted for most of the modifying and supportive differences that fell in the predicted direction, in these PSTS cases. Their intervention tended to accord to some extent with the prescriptions. The differences for the remaining workers were either negligible or reversed the predicted direction.

In general, techniques to enhance the client's self-understanding (7 through 10) were used to some extent in most cases rather than extensively in some and little in others. These techniques accounted for a total of 16 per cent of caseworker responses in the 12 cases examined. In only 2 cases (one supportive and one modifying) was this figure less than 10 per cent and in only 3 cases (2 modifying and one supportive) did it exceed 20 per cent.

Although a similar comparison of interviews drawn from modifying and supportive cases within CS yielded similar results, the comparison was largely confined to early interviews.[21] Since there were theoretical reasons for expecting greatest use of modifying techniques in extended treatment, after the worker-client relationship had been fairly well established, further testing of modifying-supportive differences within later phases of CS cases seemed warranted.

A related study by Edward Mullen provided the needed test of differences in casework intervention in later interviews in CS modifying and supportive cases.[22] Mullen analyzed casework intervention in 87 interviews drawn from work of six caseworkers with 35 CS clients. Supportive and modifying assignments were represented in about equal numbers. The majority of interviews analyzed occurred well along in treatment beyond the seventh interview. Mullen listened to tapes of each interview and categorized the caseworker's activities in accordance with a treatment classification system developed by Florence Hollis.[23] The Hollis system contains categories analogous to the categories of modifying treatment as defined in our system.

In addition to providing a test of differences in casework intervention between modifying and supportive prescriptions with a sample of later interviews, the Mullen study brought a different method of analysis to bear upon the question of modifying-

---

21. An adequate number of taped interviews in later phases of modifying and supportive cases were not yet available when this aspect of our investigation was conducted, one of the consequences of the slowness of the flow of cases into the project.

22. Edward J. Mullen, "Casework Treatment Procedures as a Function of Client-Diagnostic Variables."

23. See Hollis, *Social Casework*, XLVIII (June 1967), 338-39.

supportive differences. In applying the Hollis sytem, Mullen classified each independent clause uttered by the caseworker. A caseworker's response, as we defined it, usually contained several such clauses. Thus, in our system a lengthy interpretation containing several clauses would receive no more weight than a brief question consisting of a single clause. In the Hollis system the interpretation would receive more weight since each clause within it would be counted. If modifying treatment were characterized by such interpretations, the Hollis system would be more likely to detect modifying-supportive differences.

Mullen found no significant differences in his overall comparison of casework intervention in supportive and modifying CS cases, although he reported slight differences in the predicted direction. There was some evidence that three caseworkers (*A, B, F*) used a type of intervention comparable to clarifying developmental causation more in modifying than supportive interviews, but the amount of use in either pattern was extremely low. (Our findings for two of these caseworkers, *B* and *F*, were in a similar direction.) As in our investigations, Mullen found that style differences among caseworkers were a dominant feature of the treatment process. For our immediate purposes, the main point to be drawn from the Mullen study is the essential lack of differentiation between modifying and supportive treatment within CS.

While the content analysis of the casework interview tapes revealed no consistent or appreciable differences in treatment between modifying and supportive cases, quite a different result was obtained from data supplied by the caseworkers themselves in the schedules completed after each interview.

First, treatment in modifying and supportive cases varied appreciably in expected directions, according to the caseworkers' estimates. Second, differentiation in treatment approach was more marked in PSTS than in CS. Thus in PSTS caseworkers reported major use of key modifying techniques in 42 per cent of the interviews in the modifying prescription, but not at all in interviews in the supportive prescription. In CS, these modifying techniques were reported used to a major extent in 17 per cent of the interviews in the modifying prescription but in only 2 per cent of those in supportive prescription.

Although implementation of the modifying pattern was far from perfect, according to these estimates, they would at least lead one to conclude that modifying and supportive cases received substantially different service inputs. Such a conclusion of course is quite at variance with findings presented up to this point from the content analysis of tapes.

These contradictory results led us to an interview-by-interview comparison between the caseworker's estimates and the judgments of the interview analysts for the 121 taped interviews that the analysts had judged. The results of this comparison provided a fairly cogent explanation of the discrepancy between data obtained from the tapes and data supplied by the caseworkers. Using the presumably more precise and objective judgments of the analysts as a standard, we found the caseworkers tended to "overestimate" use of key modifying techniques in interviews within the modifying prescription and to underestimate use of these techniques in interviews in the supportive prescription.[24] The tendency to underestimate in supportive cases was particularly striking. Thus, in 52 per cent of the interviews occurring within the supportive pattern, the analysts detected some use of core modifying techniques (9. and 10.) but caseworkers reported *no* use of these techniques. In only 3 per cent of these interviews did the opposite occur, that is, analysts not detecting

24. To use the caseworker's estimate as the standard would mean, for example, that the interview analysts, who were unaware of the case prescriptions, systematically under- and over-reported according to prescription, an unlikely hypothesis.

use and caseworkers reporting it. In the remainder there was usually agreement between caseworkers and judges that no modifying techniques were used. It seems likely that our caseworkers, under some pressure to conform to prescription requirements, tended to underestimate use of modifying techniques in interviews in which they were not supposed to be used.[25] It is still possible, however, that the modifying-supportive differences in techniques reported by the caseworkers reflected real differences in treatment approach that did not emerge from the analysis of tapes.

In summary, it appears that differences in casework intervention between the modifying and supportive prescriptions were slight at best. The data suggest that certain caseworkers may have altered certain of their techniques according to those prescriptions and that the caseworkers thought they were doing something special in modifying cases. There was no hard evidence, however, of any consistent differences of any magnitude.

What can be learned from this failure? The first lesson perhaps is that any effort to control what the caseworker does within the treatment hour requires far better specification and monitoring of the operations to be controlled and possibly better training of the caseworker, than we were able to achieve. The original definitions of modifying and supportive treatment that the caseworkers were asked to follow were not sufficiently precise to guide their practice, and efforts to refine the definitions came too late. Caseworkers could not be expected to implement a kind of practice they could not properly define. Relying on the caseworkers' reports as indications of success in implementation proved to be grossly misleading.

25. This pattern of over- and underestimation by the caseworkers was particularly marked in PSTS cases. Other techniques, such as advice and logical discussion, did not seem to be affected. Additional data on agreement between caseworkers and interview analysts are given in Appendix II, p. 244.

Second, lack of differentiation between the prescriptions was due in large part to the infrequent use in modifying cases of the key techniques of modifying treatment, clarifying intrapsychic and developmental causation. These techniques were seldom used, even though the caseworkers were supposed to use them and were treating clients who were certainly better-than-average candidates for this type of treatment. If these techniques were so rarely employed under these conditions, one must question whether they occur very much at all in family casework.

Third, the findings suggest that the division of casework into "modifying" and "supportive" methods artificially splits apart an interlocking set of techniques, notably exploration, logical discussion, and confrontation. These techniques may be better seen as constituting the core of the casework method rather than as representing different methods of casework. A similar conclusion was reached by Florence Hollis on the basis of a study, that, like ours, compared cases supposedly receiving supportive treatment with cases supposedly treated primarily through the method of clarification (similar to modifying treatment).[26] In her study, as in ours, this kind of dichotomy proved of little value in defining the realities of casework practice.

Finally, our conceptions of the caseworker's efforts to help the client develop self-understanding are very poor reflections of the complex and elusive realities of those efforts in practice. We came away with no need to be reminded of the complexity and elusiveness of this aspect of casework practice. Attempts made in this and other studies to specify these operations have not yet succeeded in solving basic problems of measurement. How, for example, does one break up caseworker communication into units for analysis without destroying meaningful Gestalts? Counting different types of insight-oriented responses does not guarantee that general patterns in use of such techniques can be

26. Florence Hollis, *Casework, a Psychosocial Therapy*, p. 67.

identified, and taking certain operations out of their communicative contexts, as was done with "exploration" in our system, may lead to spurious distinctions.

In conclusion, we may have captured enough of the reality of our caseworkers' operations to say with some confidence that treatment in modifying and supportive prescriptions was pretty much the same, but certainly not enough to make any definitive assertions about the nature of insight-oriented treatment.

TWO INTERVENTION PROFILES

Up to now the analysis of casework intervention has been confined to differences between particular service patterns in the use of particular techniques. We now consider some of the general characteristics of casework intervention in the project as a whole, using as a basis a profile of intervention derived from the total sample of 121 interviews analyzed by the field work instructors (Table 4.3). This profile is then compared with a profile of casework intervention (also given in the table) from a related investigation.

The technique by far most frequently used by our caseworkers was exploration. On the whole, 46 per cent of the caseworkers' responses were classified as exploratory (that is, roughly 46 responses per interview on the average). As all interviews in the sample occurred beyond the intake phase, it is apparent that inquiry about the client's milieu and his behavior, especially his milieu, was a major part of the fabric of treatment in these cases.

Turning to the group of techniques more directly concerned with stimulating client change, the "pay-off" techniques, so to speak, we find logical discussion predominant, accounting for 22 per cent of total responses. In fact, of all "messages" explicitly directed at changing the client's perception, attitudes, feelings, or behavior (categories 4. through 10.) logical discussion accounted for nearly half.

Table 4.3. Two profiles of casework intervention

	Per cent of responses	
Response categories	Project caseworkers (121 interviews)	Caseworkers in psychiatric clinics and family agencies* (111 interviews)
Exploration—milieu (1)	34	41
Exploration—client's behavior (2)	12	10
Structuring (3)	7	5
Reassurance (4)	4	5
Advice (5)	4	1
Logical discussion (6)	22	25
Identifying specific reactions (7)	2	2
Confrontation (8)	11	5
Clarifying current intrapsychic causation (9)	1	5
Clarifying developmental causation (10)	2	2
Total	100	100

* Helen Pinkus, "A Study of the Use of Casework Treatment as Related to Select Client and Worker Characteristics."

Confrontation was the next most frequent change-oriented technique (11 per cent of all responses). Of particular interest are the breakdowns which specify what the confrontation was about. Three-fourths of the responses classified as confrontation consisted of caseworker formulations designed to enhance the client's understanding of his own functioning within a particular family role. Less than one in ten of these responses were formulations in which the caseworker called to the client's attention patterns of personality functioning *per se.* The relatively infrequent use of techniques 9. and 10. has already been discussed in relation to the use of modifying treatment.

Finally, some may be puzzled at the low frequency of reassurance (4 per cent). Usually reassuring comments were minor themes of responses whose dominant focus reflected other techniques. Thus a reassuring phrase might be used to soften a confrontation. Furthermore, as the analysts commented, the caseworkers tended to convey their concern and understanding more through their voices than their words.

In Table 4.3, the profile of casework intervention in the present experiment is compared with a profile obtained in a related study conducted by Helen Pinkus of a rather different sample of casework practice. The primary purpose of this comparison is to place the project casework practice in the broader context of casework carried on in other agencies. An important question to answer is: "Did casework intervention in the project—because of research requirements or because of the samples of caseworkers and clients used—turn out to be a special brand of casework?" If so, this fact would need to be taken into account in any generalization based on the findings of the project.

The profile used for comparison was based on 111 continued service interviews conducted by 59 experienced caseworkers, all graduates of the Smith College School for Social Work. Eighty-two per cent were employed in psychiatric settings; the remaining 18 per cent, in family agencies. The interviews were drawn from later phases of treatment, usually beyond the fifteenth interview. Pinkus used the same classification system and coding instructions employed in our own analysis of interview tapes.

The overall similarity between the two profiles suggests that the general characteristics of casework intervention in the project bear a reasonably close resemblance to the practice of a much larger group of caseworkers located primarily in psychiatric settings. Some points of difference, however, may be noted. The greater use of exploration and lesser use of advice reported by

Pinkus may have been a result of the special characteristics of intervention in PSTS in our project. Caseworkers in the Pinkus study were reported as making less use of confrontation but greater use of clarifying intrapsychic causation. This difference seemed likely to reflect differences in judging criteria, although it is possible that it may reflect greater attention to intrapsychic factors by caseworkers in psychiatric settings.[27]

The two profiles offer a basis for some hypotheses about a fairly large segment of casework practice, that is, casework treatment of family problems carried on through the medium of individual interviews with family members. They suggest that caseworkers' activities in this type of treatment may consist largely of the processes of securing data about the client's problems and in return feeding back to the client formulations to improve his understanding of these problems. Over three-fourths of the caseworkers' communications in these profiles could be so described. The problems of concern in these worker-client exchanges appear to be distinctly psychosocial, with major emphasis on the functioning of the client and others in family roles. The caseworker's formulations appear mostly directed toward helping the client achieve a better understanding of the behavior of others within their roles, and of interactions between himself and other family members.

COMBINATION VERSUS INDIVIDUAL PRESCRIPTIONS

It will be recalled that the "combination" prescription called for use of both individual and joint interviews as the medium of

27. Combining percentages for techniques 8. and 9. yields similar totals for the two studies. According to one judge who participated in both studies, responses usually classified as confrontation in our study were often classified as clarifying intrapsychic causation in hers.

service. The joint interviews were to be with the spouses, if possible. The individual prescription restricted the caseworker to individual interviews only.

It was easy enough to establish that the combination and individual prescription differed statistically in respect to type of interview. Joint interviews with the spouses were used to some extent in the great majority (75 per cent) of the cases assigned to the combination prescription and in only a few (7 per cent) of the cases assigned to individual interviewing only. In only a minority of cases in the combination prescriptions, however, did joint interviews constitute over half of the total. Consequently it was difficult to establish the adequacy of the input differences between the two prescriptions.

It would be stretching a point to say that an occasional joint interview in a case consisting primarily of individual interviews would qualify the case as "combination" treatment in any meaningful sense. Unfortunately, there was no way of knowing what proportion of joint interviews was needed to make any substantial difference in input. Because of various uncertainties in implementation, such as the chance that one partner might drop out of treatment, the proportion of joint interviews expected for the combination prescription was not specified in advance of the project. As these uncertainties began to become realities within the early months of the service phase, caseworkers were asked to try for at least 25 per cent joint interviews in combination prescriptions. Any case with at least this proportion of joint interviews was arbitrarily regarded as having received combination treatment.[28]

The combination prescription was much better implemented

28. No maximum was placed on the proportion of joint interviews. In only one case was the proportion of joint interviews in excess of 90 per cent.

within PSTS than CS. In all but 4 of the 30 PSTS combination cases at least 25 per cent of the interviews were joint. By contrast only 12 of the 30 CS combination cases met this criterion. The median number of joint interviews within the combination patterns was actually greater for PSTS cases (3) than CS cases (2.5).

On the basis of these data we concluded that the combination prescription was adequately implemented within PSTS but not CS. If so, differences in effects between the combination and individual prescriptions can be legitimately tested within PSTS but not within CS.

Even though use of joint interviews increased as a result of individual and group conferences with the caseworkers, it was not possible to raise the level in continued service cases to that achieved in short-term cases. One reason seems to have been the greater success in maintaining involvement of both partners in PSTS. As noted, husbands tended to drop out of CS, leaving the caseworker with no other choice but to carry on through individual interviews with the wife. Another reason was given by the caseworkers themselves: joint interviews in PSTS proved to be one means of providing as much service as possible to both husband and wife within the limits of a prescribed number of interviews. Unused to using joint interviews as the major medium of ongoing service, the caseworkers were inclined to gravitate to the individual interview, as they did in CS. The limits of PSTS apparently forced a change in habit.

FIVE · OUTCOMES AT CLOSING

MEASURES OF CHANGE

The principal test of differences in outcome among the service prescriptions in the experiment consisted of measures of family and individual change between the beginning and the end of service. We certainly did not lack for such measures. We had resolved our initial uncertainty about the kind of changes to look for by measuring just about everything that service could conceivably affect, from use of the local "Y" to family adequacy. The advantage of this approach was that little was missed. On the other hand, it resulted in an unmanageable array of measurements, many of which turned out to be unrelated to the problems of the families or to the course of treatment. In order to develop a logical and feasible test of treatment outcomes, it was necessary to select from this assortment a limited number of critical measures.

Accordingly, sixteen key ratings were chosen. These ratings were to constitute the major test of differences in outcomes among the service prescriptions. Remaining ratings were to be taken into account as secondary evidence.

The key ratings were selected principally on the basis of their logical connection with the objectives of the experiment.[1] Since the major goal of the experiment, as stated in the original proposal, was "to contribute to the improvement of casework practice . . . in alleviating problems in family functioning and contributing to healthier family life," it seemed sensible to stress

1. A factor analysis of the change ratings was also used as a guide in selecting key items (see Appendix II, pp. 229–33).

change in *family* problems and functioning as outcome measures. Consequently five measures of change in family problems were chosen. One was a rating of change in the family's overall problem situation. Observers were asked to make a single rating to express changes in the family's problems considered as a whole. In arriving at this judgment they normally gave greater weight to the more important problems, generally marital and parent-child relationship difficulties. The remaining four measures in this group comprised all the particular family problems reported as occurring with enough frequency to warrant analysis: ratings of change in marital problems, problems in parent-child relations, problems of the school adjustment of children, and problems resulting from the emotional distress of family members.

To this group of items were added three ratings of change in various aspects of family functioning: the functional adequacy of the family, the quality of marriage, and the emotional climate of the home. The functional adequacy of the family took into account fourteen dimensions of family functioning including such factors as the degree of family organization, mutuality of activities and interests of family members, effectiveness of communication within family, and family's ability to cope with stress. It was decided to include ratings of change in the quality of the marriage because marital conflict constituted the most common source of family problems in our caseload. The emotional climate of the home was selected largely because it was our only family level measure that was not necessarily rated negatively in cases where parents separated. Since the "home" (as we defined it) could consist of the children and only one parent, its emotional climate could in fact be improved by the break-up of a quarrelsome marriage.

Since the primary clients in each case were the husband and wife, we included a set of ratings to measure changes in the individual functioning of each: (*a*) *Functioning as spouse* consisted of the affectional, sexual, and decision-making aspects of the marital role. (*b*) *Functioning as parent* included such aspects as the physical care, emotional nurture, and socialization of children. (*c*) *Ego-functioning* comprised various aspects of the client's psychological adaptation, such as his perception of reality and self, his capacity to tolerate frustration, the quality of his interpersonal relations, and the adequacy of his defenses. (*d*) *Feelings about self* related to the client's general sense of personal well-being, regardless of the status of his presenting problems and the level of his functioning. Changes in husbands and wives were rated along each of these four dimensions, yielding a total of eight individual client ratings for each case.

Half these items (the overall problem situation, functional adequacy of the family, functioning as spouse and as parent, and ego-functioning of husband and wife) were summary ratings that took into account, in all, some fifty separate ratings of family and individual change in the areas most directly related to the service goals of the project. These summary ratings may be regarded as the nucleus of the key measures of change.

As noted previously, ratings of change during the service period were made by research interviewers at case closing. Review judges, who listened to the tapes of the research interviews, made comparable ratings. For the sake of greater economy and precision in analysis of data, ratings of the two research observers were averaged.[2]

The caseworker's closing ratings of families and individuals on key items were also used in the assessment of outcomes. Be-

2. The expression "research observers' ratings" will always refer to the mean ratings of the research interviewers and review judges. Construction of change categories for these ratings is discussed in Appendix II, pp. 233–34.

cause of possibilities of bias resulting from her knowledge of the prescription and from her personal stake in the outcome of a case, the caseworker ratings were treated as secondary to the ratings of the research observers.

Certain characteristics of these change ratings need to be made clear if the findings to follow are to be properly understood. In rating change, observers used 5-point scales, usually ranging from considerably improved to considerably worse. Definitions of dimensions to be rated and categories of change were stated in relatively abstract terms. It was left to the observers to apply these definitions in given instances. Although observers tended to agree with one another as to the direction and amount of change, the precise nature and degree of these changes are not specified. Thus, we can say that a certain proportion of wives were rated as improved in their functioning as parents, but we cannot say specifically how they improved nor can we be very exact in determining how much they improved. We *can* say that not very much needed to happen in order for a change to be recorded. For example, a little less quarreling (or a little more) would normally be rated as a slight improvement (or as a slight deterioration) in the quality of the marriage, other things being equal. In short, almost any shift in behavior could qualify as a change. This all-encompassing definition of change was adopted by design. For this group of families with deeply entrenched, long-standing problems, any noticeable trend for better or worse we felt was worth recording. Finally, measures of change, regardless of who recorded them, were based in a very fundamental sense on information supplied by the client. We asked clients to "tell it like it is" and we had to rely on what they said. Our observers could listen with their third ears and they could check the reports of one spouse against the reports of the other, but in the final analysis, the client's version of the truth became our own.

FOCUS OF THE CHAPTER

Findings of interest relating to outcomes at case closing concerned mainly differences between PSTS and CS. Consequently this chapter is devoted primarily to outcome comparisons between PSTS and CS, with particular attention to differences in individual and family change. These differences conform to a certain pattern. This pattern is first exemplified in a detailed analysis of perhaps the single most important key measure, change in the family's problem situation from the point of view of the research observers, and is then examined in relation to the key measures as a whole. The remainder of the chapter is devoted largely to further investigation of PSTS-CS differences in relation to other data and to examination of client progress during the course of CS. (Discussion of these findings is deferred, however, until after the follow-up data have been presented.) The chapter concludes with a brief presentation and discussion of our rather meager results relating to outcome differences between other pairs of prescriptions.

CHANGE IN THE FAMILY'S OVERALL PROBLEM SITUATION

As is apparent from Table 5.1, the problems of families receiving PSTS were more likely to change for the better, less likely to change for the worse, than the problems of families receiving CS. While outcomes for this measure favor PSTS on balance, it is obvious from the table that two outcome categories, "slightly alleviated" and "aggravated," account for most of the differences. The lack of difference in the proportion of families whose problems were considerably alleviated qualifies in an important sense any summary statements about the outcome superiority of PSTS in respect to this measure. Still, if the two categories of alleviation are combined, the overall problem situation of 83 per cent of the PSTS families was alleviated at least to some degree; the comparable figure for CS families was 63 per cent.

Table 5.1. Change in the family's overall problem situation during the service period, PSTS and CS, from the viewpoint of the research observers*

	Families			
	PSTS		CS	
Categories of change	N	%	N	%
Considerably alleviated	(16)	27	(16)	27
Slightly alleviated	(34)	57	(22)	37
No change	(9)	15	(12)	20
Aggravated	(1)	2	(10)	17
Total	60	100	60	100

* PSTS versus CS, Chi Square, $p < .02$

Although it was somewhat surprising to find such a high rate of problem alleviation among families receiving PSTS, the fact that alleviation was "slight" in most cases was consistent with the generally held expectation that this type of service is able to provide some amelioration of basic problems but is not able to effect considerable change. What was completely unexpected, however, was the failure of CS to produce a *better* alleviation rate, particularly at the upper level of alleviation. Just as PSTS has generally been equated with modest change, CS has been viewed as the medium for accomplishing substantial improvement. Thus a higher proportion of CS than PSTS families was expected in the "considerably alleviated" category. This did not occur. Since it did not, the outcome superiority of PSTS in the "slightly alleviated" range takes on added significance.

The other arresting difference between the two patterns oc-

curs in respect to deterioration rates. It was certainly not anticipated that in a higher proportion of CS cases the problem
situation would be rated as "aggravated" at closing. If anything,
the reverse was expected. It was thought that a certain proportion of PSTS cases might be terminated prior to the resolution
of worsening problems, but that CS cases could be carried at
least to the point of reversing any deterioration.

PSTS VERSUS CS: THE GENERAL PATTERN OF DIFFERENCE IN FAMILY AND INDIVIDUAL CHANGE

The PSTS-CS differences observed for change in the family's
problem situation reflected differences found generally in the 16
key ratings of research observers and caseworkers.[3] The differences for most other key ratings, however, were not so great. Of
the 32 comparisons between PSTS and CS provided by the two
sets of key ratings, 10 comparisons yielded statistically significant
differences in outcome, that is, differences too large to be attributed to chance. Nine of these differences were in favor of
PSTS.[4] Four of the differences favoring PSTS were found in
the ratings of the research observers; 5, in the ratings of the
caseworkers. Either research observers or caseworkers, or both,
reported significantly better outcomes for PSTS in respect to the
family's overall problem situation (as already noted); problems
of parent-child relations and emotional distress of family members; the emotional climate of the home; husbands' and wives'
functioning as spouse; and husbands' feelings about self. The

3. These data are presented in Appendix I, Tables 2–4.
4. A 2 x 2 x 2 analysis of variance for key ratings yielded a similar
pattern of significant differences in favor of PSTS, although the appropriateness of this method of analysis for such data is questionable (see
Appendix II, pp. 250–51).

tenth difference (the research observers' rating of change in husbands' functioning as parent) clearly favored neither pattern since higher proportions of CS than PSTS husbands were rated as improved *and* worse.[5]

One item not included in our key measures of change deserves comment, because the findings were so completely unexpected.[6] According to the caseworkers' ratings of change, both husbands ($p<.01$) and wives ($p<.02$) made significantly greater gains in "perception of self" in PSTS than CS. Since practitioners tend to regard a lengthy period of service as necessary to effect changes in self-understanding, outcome differences in favor of CS were a logical expectation, particularly in the ratings of the caseworkers. At least here, of all places, one would not expect strong differences in favor of PSTS. Although the ratings of the research observers were in the same direction, it should be noted that the differences between PSTS and CS were not significant.

The significant differences between PSTS and CS in the key ratings conformed to the pattern observed for changes in the problem situation (Table 5.1). This pattern may be outlined as follows:

1. There was little difference between PSTS and CS at the higher levels of positive change, that is, problems rated as *considerably* alleviated or functioning *considerably* improved.

2. There were usually substantial differences in favor of PSTS at the lower level of positive change, that is, problems *slightly* alleviated or functioning *slightly* improved. The great majority

---

5. The basis for deciding if outcomes generally favored one pattern over another in the case of contradictory differences is discussed in Appendix II, pp. 252–53.

6. In general, secondary ratings of change present about the same picture as do the key measures. All significant differences found in these ratings favored PSTS, except for a very small number that clearly favored neither pattern.

of positive changes were at this level for both services. Combining the two levels of positive change, a procedure normally followed in the analysis, resulted in appreciably higher rates of improvement or alleviation for PSTS.[7]

3. Usually a higher proportion of CS cases fell into "no change" categories.

4. In most instances a substantially higher proportion of CS cases were given negative ratings, that is, problems aggravated or functioning worse.

Minor differences between PSTS and CS, those that did not prove to be statistically significant and so might arise by chance in a sample of this size, tended to approach the pattern outlined above. Several were close to significance. All but two of the nonsignificant differences favored PSTS.

Perhaps the most arresting feature of this pattern is the consistently higher proportion of CS cases showing deterioration, that is, some aspect of functioning rated as worse or a problem rated as aggravated. This phenomenon emerges more starkly when one compares cases in which there was no evidence of deterioration in any of the key ratings and those in which at least one key rating showed some deterioration. When this is done, one finds that only 6, or 10 per cent, of PSTS cases had experienced some deterioration between opening and closing as opposed to 21, or 35 per cent, of CS cases. It is true that in most cases at least one key change rating was also positive and in some, positive changes outnumbered the negative. Even so, this is possibly the single, most impressive difference found in outcomes between the two service patterns.[8]

---

7. This procedure, which can be justified on various grounds, such as the infrequency or absence of ratings at the higher level for a number of variables, had little effect on the number of statistically significant differences. If the levels are not combined, eight rather than ten significant differences are found, all in favor of PSTS.

8. The difference is significant at the .01 level, Chi Square, 1 d.f.

On the whole, then, PSTS clients did a little better. That statement pretty well sums up the major conclusion to be drawn from the findings presented thus far. For that matter, it is about as good a statement as any to summarize the major findings of the experiment. We want, of course, to know more than this. For example, did they do better in some ways, but not others? We shall consider this question presently.

MARITAL VERSUS PARENTAL ROLES

Fairly consistent and strong differences in favor of PSTS were obtained in respect to the client's functioning as spouse.[9] The research observers reported significant differences for husbands, with differences close to significance for wives. The caseworkers' ratings for this item showed a significant outcome advantage for PSTS for both husbands and wives. Such differences did not obtain in respect to functioning as parent. Either PSTS had only a slight edge (caseworker ratings) or both improvement and deterioration rates were higher for CS (research observer ratings). Thus, whether clients received PSTS or CS seemed to make a clear-cut difference in respect to marital functioning but not in respect to parental functioning.

A major factor in this difference in respect to functioning as spouse was the higher incidence of deterioration among CS clients. For example, 22 CS clients were rated by the research observers as worse in this aspect of functioning as opposed to only 5 PSTS clients.

In digging further, it was discovered that marital separations played an important role in this finding. Seven couples separated during the course of service, and 6 of these couples were recipients of CS. Since observers were instructed to give negative weight to a separation in assessing changes in functioning as spouse, all of the separated clients were rated as having deteri-

9. See Appendix I, Table 4.

orated in their performance of marital roles.[10] Thus, of the 22 CS clients rated as worse in this respect by the research observers, 12 had undergone marital separations.

Data on marital separations specify a major source of the PSTS-CS difference in respect to marital functioning. They do not explain away the difference. Even eliminating the separated couples leaves CS with more clients whose marital functioning had worsened.

MARITAL VERSUS CHILD-RELATED PROBLEMS

The pattern of findings for functioning as spouse and parent did not extend in any direct way to marital and child-related problems.[11] Outcome differences for both types of problem favored PSTS. However, the greatest differences, oddly enough, occurred in respect not to marital problems but to child-related problems. Both research observers and caseworkers reported close to significantly better outcomes for PSTS in respect to problems of the school adjustment of children. Changes in problems of parent-child relations significantly favored PSTS according to the ratings of research observers.

In the caseworkers' data (though not the research observers') the differences in respect to school adjustment problems were affected by a larger number of problems reported dealt with in CS. Thus, caseworkers reported treating such problems in 36 CS cases, and improvement was observed in 15, or 42 per cent. In PSTS there were fewer cases (24) in which such problems

10. These instructions were based on the assumption that a marital separation is a sign of a worsening in functioning in the marital *role*. Observers were free to rate the clients as having improved in other respects. It should also be noted that the caseworkers' goals in these cases (Caseworker's Diagnostic Schedule) were almost always in the direction of strengthening the marriage. In none was helping a couple to separate a stated goal.

11. See Appendix I, Table 2.

were reported. In 17, or 71 per cent, of these cases the problem was rated as alleviated. Thus, the numbers of PSTS and CS cases in which such problems were alleviated were very close but the proportion alleviated of those reported was higher for PSTS. A similar tendency (to deal with a large number of problems in CS with relatively less success) was also noted in the research observers' ratings of parent-child problems. The evidence that more emphasis was placed on child-related problems in CS than PSTS is consistent with previous data on service inputs. This greater emphasis apparently did not lead, however, to more successful outcomes.

As these findings illustrate, outcome comparisons between the two services in respect to child-related problems are clouded by the possibility that more such problems were dealt with in CS. Also one does not know how crucial changes in these or other specific problems may have been for the case as a whole. In one case a child-related problem may have been primary, in another, secondary. A rating of "no change" would mean something quite different in the two cases.

Accordingly cases were grouped according to the primary problem for which help was initially sought, that is, marital, child-related, or a combination of both.[12] Within each problem type the research interviewers' rating of change in the family's overall problem situation was compared for PSTS and CS cases. For families initially classified as having primarily marital problems, outcomes were strongly in favor of PSTS. The problem situations of 25 of the 30 marital cases assigned to this pattern, or 83 per cent, were judged to be alleviated. For the CS marital cases, only 56 per cent (15 out of 27) were reported eased.[13] A similar statistically significant advantage for PSTS was found for families with both marital and child-related problems. For

12. *Supra*, p. 46.
13. The difference was statistically significant $p < .05$, Chi Square, 1 d.f.

families with primarily child-related problems, however, outcomes for the two services were more nearly equal: PSTS, 84 per cent ameliorated (16 out of 19); CS, 74 per cent (17 out of 23). Proportionately more CS cases (7) than PSTS cases (4) were reported as substantially alleviated. The pattern for the case-worker ratings for changes in the problem situation was similar. For cases seeking help for primarily marital problems the alleviation rate was 73 per cent for PSTS, as opposed to 55 per cent for CS. For families with primarily child-related problems, the rates for PSTS and CS were much closer (84 per cent versus 78 per cent).

The evidence relating to outcome differences for PSTS and CS is obviously not consistent for different types of problems. Nevertheless, it may be said that PSTS had clearly the better outcomes in cases in which marital problems predominated, or in which marital problems appeared in combination with child-related problems. For families seeking help for primarily child-related problems, it made little difference in outcome whether assignment was to PSTS or CS. Viewed in this way the findings are consistent with the earlier conclusion that PSTS had a definite outcome advantage over CS in respect to marital functioning but not necessarily in respect to parental functioning.

HUSBANDS VERSUS WIVES

Although both husbands and wives generally did better in PSTS, the differences in outcome between the two services tended to be somewhat more pronounced for husbands. For example, four of the five significant differences favoring PSTS in the functioning of the partners as individuals were found in the husbands' ratings.[14] This tendency for husbands to do well in PSTS may be noted in the research observers' ratings of change on

14. See Appendix I, Tables 4 and 5.

psychological dimensions (ego-functioning and feelings about self). On ego-functioning the difference shows up not so much in improvement rate as in deterioration rate, with 3 PSTS wives and 3 PSTS husbands rated as worse on ego-functioning as opposed to one CS wife and 9 CS husbands. With respect to feelings about self, the improvement rate shows the main difference. The improvement rate for wives was only slightly higher in PSTS than in CS (77 per cent versus 73 per cent); by contrast the improvement rates for husbands in this variable differed greatly (79 per cent for PSTS, 60 per cent for CS). The differences were significant for husbands but not for wives.

Up to this point we have compared outcomes for PSTS and CS husbands on the one hand, and outcomes for PSTS and CS wives on the other hand. We may also ask a quite different question: Did wives in general tend to have more favorable outcomes than their husbands, or vice versa? An answer may be obtained by determining couple by couple, whether one partner achieved more positive change than the other. The four key change ratings pertaining to individual client functioning were examined in this manner. According to the research observers ratings, husbands and wives did about equally well in respect to changes in functioning as spouse and parent. In the majority of cases ratings for the two partners were identical. In cases where the ratings differed, about as many husbands as wives had the more positive rating. In respect to changes in ego-functioning and feelings about self, however, wives did significantly better than husbands. Although ratings were equal in approximately 40 per cent of the cases, where differences occurred, the higher rating was given the wife about twice as often as the husband. The caseworker's ratings showed a quite similar pattern.[15]

---

15. Husband-wife differences were statistically significant for both *feelings about self* and *ego-functioning*, research observers' ($p < .01$) and caseworker ratings ($p < .05$), Sign Test.

The lack of difference in ratings between husbands and wives in respect to functioning as spouse and parent may be explained in part by the complementarity of these family roles. Thus the extent of change in one marital partner may be dependent upon the extent of change in the other. Interdependency between husband and wife may not have been as strong in respect to the more psychological variables, *ego-functioning* and *feelings about self*. That wives did better in these respects may be related to their having received more service (in both PSTS and CS) and to their apparently greater motivation for change.

It is also of interest that the pattern of husband-wife differences described above held for both PSTS and CS cases. Wives did better than their husbands in respect to the more psychological aspects of change regardless of which of the two services they received, even though the spread between PSTS and CS for these measures was greater for husbands than wives. While distressingly complex, these findings are not contradictory To use a simple analogy, regardless of type of instruction, first grade girls may make greater progress in reading than first grade boys; the type of instruction, however, may have a greater impact on the boys than the girls.

INITIAL CHARACTERISTICS AND OUTCOME: THE SEARCH FOR DIAGNOSTIC CRITERIA

In the findings presented thus far, two initial characteristics, the type of problem and, to a lesser extent, the sex of the client, have been shown to affect the outcome differences between PSTS and CS. There was interest in learning if these differences were affected by other initial characteristics of families and individuals, such as social class, level of adjustment, motivation to use casework help, and the like. In particular, we wanted to determine if there were any constellations of initial characteristics that might be associated with favorable outcomes in PSTS and un-favorable outcomes in CS, or vice versa. The identification of such characteristics could provide the practitioner with criteria to guide him in selecting the pattern of service most likely to benefit a particular individual or family.

Extensive analyses of the relation between initial characteristics and outcome added little to what already has been suggested: that PSTS outcomes were generally more favorable than CS outcomes, with a tendency for families with marital problems and for husbands to do particularly well. There proved to be no type of family or individual who did well when assigned to one pattern but poorly when assigned to the other. The most successful PSTS cases were similar in initial characteristics to the most successful CS cases. A similar correspondence in initial characteristics obtained for the least successful cases in each pattern. There were just more cases that were successful and fewer that were unsuccessful in PSTS. For example, a couple whose marriage was rated as poor in quality at the beginning of service proved less likely to experience positive change than a couple whose marriage was rated as good in quality at the outset. In each case, assignment to PSTS increased the couple's chances of getting a better outcome rating, assignment to CS lowered them. But the initial rating of the quality of the marriage would have been, in itself, of no particular use in predicting whether a case would do better in PSTS or CS. Much the same observations could be made for most initial characteristics, whether taken singly or in combination.

Our search for diagnostic criteria was handicapped by two factors. First, there were too few PSTS families or individuals with distinctively negative outcomes to form an adequate basis for determining the type of case for which PSTS might be contra-indicated. Second, the level of association between initial characteristics and outcomes was generally quite low.[16] Consequently there was little room for variation between PSTS and CS in patterns of association between initial and terminal measures. Thus, the family's social class, a characteristic often related to outcome in studies of treatment, proved in our study to bear little relationship to the family's progress. Upper class families did as well as lower class families, and families of all classes did better in PSTS.

The general lack of association between initial characteristics and outcome was probably due more to the homogeneity of our sample than anything else. For example, two social classes, IV and V, accounted for two-thirds of our sample, with a fairly narrow spread between these two classes. Given the lack of sizable groups of families representing sharply contrasting social classes, the lack of relation between social class and outcome in our study becomes more understandable. Similarly, differences in the degree of client motivation to use casework help bore little relationship to outcome. Since our clients were generally well motivated for help to begin with, the differences between the more and less highly motivated were perhaps not great enough to result in appreciably different outcomes.

THE CASEWORKER AND OUTCOMES FOR PSTS AND CS

Within the caseloads of each caseworker, PSTS cases had generally more favorable outcomes than CS, as measured by the key change ratings. Thus each caseworker did somewhat better with his PSTS than CS cases. Furthermore, it made little difference whether the caseworker preferred PSTS or CS at the outset. As it turned out, caseworkers expressed an initial preference for

16. Of 496 correlations between initial characteristics and key outcome measures (done separately for PSTS and CS) only 10 exceeded .30.

CS in 85 per cent of the cases.[17] Their expressions of preference for PSTS, which usually occurred in cases already assigned to that pattern, did not seem to add to its success.

That caseworkers showed greater preference for the service pattern that, according to their own estimates, yielded less favorable outcomes presented an anomaly that begged to be investigated. Accordingly, at the end of the service phase, we obtained some additional data on the caseworkers' perceptions of the service patterns. The caseworkers were first asked to order the eight prescriptions from most to least effective, on the basis of their project experience. They were then asked to reorder them according to the degree of comfort or ease they felt in carrying them out.

There was little agreement among the practitioners in their rank ordering of effectiveness of the prescriptions, although the PSTS prescriptions on the whole were ranked slightly higher than their CS counterparts. In respect to ease of execution, however, the difference was clear. With only scattered exceptions, the prescriptions ranked as the two *easiest* to carry out were CS. Conversely the prescriptions ranked as the two most difficult were almost always forms of PSTS.

The caseworkers' comments in a final group session, at the end of the service phase, supported these rankings. Most thought that their PSTS cases had turned out better than expected, though there was disagreement about the relative effectiveness of PSTS and CS, with some of the opinion that the issue could not be decided before completion of the follow-up. There was general agreement, however, that PSTS was more challenging, placed the worker under greater pressure, allowed less oppor-

17. The caseworkers were asked on the Caseworker's Diagnostic Schedule to indicate the service pattern they would have preferred, regardless of the pattern to which the case was assigned.

tunity to make up for errors, and required more energy per interview, all factors contributing to the greater sense of strain the caseworkers apparently felt in conducting this type of treatment.

It is not surprising then that caseworkers, uncertain about the relative effectiveness of the two patterns, would prefer the one easier to carry out. The upshot of all this, of course, is an obvious paradox: the more stressful pattern for the caseworker was the apparently more beneficial pattern for the client.

NUMBER OF INTERVIEWS AND OUTCOMES

The number of interviews constitutes an important variable in this experiment for at least two reasons: first, the distinction between CS and PSTS rests in part on the number of interviews; second, any analysis of outcomes within CS must take into account the great variation in amount of service received.

We were particularly interested to see if outcomes in CS were associated with the number of interviews families received. If families leaving treatment early had poorer outcomes than families remaining in treatment, a reasonable assumption, then one would expect a positive association between outcomes and numbers of interviews.

As it turned out, the number of interviews received by CS cases was not strongly associated with key measures of change in family functioning or problems.[18] None of the correlations exceeded .20 and none was statistically significant. In other words, there was no general tendency for family functioning or problems to improve as the number of interviews increased.[19] The

18. Only research observers' ratings for key items were used in the analysis reported in this section.

19. The obvious conclusion is that PSTS-CS differences in respect to these variables were not dependent upon the number of interviews received by families in CS. For example, when CS families receiving fewer than ten interviews are dropped from Table 5.1, the differences are still significantly in favor of PSTS ($p < .02$).

correlations rise somewhat (.26 to .48 for key ratings) when change in the functioning of husbands receiving CS is related to the number of interviews each received. These correlations are all significant. For CS wives, all correlations are low, though at least two are significant (functioning as parent, $r = .32$, ego-functioning, $r = .35$).

Interestingly enough, correlations between the number of interviews and changes in family functioning and problems were higher for PSTS than CS. All the PSTS correlations for these measures fell between .26 and .40, and all were statistically significant. Correlations between interview input and outcome were also generally higher in PSTS than CS in respect to measures of functioning of husbands and wives. These differences were unexpected in view of the narrower range in the number of interviews in PSTS. For example, one would have expected that a difference of between two and eighteen interviews in CS would have yielded a greater difference in outcome than a difference between two interviews and six in PSTS.

An association between number of interviews received and outcome does not establish a causal connection between the two variables. It is possible that PSTS interviews had a greater impact or that CS husbands tended to profit more than wives from the interviews they received. It is also possible, however, that in PSTS clients who were more likely to change in a positive direction were more likely to stay in treatment. The same logic could be applied to husbands in CS. In general, the amount of service received may be regarded as much a consequence as a cause of change, if the only evidence is a statistical correlation.

Be that as it may, the pattern of correlations between number of interviews and change in CS, particularly in respect to families and wives, gives one pause. Whether the amount of service received is interpreted as cause or effect, CS families and wives receiving a substantial amount of service terminated with outcomes no better than those receiving only a modest amount. It seems likely that service in some CS cases was carried beyond the point of diminishing returns.

ASSESSMENTS OF HELPFULNESS OF SERVICE AT CLOSING

Assessments of helpfulness of service provide a somewhat difference evaluation of outcome from measures of change in problems or functioning. For example, a family's problems or functioning may have worsened during the course of service, but service may still have been perceived as helpful on grounds that things would have been even worse without it. Conversely, a family's problems or functioning may have changed in a positive direction for reasons unrelated to service. If so, the family may have been better off at closing but service may not have been rated as helpful. Ratings of helpfulness of service may offer then a measure of control for the impact of extraneous variables on the effects of service.

Ratings of helpfulness of service, on the other hand, may be subject to various kinds of bias. Service may be rated as helpful simply because positive change has occurred or because of a need to justify the client's investment of time, money, and energy. They are by no means ideal measures of service effects.

Table 5.2 presents ratings of the overall helpfulness of service to the family from the point of view of the research observers, caseworkers, and clients. The shape of the data resembles the pattern of PSTS-CS outcome differences observed in the ratings of change. Differences at the most positive level are small, though all but the caseworkers report a slight edge for CS. The major differences occur in the remaining categories, "helped a little" and "no positive effect." Those differences are analogous to the consistently more favorable PSTS change ratings of

OUTCOMES AT CLOSING · 117

Table 5.2. Closing ratings of the overall helpfulness of service to the family, PSTS and CS

	Families							
	Helped considerably		Helped a little		No positive effect		N†	p<‡
From point of view of:	N	%	N	%	N	%		
Research observers								
PSTS	(19)	32	(31)	52	(10)	17	60	.02
CS	(22)	37	(17)	28	(21)	35	60	
Caseworkers								
PSTS	(12)	20	(39)	65	(9)	15	60	
CS	(11)	18	(34)	57	(15)	25	60	
Husbands*								
PSTS	(21)	39	(29)	54	(4)	7	54	.01
CS	(22)	42	(11)	21	(19)	37	52	
Wives*								
PSTS	(27)	47	(20)	35	(10)	18	57	
CS	(26)	49	(13)	25	(14)	26	53	

* Clients were asked in the research interview to rate the helpfulness of service to the family. The ratings were recorded by the research interviewers and review judges and then averaged (see Appendix II, p. 236).

† Here and elsewhere totals reflect the number of cases or clients on which data were obtained. Failure to secure or complete research interviews with a number of husbands and wives is largely responsible for client totals of less than 60 for PSTS and CS (see Appendix II, p. 227).

‡ Chi Square tests, 2 d.f. The slight superiority of CS in the "helped considerably" category did not contribute materially to the statistical significance of the differences (see Appendix II, p. 252).

"slightly improved" and "worse." Again the PSTS-CS differences are slightly stronger for husbands than for wives.

The least favorable category, "no positive effect," consists of ratings of "service neither helped nor harmed" and "would have been better off without contact." There were only six of the latter ratings (all made by CS clients). In general, then, service was not reported as contributing to the changes for the worse observed for the CS cases.

On the whole, PSTS was the service more likely to be rated as providing at least some help. From 82 to 93 per cent of the cases (depending on the rater) were so rated. The comparable range for CS cases was 63 to 75 per cent. The slight advantage for CS in the upper level of helpfulness qualifies, but does not invalidate, the generalization that PSTS was perceived as generally the more helpful of the two services.

THE CLIENT'S VIEW OF THE COMPONENTS OF SERVICE

The data presented thus far have pertained to changes associated with service or to assessments of the helpfulness of service. In this section we are concerned with the clients' evaluation of the components of service: what they saw it consisting of, what they liked and disliked about it, their attitudes toward the caseworker, and so on, as expressed to the research interviewers at closing. These evaluations may shed light on some of the PSTS-CS outcome differences previously observed. They also point to some of the factors in the client's view of service that need to be taken into account in both PSTS and CS.

Table 5.3 presents husbands' and wives' reactions to selected components of service, including all in which significant PSTS-CS differences occurred and some in which such differences might have been expected but did not occur. Clients were permitted multiple choices in these check-list items. The table gives the percentages of clients interviewed who responded to particular items in the ways indicated.[20]

Several points in Table 5.3 are of interest. With the one notable

20. The data in this section were supplied by the research interviewers only.

Table 5.3. Client's perception of service, aspects liked and disliked, PSTS-CS

	Husbands			Wives		
	PSTS	CS		PSTS	CS	
	(N/52)	(N/48)		(N/58)	(N/56)	
	%	%	p*	%	%	p<*
Client's perception of service						
Nothing but talk	4	13		3	16	.05
Chance to express concerns	54	54		60	68	
Gave support, understanding, and reassurance	31	23		40	48	
Helped think out problems	46	31		48	46	
Helped understand self	62	42		76	59	
	PSTS	CS		PSTS	CS	
	(N/49)	(N/47)		(N/57)	(N/54)	
	%	%		%	%	
Aspects client liked						
Content of interviews	39	15	.02	33	17	
Worker's personality or attitude	61	43		75	48	.01
Aspects client disliked						
Worker gave little advice	16	26		14	28	
Worker talked little	4	11		4	17	.01
Brevity of service	22	2	.01	42	7	.001

* Chi Square tests, 2 x 2 tables, item checked versus not checked, PSTS and CS.

exception of brevity of service, PSTS clients tended to give more positive evaluations to the components of service than did CS clients. CS husbands and wives were more likely to see service as "nothing but talk," more likely to dislike lack of caseworker talk, and less likely to express liking for the content of the interviews and for the caseworker's personality and attitude.

Differences were statistically significant for at least one partner for each of these items, with differences for wives more numerous than for husbands. The clients' reactions to brevity of service point up one feature of PSTS that a significant proportion of clients, mostly wives, did not like. As might be expected, few CS clients complained of this aspect. This finding merits special attention, not only because it runs counter to the general trend of PSTS-CS differences, but also because it may point to some special problems in carrying out brief, time-limited treatment.

Responses to open-ended questions, in which clients were asked to express their feelings about termination, were analyzed. Of the 35 clients (24 wives and 11 husbands) who had expressed dislike of the brevity of service, the great majority (29) also commented on the brevity of service in their free responses. Twelve of these 29 clients qualified their dislike in one of two ways. Eight expressed a wish for a "few more interviews"; they were apparently content with relatively brief treatment but wanted somewhat more of it than they received. Four had mixed feelings about the brevity of service, indicating on the one hand that they had wanted more service but on the other hand that perhaps what they had received was enough. The remaining 17, mostly wives, were fairly clear in expressing their reservations about service brevity, though they varied in the intensity of feeling expressed. Interestingly enough, there proved to be no relation between the client's dislike of the brevity of service and the client's assessment of the helpfulness of service. About half the 35 clients expressing dislike of brevity of service on the check-list item rated service as helping considerably, about the same proportion as found for clients who did *not* complain that service was too brief.

Although negative reactions to the limits of service in PSTS may be qualified by the above and must also be seen in relation to the fact that the majority of PSTS clients did not react in this way, still one is left with the impression that a noteworthy proportion of PSTS clients did feel a need for more service than they received. This finding is not necessarily inconsistent with the more positive evaluations given PSTS in other respects. In fact some clients may have reacted adversely to termination in part because they liked the service and thought it was helpful. They might just have wanted more of it.

Table 5.3 also suggests certain links between the client's assessment of service components and the nature of these components, as measured in investigations of service characteristics. These investigations, it will be recalled, suggested that caseworkers were more active in PSTS. In the average PSTS interview, caseworkers made less use of exploration and were more likely to provide the client with advice and formulations of his problems.

The data in the present table suggest that clients were not only sensitive to these differences but also preferred the approach caseworkers used in PSTS. Thus clients were more likely to dislike lack of caseworker advice and talk in CS, and to perceive PSTS more than CS (though not to a significant degree) as helping them to think through their problems and to increase their self-understanding. In the client's judgment, at any rate, the greater worker activity perceived in PSTS cases did not deprive them of the opportunity to express their concerns or to receive understanding and reassurance, although CS wives were a little more likely to cite these aspects of service than their PSTS counterparts.

The finding that PSTS clients were more apt than CS clients to like the caseworker's personality and attitude suggests the two services may have had different effects on the client's feelings toward the caseworker. The two groups of clients, it should be recalled, were reacting to the same caseworkers, since the caseload of each worker was evenly divided between PSTS and CS clients.

The research interviewers rated the client's feeling toward the caseworker prior to service and at closing. In general clients in both services were found to have positive feelings toward their caseworkers at both points of time. Within PSTS the attitudes of both husbands and wives toward the caseworker became more positive during service, as may be seen in Table 5.4. Most shifts were from moderately positive at opening to strongly positive at closing. Within CS, there was no consistent direction to shifts in attitudes, although there were slightly more downward than upward changes.

Table 5.4. Changes in the client's feeling toward caseworker from opening to closing, PSTS and CS

Direction of shift in feelings toward caseworker, opening to closing	Wives				Husbands			
	PSTS		CS		PSTS		CS	
	N	%	N	%	N	%	N	%
Positive (rating higher at closing)	21	41	16	33	28	47	15	29
No change	25	49	15	31	26	44	20	38
Negative (rating lower at closing)	5	10	18	37	5	8	17	33
Total	51	100	49	100	59	100	52	100

PSTS-CS differences, husbands and wives, $p <.01$, Chi Square, 2 d.f.

The client's feeling toward the caseworker was positively associated with his view of the caseworker's feelings toward him ($r = .67$ for wives, .43 for husbands). On the whole, a greater proportion of PSTS clients than CS clients viewed their caseworkers as having moderately or very positive feelings toward them (65 versus 47 per cent). The difference was statistically significant for husbands.

The findings leave little doubt that PSTS clients were more apt to "warm up" to their caseworkers than CS clients. They also suggest that there may have been more strain in the treatment relationship in CS. A sizable proportion of CS clients (about a third) came away from treatment feeling less positively toward the caseworker than they had at the outset (Table 5.4) and at closing only a minority thought their caseworkers had clearly positive feelings toward them. Such indicators of strain were much less likely to be found in the feelings and perceptions of PSTS clients.

THE CLIENTS' REASONS FOR TERMINATING SERVICE

The reasons clients gave the research interviewers for terminating service provide further insight into differences in client reactions to PSTS and CS. A slightly higher proportion of CS clients (32 per cent) than of PSTS clients (25 per cent) said they left treatment because of improvement in the problem situation. It is a little curious that as many as a quarter of the PSTS clients gave this as a reason for leaving treatment that was set up in advance to end at a certain point. It is also a little dismaying that less than a third of the CS clients, who could continue about as long as they felt the need, said they left treatment for what might be considered the optimum reason. Still CS emerges with a slight advantage over PSTS in this respect.

About 30 per cent of the PSTS clients gave reasons for terminating that had somewhat "negative" connotations. The majority of these clients said they had wished to continue but stopped because the caseworkers wanted them to; however, some left because of dissatisfaction with progress. A higher proportion of CS clients (45 per cent) gave "negative" reasons for terminating. Most of these clients (31 of 44) said they quit because of dissatisfaction with progress. Only 9 said they wanted to continue but the caseworker wanted them to stop. Finally, the reason for termination given most often by PSTS clients (36 per cent) had neither clearly negative or positive connotations. It was simply that "service was set up to stop at a certain point." This reason was seldom given by CS clients.[21]

Perhaps the main point here is that PSTS clients were more apt to see termination in neutral terms, as part of the structure of service. CS clients were more likely to see the end of service in negative terms, as having come about because sufficient progress was no longer being made. A CS client could say this, of course, and still feel that service was helpful. For example, one woman assigned to CS felt that service helped considerably in alleviating the family problem for which help was sought, in fact the family couldn't have gotten along without this help in her judgment. Asked why she had decided to leave treatment, she gave "dissatisfaction with progress" as the reason. The two answers are not necessarily inconsistent.

The data support our earlier observation that many CS clients, like the woman in the example, did stay on in treatment until after a point of diminishing returns had been reached. Although termination in PSTS may have been frustrating for some clients, their frustration was not of the same kind apparently experienced by a good share of CS clients. If CS clients continued treatment with the *expectation* of progressive alleviation of their problems, then the data suggest that after a point treatment could no longer fulfill these expectations.

CLIENT PROGRESS DURING THE COURSE OF CS

Findings presented thus far have raised a number of questions about client progress during the course of CS. As implied above, did some clients reach their peak of progress considerably prior

21. Remaining reasons for both services had to do with "practical difficulties" in keeping appointments or "unwillingness of spouse to continue." It is of interest that a higher proportion of clients in CS (15 per cent) than in PSTS (8 per cent) gave reasons in this category.

to the ending of treatment? In general, did most progress in CS cases tend to come rather early? Such questions obviously could not be satisfactorily answered from measures obtained at closing. We were also troubled by another kind of question. Did our closing measures of outcome tend to underestimate progress in CS cases? These measures after all were rather gross. A rating of slight or substantial change on given aspects of functioning might not have done justice to the amounts of improvement that might have occurred in the longer CS cases.

We attempted to answer these questions through further analyses of the tape recordings of casework interviews. In addition to providing data on the treatment process, the tapes presented evidence on client movement over the life of a case. It was assumed that in each interview the client would reveal enough about his current problems and functioning, so that a comparison of interviews from different points in his course of treatment would yield a longitudinal picture of his progress. If so, comparisons of CS interviews could provide clues as to when progress occurred in treatment and also might offer a check on closing measures of change based on ratings of the research observers and caseworkers. If clients showed steady progress from one stage to the next in a course of long-term treatment, one might then have grounds for questioning the assumption that terminal ratings of change for PSTS and CS clients can be compared on the same scale.

Accordingly, all CS clients who continued beyond a fifth interview and whose interviews were taped, were selected for analysis. The 32 CS clients in this group consisted of 14 husbands and 18 wives representing 20 families. Outcomes for clients and cases selected, in respect to such measures as change in the problem situation and ego-functioning, were comparable to the outcomes for remaining CS cases and clients.

Treatment was divided arbitrarily into five phases, taking into account the pattern of attrition characteristic of this sub-sample. A target interview was designated for each phase. These interviews were the second, seventh, twelfth, twenty-second, and thirty-seventh with the client. If the target interview turned out to be joint or inaudible, another interview in the phase, usually not more than one or two removed from the target interview was chosen.

The second and seventh interviews or close substitutes were available for all 33 clients; 23 clients continued to the point of the twelfth interview; 13 to the point of the twenty-second, and nine to the point of the thirty-seventh. Thus, for each client a set of from two to five interviews was selected, representing his progress in treatment at various stages.

Within each set all possible pairs of interviews were compared; that is, if a set consisted of the second, seventh, twelfth interviews, the second was compared with the seventh and twelfth, and the seventh with the twelfth. Through this method 148 pairs of interviews were designated for comparison. A judge compared a pair of interviews after listening to portions of each, approximately the middle third. About half the time the later interview was presented to the judge first and the rest of the time the earlier interview was presented first. The judge, a highly experienced caseworker from outside the agency, was given no identifying information about the clients or the interviews, and, in fact, was ignorant of the purpose and design of the project as a whole. After listening to the segments of the two interviews, she was asked to compare them on nine items such as the following:

The client seemed to accept more responsibility for problem-solving.

The client seemed to be coping more effectively with his problems

The client's problems seemed less critical.

The client seemed less anxious or depressed.

The client displayed a better understanding of his own behavior.

Her task was to indicate which interview better fitted each statement. A second judge, also a highly experienced caseworker, independently compared approximately one-half of the interview pairs.

As can be seen from the examples, the comparisons yielded a measure of client progression or movement in such respects as problem-solving, insight, and psychological symptoms. Perfect progression could be said to occur if the interview selected in each paired comparison turned out to be the later one. For example, in a comparison of the second and twelfth interviews, if the interview selected by the judge as the one in which the client's problems seemed less critical was the twelfth, then one would have evidence of positive movement between an earlier and later stage of treatment. If the client's movement was consistently upward it might be expected that the twelfth interview would be chosen over the second but the twenty-second and thirty-seventh would each be selected in preference to the twelfth. Since treatment inevitably has its vicissitudes, a perfect progression would not be expected. But most would assume that for the majority of clients the later interviews would have the more positive indicators and hence would be chosen more frequently.

The results will be summarized briefly. In general, no clear pattern of progression emerged; in fact, there was a slight tendency for *earlier* interviews to be chosen over *later* interviews. Both judges showed a marked tendency to *perceive* the later interviews as best fitting the statements in the instrument, indicating that both were operating under the assumption that the interviews showing greater sign of positive movement were the later ones, but about as often as not, their perception of which interview was the later one turned out to be in error.

Agreement between the two judges in respect to particular items was not generally beyond chance expectations, but agreement beyond chance would be difficult to achieve if interviews from different phases revealed similar degrees of client movement.[22] There were, however, three items in which agreement between the judges exceeded chance levels. These items, the first three given in the example above, concerned aspects of the client's problems. Because of their reliability, they were selected for more intensive analysis.[23]

In general these items showed no pattern of progression in client movement. Most clients showed neither a consistent upward or downward trend. On the whole there was a slight downward drift, with earlier interviews tending to be chosen over later interviews. This trend was most noticeable with husbands in respect to the first two phases (roughly the second versus the seventh interviews). Thus, for 11 of the 14 husbands the earlier interview was chosen over the later interview in respect to at least two of the three "problem" items. No such patterns emerged for the wives.

These findings suggest that the line of client progress in CS tended to be rather wavy. There was no evidence at all that any consistent upward progression had occurred. For most of these clients, as for the majority of CS clients, as a whole, positive changes between opening and closing were reported by the research observers. The two sets of findings are not necessarily inconsistent since a client's "ups" may have been more pronounced than his "downs" over the course of treatment, result-

22. See Appendix II, pp. 244–45.
23. Since the second judge completed only a sample of the comparisons, the analysis was confined to data supplied by the first judge.

ing in some net gain at closing. The interview comparisons do not suggest a pattern of steady movement over long periods of service that may have been underestimated by the research observers. Nor do the interview comparisons indicate that clients in CS cases achieved substantial progress early in treatment that might have been lost sight of in judgments of change made at a later point in time. There is some evidence, however, that progress on the part of husbands did come quite early in treatment. This tendency of husbands to do better in the first phase of treatment than the second takes on added significance when one recalls that most husbands in the project did not reach the third phase or twelfth in-person interview. Husbands, in particular, may have achieved their maximum benefits from CS quite early in the relatively short period of time that they remained in treatment.

These findings must be weighed cautiously, however. They are based on only samples of work from a portion of the CS caseload. More important, the method of assessment used (paired comparisons of interviews) involved some untried procedures and presented some unresolved reliability problems.

MODIFYING VERSUS SUPPORTIVE TREATMENT

No significant differences in outcome emerged in comparisons between the total samples of families (or individuals) assigned to modifying as opposed to supportive prescriptions. This statement holds, regardless of observer or method of analysis. Considering the uncertain implementation of this service variable, such negative findings are not surprising. Within the short-term service pattern, however, husbands assigned to modifying treatment had significantly more favorable outcomes than husbands assigned to supportive treatment in respect to functioning as a spouse and ego-functioning.

Other ratings for PSTS husbands tended also to favor modifying treatment, as did ratings for PSTS wives and families, though to a lesser extent and with less consistency. Given the fact that only two significant differences were found on only one set of measures, one is hard put to say whether modifying PSTS did in fact achieve distinctly better results. When a large number of variables and measures are examined, and only occasional statistically significant differences are found, as was the case here, one cannot reject the possibility that these differences themselves are the result of chance variation. In this kind of multi-variable and multi-measurement situation, it is perhaps best to insist upon a *pattern* of significant differences, such as is found between PSTS and CS outcomes, before taking any of the differences seriously.

The relationship between the use of modifying techniques and outcome was further investigated through correlational methods. If the application of modifying treatment had specific effects, one would expect some association between the extent of its application and outcome. Clients with whom modifying techniques were used extensively might be expected to experience greater change in certain respects than clients receiving this kind of treatment in only minimal amounts.

In this analysis a gross measure of the use of modifying techniques for each client was determined from the caseworkers' own estimates.[24] Although of dubious reliability these "scores" were available for each case, whereas the presumably more reliable data derived from the analysis of tapes were available for only a sample.

---

24. The measure consisted of the ratio of the number of uses checked by the caseworker on the Caseworker's Interview Schedule of any of the steps of modifying treatment, over the number of interviews with the client.

Since both employment of modifying treatment techniques and outcome were found to be positively associated with the number of interviews with a client, use was made of partial correlation to remove the effect of number of interviews. Modifying technique "scores" and change ratings for each client were thus correlated, with the number of interviews controlled. Only two of these correlations proved to be statistically significant, but these two are of some interest. First, the use of modifying techniques was significantly correlated with change in ego-functioning of PSTS husbands (partial $r = .27$). This finding provides some additional evidence in support of both the reality of modifying-supportive differences in outcome for PSTS husbands and the contribution of modifying treatment to these differences. One cannot, however, rule out the possibility that, as the client's ego-functioning improved, the worker was more inclined to use modifying treatment. Moreover, the low degree of correlation indicates only a weak relationship at best.

The other significant correlation concerned use of modifying treatment with wives in CS cases and changes in their feelings about themselves. Contrary to expectation the correlation was negative (partial $r = -.27$). That is, there was a tendency for greater use of modifying treatment to be accompanied by a decline in the wives' feelings about themselves. Although the degree of association is not substantial, its direction is arresting. Again a cause-effect sequence cannot be definitely established. It is possible that a worsening in feelings about the self brought forth greater use of modifying treatment. It is also possible that use of modifying treatment in CS had a depressive effect upon the wives' feelings in certain instances. Whatever the interpretation, and others are possible, the findings give no indication that modifying treatment had a beneficial effect upon the CS wives, in respect to this variable. One might add that in general correlations between use of modifying treatment and outcome variables for CS wives were in a negative direction, although no others were statistically significant.

In sum, what can be said about the special effects of modifying treatment? First, it is impossible to establish any special effects at all, either positive or negative, since there was no pattern of significant differences. Even if one assumes outcome differences for PSTS husbands or gives weight to the significant correlations, it is difficult to relate such findings to definable service inputs. It is difficult to extract possible effects on treatment resulting from the greater use of psychiatric consultation in PSTS modifying cases. Moreover, we were unable to establish clear differences between PSTS modifying and supportive treatments in respect to casework technique. It does little good to learn that a mode of treatment had certain effects if we cannot specify the nature of the treatment.

We can only speculate about ways in which treatment in modifying cases may have differed from treatment in supportive cases. Thus, perhaps it can be said that stimulating caseworkers to use an insight-oriented approach may have had a salutary effect on outcome in PSTS but not in CS. If so, once again the findings run counter to initial expectations. At the beginning of the project there were doubts about the advisability of attempting insight-oriented treatment under short-term service conditions. One leaves the project reassured on this score but with questions about use of this mode of treatment in CS. It is just possible that the structure of PSTS places certain useful limits on insight-oriented treatment.

INDIVIDUAL VERSUS JOINT INTERVIEWS

As indicated, the joint interview prescription was not successfully implemented in CS. Consequently no differences in outcome were expected and none was found. In PSTS there was sufficient differentiation between the individual and joint interview patterns to expect significant differences in outcome, if there was in fact any difference in their effectiveness. Again no differences in outcome were found. Even such items as whether or not clients liked their spouses' involvement in treatment showed no difference. Following procedures used in analysis of the modifying-supportive variable, the amount of use of joint interviews was correlated with various measures of individual and family change.[25] Essentially no relation was found between these measures and use of joint interviews, either in CS or PSTS.

The negative outcome findings in respect to type of interview within PSTS merit some discussion in view of the clear differences in input. One explanation, which has become standard in such situations, is to ascribe negative outcome findings to failure of study instruments to detect differences. This possibility cannot be dismissed, although its likelihood is diminished by the fact that the same instruments did detect differences in outcome between PSTS and CS. Perhaps it can be said that whatever differences may have occurred between PSTS individual and joint interview prescriptions did not fall within the scope of the measurements employed.

In sum, whether interviews were individual or joint made little general difference in the results of treatment under PSTS conditions. It does not follow from this that the type of interview made no difference in individual cases. For example, within the individual interview prescription there may have been cases for which joint interviews were particularly indicated but could not be used. These cases may have done less well under a regimen of individual interviews than they would have if joint interviews had been used. Conversely, the joint interview pre-

25. The proportion of joint interviews to total interviews in a case was used as the independent variable. As before, variations in total number of interviews were controlled through partial correlation.

scription may have been given to a number of cases for which individual interviews would have been more helpful. The consequent cancelling out of treatment effects could have produced the lack of differences between the two *groups* of cases. Given the design of the experiment, there is no way of really determining if this was so. The findings mean only that there was no *general tendency* for project families to do any better when service was conducted through individual interviews only than where service was conducted largely through joint interviews. Thus, the findings do not support any "across the board" claims for the superiority of individual over joint interviewing (or vice versa) with the type of families served in the project.

SIX · THE PICTURE SIX MONTHS LATER

THE ROLE OF THE SIX-MONTH FOLLOW-UP

The major purpose of the experiment as a whole was to test the relative effectiveness of different patterns of service. How the six-month follow-up relates to this purpose needs some explication.

As one group of researchers concluded, follow-up studies, conducted a period of time after cessation of service, may be a questionable means of evaluating service effectiveness:

The cumulative effect of the life experiences of psychiatric patients after the termination of treatment, coupled with the impossibility of determining what part of these experiences should be attributed to changes in the patient's behavior resulting from therapy, would make it well-nigh impossible to determine what features of the end state can be attributed to a course of treatment years before. . . . A more nearly valid evaluation of different forms of psychotherapy might be in terms of their ability to accelerate improvement. Even if the results of all forms of psychotherapy prove to be statistically undistinguishable after a sufficient lapse of time, the better therapy would be the one which achieved the greatest amount of improvement most rapidly. . . . If this view is correct, evaluation of different forms of psychotherapy should be primarily in terms of their immediate results.[1]

1. Anthony R. Stone, Jerome D. Frank, Earle H. Nash, and Stanley D. Imber, "On Intensive Five-Year Follow-Up Study of Treated Psychiatric Outpatients" in *Psychotherapy Research,* edited by Gary E. Stollak et al., p. 153.

The follow-up phase of the current experiment, albeit only six months rather than years following the end of service, provided ample evidence in support of their position. As will be shown, additional help received by families following service and the client's difficulties in recalling experiences during the service period were among the factors that limited the usefulness of the follow-up data as measures of service effectiveness.

Accordingly, data obtained at closing will constitute the primary source of evidence on service effects. The follow-up data will serve primarily to illuminate certain aspects of service effects that could not be investigated at closing, notably, the durability of closing outcomes and the presence of possible delayed effects of service. Since only the PSTS-CS comparisons yielded appreciable differences in outcomes at closing, only the comparison of these patterns will be of concern at follow-up.

FAMILY AND INDIVIDUAL CHANGE FROM CLOSING TO FOLLOW-UP

It was expected that the PSTS cases would be less likely to retain their gains than CS cases. Positive movement in the PSTS cases could have been due to the temporary relief of symptoms that often occurs, so it is said, after a brief period of service. Positive movement in CS cases could have been more "cemented in." If so, it would not be surprising to find more negative movement in the PSTS than the CS caseload between closing and follow-up.

These expectations did not materialize. The research observers' key ratings of family and individual change during the follow-up period revealed no significant differences between CS and PSTS cases.[2] The distributions of ratings for the two patterns are in fact quite similar in respect to most variables and

2. These data are presented in Appendix I, Tables 5 and 6.

categories of change. Furthermore, no significant differences were found in respect to other measures of change between closing and follow-up.

Some deterioration did occur among individuals and families receiving PSTS. From 5 to 20 per cent of the ratings on most variables fell into this category. But deterioration occurred with similar frequency within the CS caseload. There was little difference between the two patterns in respect to cases showing deterioration on one or more key measures (19 or 35 per cent for PSTS; 20 or 37 per cent for CS).

Whether or not worsening occurred seemed more a function of the variable rated than of assignment to PSTS or CS. PSTS and CS deterioration rates tended to fluctuate together across measures. The greatest losses during the follow-up period occurred in the marital area. Close to a quarter of the clients (23 per cent) were rated as worse in functioning as spouse as opposed to only 8 per cent in functioning as parent and 7 per cent in feelings about self. Similarly higher proportions of problems of marital relations were rated as aggravated than of child-related problems or problems of emotional distress.

It will be recalled that broken marriages were a factor in assessments at closing relating to the marital area. They played a much less significant role in the follow-up data. Between closing and follow-up three additional couples separated (two from PSTS, one from CS). Couples who were separated at closing were either separated or divorced at follow-up. Of 24 cases in both services in which problems of marital relations were rated as worsening between closing and follow-up, only 7 (4 CS, 3 PSTS) involved couples who were separated either at closing or follow-up.

For both services, and on all measures, proportions of families or individuals showing improvement exceeded proportions showing deterioration. For the great majority of variables, improvement rates exceeded 40 per cent; for some variables, such as feelings about self, the overall problem situation, and problems of parent-child relations and emotional distress, improvement rates exceeded 60 per cent. Most of the improvement, however, tended to be in the "slight" range.

In general, clients tended to hold on to their gains or to add to them slightly during the follow-up period. It made little difference whether these clients had received PSTS or CS.

PATTERNS OF CHANGE FROM OPENING TO FOLLOW-UP

We have seen that PSTS families were as likely to hold on to gains achieved during the service period as CS families. Since PSTS families had achieved greater gains, one might expect these families to be in a more favorable position at follow-up. In order to determine if this was so, it was necessary to combine measurements of change made at closing and follow-up. Table 6.1 presents the results of an attempt to bring these measurements together for one key variable, change in the family's problem situation.

In this table ratings of change made at closing have been adjusted by addition of ratings of change between closing and follow-up. Combining the ratings in this fashion yields an approximate measure of "net change" between opening and follow-up. Thus, if the overall problem situation was rated as alleviated for a given family at closing (+) and no change was observed during the follow-up period (o), the family's problem situation could be said to have undergone a net positive change from opening to follow-up. That is, the family would have maintained its gains during the follow-up period. Similarly, a closing rating of alleviated (+) and a follow-up rating of aggra-

Table 6.1. Net change in the family's overall problem situation, PSTS and CS.

	Research observers' rating at:		Number of families	
	Closing	Follow-up	PSTS	CS
Net change +	+	+	29	29
	+	o	14 }51	5 }41
	o	+	4	4
	+	×	4	3
Net change o	+	−	3	1
	o	o	3 }8	5 }11
	−	+	1	3
	o	×	1	2
Net change −	o	−	1	2
	−	o	0 }1	3 }8
	−	−	0	2
	−	×	0	1
		Total	60 60	60 60

Key   + Alleviated   o No change   − Aggravated
   × No rating, family not interviewed at follow-up
Differences in net change, PSTS-CS, p <.05, Chi Square.

vated (−) problem situation would yield a net rating of no change, since a change for the better from opening to closing would be cancelled out by deterioration from closing to follow-up. The various possible combinations are set forth in the table, grouped according to the type of net change yielded.[3]

It can be seen that differences in net change in the family's problem situation significantly favor PSTS. Thus the basic pattern of outcome difference between PSTS and CS observed at closing remains the same after correction is made for post-service changes. In respect to this variable, PSTS families were

3. For the 11 families not interviewed and not rated at follow-up (×), the closing rating was used as the best approximation of net change.

"better off" than CS families at closing; they remained "better off" at follow-up.

That PSTS families were in a more favorable position at follow-up cannot be taken as any kind of special evidence of the superior effectiveness of that pattern. As noted, a test of service effects is best made with closing measurements. The more that post-service changes are brought into the picture, the less we are able to say about what service *per se* was able to accomplish. Nevertheless, it is of interest that outcome advantage for PSTS at closing was strong enough to endure the follow-up period.

An additional difference between the two services is suggested by the data in Table 6.1. Within PSTS, one group of cases (17 in number) followed a particular pattern of change. Positive change occurred during the service period, followed by either no change or deterioration during the follow-up period (combinations +o and +—). Only 6 CS cases followed this pattern. This combination of changes, progress during treatment followed by lack of change or regression, is the kind normally expected in follow-up studies of treatment. One assumes that treatment will have certain positive effects, that these effects will be in evidence at the termination of treatment, that resulting gains will either remain or diminish when treatment is withdrawn. It is of interest that relatively more PSTS cases appeared to conform to this pattern.

However, the most prevalent pattern of change for families in both services is described by the ++ combination, that is, positive change during both service and follow-up periods. Almost half the project families conformed to this pattern. As can be seen, families whose problem situations were alleviated to some degree during service usually experienced additional alleviation during the follow-up period.

Net change differences for other key measures generally

showed more positive outcomes for PSTS. Differences were significantly in favor of PSTS in respect to net changes in the quality of the marriage and the emotional climate of the home. In sum, the advantage for PSTS was particularly marked for net changes in family problems and functioning.

Although no significant differences were found in favor of CS, on one set of measures, functioning of husbands and wives in the role of parent, CS did prove to have somewhat of an edge on the whole. Combining data for husbands and wives, we find that 68 per cent of CS clients showed a positive net change in functioning as parent as opposed to 52 per cent of PSTS clients. Relatively more CS clients (9 per cent) than PSTS clients (6 per cent) were rated as deteriorated, however. The higher net improvement rate for CS comes from the slightly higher proportions of clients rated as improved during both the service period and follow-up period. By contrast, net change for functioning as spouse favored PSTS, though again not to a significant degree. Here the net improvement rates for the two services were about equal (53 per cent for PSTS and 52 per cent for CS), but relatively fewer PSTS clients showed net deterioration than CS clients (10 per cent versus 23 per cent). These results support previous findings that the better outcomes generally associated with PSTS are not in evidence in 'respect to functioning in the parental role.

FOLLOW-UP ASSESSMENT INVOLVING THE CLIENT'S RECALL OF THE SERVICE PERIOD

Certain measures obtained at follow-up did not yield appreciable differences between PSTS and CS, as would have been expected from the findings presented up to this point. These measures, which involved in one way or another the client's recall of the service period, included ratings of change in family problems from the beginning of service and ratings of the helpfulness of service.[4] Two examples will be considered.

First, at follow-up the research observers assessed changes in the overall problem situation from the point of application. On these judgments differences were only marginally in favor of PSTS, and did not therefore confirm the findings with respect to the net change measure (Table 6.1). The reason for the contradiction seemed to lie in the tendency of research observers, in making their assessments of change from time of application, to give greater weight to developments during the follow-up period than during the service period. This conclusion is based on the fact that ratings of change from application to follow-up yielded a correlation of .75 with closing-to-follow-up ratings, but of only .52 with opening-to-closing ratings. This pattern of correlations, which obtained both for PSTS and CS, suggests that the more recent changes, that is, changes during the follow-up period, were given greater emphasis in assessing change from application to follow-up. Since there were minimal differences between CS and PSTS in respect to changes during the follow-up period, it is easy to see how a rating based largely on changes during this period would yield little difference. It was of course during the service period that the maximum PSTS-CS differences occurred and PSTS families achieved most of their gains. Other ratings of problem change from application to follow-up showed the same effect as ratings of change in the overall problem situation.

Follow-up ratings of the helpfulness of service to the family from the viewpoint of the research observers likewise showed no appreciable differences between PSTS and CS. Similar ratings

4. Although most follow-up measures, as well as closing measures, involved the client's memory for past events, the time spans were more limited, that is, recall of the post-service period at follow-up or of the service period at closing.

made at closing, it will be recalled, significantly favored PSTS. Now these *closing* ratings of helpfulness of service were highly correlated ($r = .72$) with *closing* ratings of change in the overall problem situation. That is, if the overall problem situation was judged to be improved at closing, service was likely to be rated as helpful and vice-versa. Interestingly enough, however, help-fulness of service ratings made at *follow-up* were correlated, *not* with closing ratings of change in the overall problem situation ($r = .19$), but with ratings of change from *closing to follow-up* ($r = .66$). Again, the more recent changes in the family's prob-lems, that is changes during the follow-up period, seemed to be exerting the greater influence on the follow-up ratings. And again this effect would tend to depress differences between PSTS and CS at follow-up. The same pattern was also found for follow-up ratings of helpfulness of service from point of view of husbands and wives.

It is not surprising that greater emphasis was placed on more recent changes in this set of follow-up ratings. Interviewers asked clients to try to take into account complex changes, usually covering a one-to-two-year period whose exact point of origin had probably been forgotten. More recent changes would well count for more in this kind of taxing recall situa-tion. Moreover, opening-to-follow-up assessments constituted a minor theme that was not strongly emphasized in an interview devoted primarily to events since closing. An interview so ori-ented would, of course, tend to highlight recent changes.

The tendency to give greater weight to recent changes has substantive implications. It suggests that the client's recall of changes occurring during the service period faded with the im-pact of subsequent events. Some would argue that this finding diminishes the significance of PSTS-CS differences in changes during the service period, since these differences were no longer detectable through the memories of the clients six months after the completion of service. This is not to say that the differences were not real or meaningful. Rather it is suggested they were not sufficiently profound to be preserved in the collective memory of our client population. We have no way of knowing, of course, how profound they would need to have been to withstand this kind of memory test.

HELP RECEIVED DURING THE FOLLOW-UP PERIOD

Whether or not families obtained additional professional help following the end of project services was of concern for two reasons. First, securing further help could possibly be seen as an "after-effect" of service. Second, further help received would need to be taken into account in assessing the stability of closing outcomes, since patterns of change during the follow-up period could be affected by additional therapeutic inputs.

A family was judged to have received help if one of its members reported at least one in-person contact with a professional person, such as a social worker, psychiatrist, clergyman, or guidance counselor, to obtain assistance with an individual or family problem. Problems for which such help was sought during the follow-up period generally involved relational or adjustment difficulties.

We expected, as did most of our practitioner colleagues, that families receiving the more limited PSTS would have greater need for further help and would be more likely to obtain it during the follow-up period. Once again, our theoretical assumptions uncannily predicted the opposite of what occurred. Significantly more CS families (24, or 44 per cent) sought help than PSTS families (12, or 22 per cent).[5]

PSTS and CS families also differed in respect to where they

5. $p < .05$, Chi Square, 1 d.f.

went for help.[6] Of the 12 PSTS families 5 returned to the Community Service Society, with the remainder using a variety of other sources, and only 2 families seeking help from a psychiatrist or mental health facility. Among the 24 CS families, the most frequent source of help was a psychiatrist or mental health facility (9 families); 4 returned to Community Service Society, the next most common source.

Further analysis revealed that direct contact with children was a factor of interest in the help received during follow-up. In none of the 9 cases returning to Community Service Society during the follow-up period was there direct contact with a child. However, in two-thirds of the cases in which help was sought from other sources, the child was seen by the therapist. It is worthy of note that all of the 9 CS families who sought help from psychiatrists or psychiatric facilities fell in this group.

The number of family members seen and the number of contacts per family member were also determined. All told, 25 PSTS and 48 CS clients were seen by a helping person; the great majority were seen at least twice and about half had over five contacts. For the individuals seen, the distribution for CS and PSTS clients in respect to number of contacts was generally similar. Since more CS clients had some contact, the total number of contacts for the CS clients was naturally greater. This was particularly true in the case of contacts with children: only 4 children seen in PSTS had two or more contacts as opposed to 13 children in CS who were seen at least twice. Finally, in the majority of cases, services received during the follow-up period were judged by the clients and research interviewers to have resulted in at least some problem alleviation.

Why should more CS families have received help during the follow-up period? A partial explanation seemed to lie in a

6. This breakdown refers to the primary source of help. Some families sought help at more than one facility.

tendency of CS families with less favorable outcomes to seek further help after the termination of service. Thus of the 24 CS families receiving post-service help, exactly half were families rated as worse at closing on one or more key measures. Only 5 of the 30 CS families not receiving help fell into this group. Further, few CS husbands and wives (6 out of 48) in families receiving additional help gave "improvement in the problem situation" as the reason for terminating regular Community Service Society help. The great majority gave reasons, such as dissatisfaction with progress, that indicated the presence of active problems at case closing. For PSTS the relation between service outcomes and receipt of additional help was similar in nature, though less strong. The small number of families (12) who secured further help placed limits on the meaningfulness of the analysis.

When data on the caseworkers' activities and attitudes in respect to post-service help for project families are brought to bear, some interesting relations emerge. To begin with, PSTS families numbered 8 of the 10 families for whom an initial goal of the caseworker was referral for further help.[7] Only one of these PSTS families actually received further help.

From analysis of the caseworkers' closing summaries, it was determined that, in half the project cases, caseworkers indicated that at least one family member needed additional help following project service. The summaries did not always specify how this was taken up with the client, although in the great majority of cases there was evidence in the record that the caseworkers encouraged these clients to seek help at a specific resource, usually at a psychiatric facility, at some point after termination of our services.

There was a slightly greater tendency for caseworkers to re-

7. Data obtained from the Caseworker's Diagnostic Schedule.

port at closing additional help needed in PSTS cases (56 per cent) than in CS cases (45 per cent). However, of the 33 PSTS families needing further help in the caseworker's judgment, only 10 families, or less than a third, actually received help during the follow-up period. By contrast, post-service help was received by 16, or over half, of the 27 CS families for whom such help was indicated.[8]

In sum, obtaining additional help during the follow-up period seemed to be associated with poorer outcomes at closing. Since CS families were more likely to have such outcomes, it would follow that families in this pattern would be more likely to secure further help. Although various interpretations of the caseworker's role are possible, there seems to have been greater agreement between caseworkers and CS families that further help was needed than between caseworkers and PSTS families. It is also of interest that relatively fewer PSTS families secured additional help despite the apparently greater caseworker emphasis on post-service help for families in this pattern, as observed in both the caseworkers' statements of initial goals and their closing summaries.

These findings must be taken into account in assessment of data describing change during the follow-up period, including measures of change from application to follow-up. It is quite possible that changes recorded during the post-project period were influenced in a positive direction by subsequent help families received. If so, then the CS change ratings would have received a disproportionate share of the benefit. As it turned out, families receiving post-project help showed about the same amount of positive change during the follow-up as families not receiving help. Unfortunately this kind of comparison is not

8. The PSTS-CS differences were statistically significant. $p < .05$, Chi Square.

conclusive since these two groups of families differed systematically, at least among CS cases. Thus, additional treatment may have enabled certain CS families whose problems had worsened by closing to achieve the same amount of positive change during the follow-up period as possibly healthier families that did not receive additional treatment. Although this may not have happened, there is no way to rule out the possibility.

THE CLIENT'S PERCEPTION OF NEED FOR HELP AT THE POINT OF FOLLOW-UP

Data on the client's felt need for help at follow-up were obtained primarily to find out if clients receiving a brief, time-limited service had greater need for additional help than clients who had the opportunity to receive as much service as they wanted.

Clients were asked whether or not they currently felt the need of additional help for personal and family problems. Overall, 38 per cent of the clients interviewed said they did, in most instances for problems of marital or parent-child relations or problems of emotional distress. The majority planned either to return to the Community Service Society or to go to a psychiatrist or mental health facility. PSTS-CS differences were not significant. A somewhat higher proportion of CS than PSTS husbands indicated a current need for help; the reverse was true for the wives. Interpretation of the clients' responses to this item was complicated, however, by the fact that a number of clients who were currently receiving help said they felt no need for additional help at the point of follow-up. In order to obtain an unduplicated picture of needs unmet by project services, we determined the proportion of clients who had either expressed a need for help at follow-up or who had received help during the follow-up period. Fifty-two per cent of the CS clients interviewed fell into one or both categories; the comparable figure for PSTS was 42 per cent. When analyzed separately for husbands and wives, the differences were not statistically significant. Nevertheless, they are at least consistent with the differences in respect to help actually received.

That almost half (47 per cent) of the project clients and at least one client in over half of the project families (56 per cent) received or wanted further help is in itself impressive. This persistence of expressed need for help must be taken into account in assessing project services as a whole. It would be naive to expect that casework treatment in the project should have provided complete or lasting solutions for the complex, long-standing problems that our families brought to us. There is evidence that families were helped in meaningful ways even though these problems may not have been resolved. It is also true that further help was sought or wished in some cases for minor or residual problems following substantial alleviation of major difficulties. Nevertheless, the continued push for help provokes some thoughts about the nature and consequences of project treatment. In retrospect, such treatment may be better seen as one of a series of help-seeking efforts by project families rather than as an ultimate resource. It may also have served to maintain or even stimulate needs for additional help for problems it could not be expected to resolve. In some cases this may have been for the good. Still, any hope that either brief or extended treatment of family problems will drastically reduce felt needs for treatment receives little encouragement from these findings.

HELP IN THE FUTURE

Toward the end of the follow-up interview, clients were asked: "If you should again feel in need of help with the kind of problems that brought you to the Community Service Society, what source do you think you would turn to?" The question, of course, was another attempt to elicit the client's evaluation of the service patterns. It was assumed that a choice of the Community Service Society as the resources the client would turn to would reflect a positive evaluation of the client's experience in the project. The results are presented in Table 6.2.

Table 6.2. "If you should again feel in need of help with the kind of problems that brought you to Community Service Society, what source would you turn to?"

	Husbands				Wives			
Source clients would turn to	PSTS		CS		PSTS		CS	
	N	%	N	%	N	%	N	%
Community Service Society	29	66	19	50	36	71	26	53
Other	9	20	9	24	7	14	13	27
Unable to specify	6	14	10	26	8	16	10	20
Total reported	44	100	38	100	51	100	49	100

First, it is gratifying to note that the majority of clients interviewed would return if they had it to do all over again. Second, although the differences between PSTS and CS are not significant, an even higher proportion of PSTS clients, both husbands and wives, would choose Community Service Society. The relatively high proportion of PSTS wives who would return is of particular interest in view of their reservations at closing about the brevity of their service experience. Although these PSTS-CS differences are not strong enough to be decisive, they are consistent with the higher valuations given PSTS at closing. It is possible that this finding represents this higher valuation in attenuated form.

SEVEN · ASSESSMENTS OF THE MAJOR RESULTS OF THE EXPERIMENT

THE PRINCIPAL FINDINGS of the experiment concern differences in outcome between continued service and planned short-term service. It was quite unexpected and rather puzzling that families receiving a service limited to eight interviews should have made more progress during treatment than families receiving a service that provided, on the whole, a far greater number of interviews. Further, as the follow-up data indicated, gains made by PSTS families proved as durable as those achieved by CS families.

When findings run counter to prevailing notions, as these findings certainly do, more is demanded in the way of an explanation than if expectations are confirmed. Moreover, the findings have some provocative implications for casework practice. This chapter is therefore primarily devoted to an analysis of why outcomes for PSTS families proved more favorable.

In the course of this analysis some general hypotheses relating to the treatment of family problems and to family change are suggested. The results of the experiment have greatest relevance for casework treatment of the problems of intact, middle-income families. The relevance of the findings progressively diminish with each further departure from our particular samples of clients, problems, services, and practitioners. In an experiment with selective samples such as ours, any generalizations that exceed the boundaries of whatever has been actually studied assume the status of conjectures for the reader's consideration. The limits of such conjectures are a matter of judgment, if not of taste.

The straightforward approach to interpreting the differences in outcome between PSTS and CS is to assume that they were the result of differences in the effects of the two services. If this assumption is granted, then attention can be turned to why PSTS may have been more effective. We shall grant this assumption for the time being and proceed accordingly, even though, as shown, it is possible to explain the differences in outcome without recourse to explanations involving differences in service effects.

If we assume that PSTS was the more effective of the two patterns, then the reason for its greater effectiveness should logically lie in the characteristics that distinguish it from CS. If so, then how might the differing service characteristics have resulted in the differing outcomes? In developing some possible answer to this question, we view the difference in service inputs as having their origins in contrasting features of the *structures* of the two services: PSTS is structured as a brief service with a predetermined end-point, and CS as an open-ended service of frequently long duration. One may then assume that the structure of PSTS had different effects on both the caseworker and the client from the structure of CS, and that these dissimilar effects in turn led to differences in outcome. In these terms the structure of service would presumably shape the caseworker's operation in certain ways, which in turn would have their effects on the client. At the same time the clients themselves may be affected in certain ways by the structure of service, whether or not the caseworker is operating in a special way. For example, a client may have liked PSTS, because the caseworker was active or simply because the service was short.

THE ROLE OF THE CASEWORKER

Whether a case was assigned to PSTS or CS made a difference in the caseworker's performance. The distinctive characteristics of caseworker intervention in PSTS may then have been a factor in the relative success of this service pattern. The structure of PSTS appears to have affected the caseworker's level and timing of activity, her goals, her treatment planning, and perhaps her general performance.

The more active treatment approach used by caseworkers in PSTS was a major point of input difference between the two services. It is possible that the higher level of caseworker activity in PSTS accomplished its purpose, that is, to effect changes through greater use of more overt, direct attempts to influence the client's thinking and actions. Since CS clients, in the long run, received more of this kind of communication simply because they received a greater number of interviews, the question of dosage becomes important. The concentration of more active types of intervention during a small number of interviews may have provided greater stimulus for change than the more numerous but less intensive CS interviews. It was not possible to link up specific kinds of worker interventions and specific client changes, although there was evidence that clients liked the more active style of PSTS.

The findings suggest that the more active casework techniques characteristic of PSTS may be more efficacious than the techniques characteristic of CS. This statement is practically meaningless unless we can specify the nature and level of activity that produces the better result. Yet the mix of techniques used in PSTS did not differ in any radical way from the mix used in CS. Also, as we have learned, hypotheses regarding technique must take caseworker styles into account. Thus, if the level of advice-giving characteristic of PSTS were to be used as a guide to establish an optimum level for this technique, one might suggest that an average of six or so advice-giving responses per interview was somewhere in the right range. Such a level would probably be higher, but not a great deal higher, than is customary in casework, and it is also certainly lower than the level used by some caseworkers. Since a certain level of advice per interview was used in the more successful PSTS pattern, it may follow that this level is associated with good treatment results. It does not follow, however, that an even higher level would yield better results or that advice should be used "extensively."

The same line of reasoning can be applied to other techniques used in a distinctive way in PSTS, as well as to the greater general activity level of caseworkers in that pattern. Clearly it would be foolish to strive to establish recommended doses of this or that approach. But there should be a place for some reasonable precision in linking up techniques and outcomes.

Another consideration is timing of activity. The relative success of PSTS suggests that there may be special advantages to be gained from greater caseworker activity early in treatment, whether treatment is planned and brief or open-ended and long. Although the first interview within the two patterns was not the first with the family, it did represent the beginning of a particular course of treatment and was, in any event, an early interview in work with a particular client. There is some division of opinion about what the caseworker's objectives and approach should be this early in treatment. Some practitioners would hold (as apparently our practitioners did in CS) that such an interview should be primarily exploratory, with emphasis upon obtaining a more thorough understanding of the client and his problem. Others would combine further exploration of the problem with beginning efforts to stimulate specific changes through advice, logical discussion, confrontation, and the like (the practice followed by our caseworkers in PSTS). Our findings, of course, would tend to support the latter position. An active first interview, in which exploratory responses made up less than half the worker's communications, not only occurred in the more successful pattern but it also may have been a factor in bringing clients back for a second interview. To put it negatively, the findings offer little endorsement for the greater emphasis on an exploratory approach in the early CS interviews following intake and no support whatsoever for the notion that the kind of active approach described for the first interview in PSTS promotes client discontinuance.[1]

The caseworker's treatment approach differed between the two services, not only in respect to technique but also in respect to goals. It is hard to say what part the more specific goal formulation in PSTS may have played in its greater success. As Phillips has said, "A time limit for treatment lends an immediacy and sharpness, and it brings an urgency that makes structuring inevitable, so that there is less improvisation and drift in therapy."[2] The broader the treatment goals, the greater the tendency, perhaps, for treatment to become overly diffuse and thereby less effective. Moreover, in CS, caseworkers may have tended to concentrate excessive attention on underlying or re-

---

1. An opposite conclusion was reached by Hollis in a study of the relationship between continuance and the caseworkers' techniques in the first intake interview. See Florence Hollis "Continuance and Discontinuance in Marital Counseling and Some Observations on Joint Interviews," *Social Casework,* Vol. XLIX, No. 3, (March 1968), 169, 171. The difference between the very first interview with a client and the second or third may account for the difference in results.

2. E. Lakin Phillips and Daniel N. Wiener, *Short-Term Psychotherapy and Structured Behavior Change,* p. 5.

fractory problems not susceptible to modification through case-work treatment. For example, caseworkers (according to their own reports) *dealt* with more problems of school adjustment of children in CS than in PSTS but did not succeed in *alleviating* more problems of this type. Possibly caseworkers here and else-where were more selective in the treatment objectives in PSTS, with the result not only of greater economy in effort but also of the choice of objectives whose attainment was more likely.

For example, in one PSTS case involving a parent-child prob-lem, the caseworker outlined in her diagnostic assessment the various objectives she would have liked to pursue had the case been CS. Most of these objectives had to do with altering under-lying patterns in a relationship between an anxious, overprotec-tive mother and her underachieving child. The caseworker then commented rather ruefully that, since the case had been assigned to PSTS, she would have to settle for a more modest goal, namely to help the mother "get off the kid's back," particularly in respect to his situation at school. The caseworker succeeded in getting the father to take over the mother's responsibility for supervising the child's homework and in getting the mother to let him work out some minor problems with his teacher on his own. The mother's reluctance to let her son take appropriate responsibility for his own actions was pointed out, and she was helped to see how this reluctance was a reflection of her need to have a "perfect child." By the seventh interview both the mother and the caseworker agreed (judging from the taped comments) that her relationship with her son was better. The mother wanted to quit at that point but came in for one more interview, because eight interviews had been planned.

In this case at least, the gearing-down and focusing of the caseworker's goals may have had a beneficial effect on the course and outcome of treatment. Had the case been assigned to CS and had the caseworker pursued her more far-reaching objectives, it is possible that what was sought would have proved unattainable and what was attainable would have been overlooked.

Because of its limited, predictable length, PSTS doubtless facilitated the caseworker's planning of treatment. Treatment objectives and approach, and possibly the topics of certain interviews, could be mapped out in advance with greater ease. There was also greater certainty that the family would complete the projected course of treatment, and that husbands in particular would be around at the finish. In the combination prescription, for example, the caseworkers could plan with a fair degree of certainty on conducting PSTS through joint interviews, whereas such plans were likely to go awry in CS. We do not know to what extent the course of treatment in PSTS was planned out or how such planning may have influenced outcomes. A certain amount of planning would enable the practitioner to work out in advance the more effective treatment strategies in a given case; over-planning could of course result in excessive rigidity. Possibly the limits of PSTS opened the way for the kind of planning that could add to the effectiveness of treatment.

Finally, the limits of PSTS may have had a certain mobilizing effect on the caseworker's motivation and general performance. Her more active and focused approach may have been one reflection of this effect, but there may have been others. If the time in which certain operations are to be carried out is limited, a person may try harder and work more efficiently, with the result that as much, if not more, is accomplished than if he has an unlimited amount of time at his disposal. In PSTS caseworkers may have been more attentive, energetic, faster-moving, and all of this may have provided the client with greater stimulus for change. We cannot say for sure how great this mobilizing effect and its consequences may have been. There is little real evidence to go on. One specific connection comes to mind, however. The fact that caseworkers felt less comfortable in PSTS may be an indicator of the time pressures they felt in this pattern, but clients had a more positive attitude toward the caseworker's attitude and personality, possibly an indicator of the client's reaction to a more energized practitioner.

It is possible, of course, that the caseworker's motivation and performance in PSTS may have been enhanced by the challenge of carrying out an unfamiliar form of treatment. If so (and if we are willing to discount the values of added experience) her effectiveness in PSTS might be expected to diminish as she became more familiar with this pattern. Thus in his study of short-term therapy Malan found "some slight evidence" that the therapists were more successful with earlier than later cases.[3] Although we did not find such a tendency in the present experiment, it may be argued that no caseworker treated a large enough number of cases in PSTS to permit a wearing off of its novelty. Also, the challenge posed by PSTS may have been heightened by the research component of the experiment, with its scrutiny of service characteristics and outcomes.

For these reasons, among others, a service innovation may prove more efficacious in an experimental trial than after it has been incorporated as an established part of a program. Should this be true of PSTS in the present instance, its superiority over CS might not obtain under normal practice conditions. This possibility should introduce a note of caution in using the results of the experiment as the basis for modifying ongoing programs. On the other hand, it must be recognized that further experimental trials of PSTS as an innovation could provide no definitive answers on this score. Inevitably such experiments would be subject to the kind of effects just described.

3. D.H. Malan, *Brief Psychotherapy*, p. 274.

THE EFFECTS OF SERVICE STRUCTURE ON THE CLIENT

The structure of PSTS and CS may have had quite different effects on the clients and these effects may have contributed to the differences in outcome. We are referring here to client responses to a service with a brief, fixed duration, on the one hand, and to a service of indeterminate length, on the other. Such effects may have occurred regardless of the specific characteristics of the caseworker's approach.

Turning first to PSTS, the structure of the service may have conveyed to the client the expectancy of positive change within a brief period, with a resulting elevation of motivation and hope. The brevity of the service period may have brought forth an extra effort from the client as it may have from the caseworker. The predetermined end-point in PSTS may have enabled the client to contract his expectations of change, so that he could end treatment with a feeling of having made some progress within the allotted period. In a way termination in PSTS might have served a psychological function similar to that served by a school graduation, which, after all, is just another instance of a pre-planned ending. Graduation from a prescribed program of instruction, whether elementary school or college, usually gives the student some feeling of mastery, since graduation itself is set forth as an achievement and since considerable emphasis is placed on what was accomplished during the program. At the end of PSTS clients may have felt an analogous sense of accomplishment, while their CS counterparts were perhaps more likely to have doubts about the rightness of ending when they did.

In general, the PSTS client's expectancy that positive changes might occur within a brief period of time may have generated a set of conditions that helped to bring such changes about. A similar hypothesis was developed by Frank following a review of several investigations of time-limited treatment. "These studies suggest that the speed of improvement may often be largely determined by the patient's expectancies as conveyed to him by the therapist, as to duration of treatment, and that a favorable response to brief treatment may be enduring."[4]

Notions from crisis theory may also shed some light on the client's response to the structure of PSTS. As crisis theorists suggest, considerable change in family and individual functioning may occur in reaction to a crisis situation.[5] In fact the crisis situation is presumably an optimal period for change since established patterns have been upset and new modes of response are demanded. The client's willingness to experiment with new ways of coping, and consequently his openness to help, may be at a peak. Although families treated in the experiment did not come for help with clear-cut, time-limited crises, they were, nonetheless, experiencing problems that had upset existing balances to the point where professional assistance was sought. Their turning for help perhaps signalled both a crisis in coping with chronic strains and an effort at resolution. If propositions from crisis theory are applicable to this group, then the greatest push for change within the families probably occurred when problems reached a point of unmanageability. As problems once again became more manageable, possibly quite soon in most cases, motivation for change may have diminished.

The mobilization of client effort stimulated by the limits of PSTS may have coincided with, and may possibly have reinforced, the push for change induced by the crisis. Quite possi-

4. Jerome Frank, "The Dynamics of the Psychotherapeutic Relationship," *Psychiatry*, XXII (February 1959), 33.
5. See, for example, Lydia Rapoport, "The State of Crisis: Some Theoretical Considerations." *Social Service Review*, XXXVI (June 1962), 211-17.

bly the span of PSTS fell within the period of greatest client susceptibility to change and to help. Since her goals had to be limited, the caseworker may have concentrated her attention on more immediate, resolvable problems. In sum, PSTS may have been particularly well suited to the kind of family crises dealt with in the project.

Client reactions to the structure of PSTS were not, however, so overwhelmingly positive as the foregoing analysis might imply. We must not forget that a third of the clients in PSTS expressed a dislike of the brevity of service. That these clients may still have benefited from various aspects of the structure of PSTS is suggested by the fact that most who thought PSTS too brief also thought it helpful. Nevertheless, this discontent with the limits of service is in itself a matter of concern. Since some clients seem to have been taken a little by surprise at the suddenness of service termination, it is possible that the prescribed limits of service were not always sufficiently well explained or understood. Also, the time lapse of three months (median) between initial application and the beginning of service may have created the impression among future PSTS clients that treatment would be a long-term affair. A more thorough interpretation of service limits and a more rapid delivery of service could possibly have reduced the proportion of clients who felt they were given too few interviews.

Our finding that wives were more likely to complain about the brevity of service than husbands merits some comment. Not only were husbands less likely to complain about this feature of PSTS, but they were also more likely to fade out of CS cases. Men may be less accepting of a continuing casework relationship, which represents among other things a threat to their sense of adequacy as "head of the house." Women may have a greater concern over family problems, may feel more responsible for their solutions, or may have greater need to talk things out with a sympathetic listener.

The structure of CS may have had a quite different impact on the client from that of PSTS. If we assume that differences in the service patterns themselves played a part in the differences in outcome, then it would follow that the structure of CS had fewer positive and more negative consequences for the client.

One way of putting it would be to say that the structure of CS was not able to produce certain special effects that may have occurred in PSTS. Its open-endedness, with intimations that the end might be rather far off, may have conveyed expectations that change would be slow in coming and difficult to achieve. The elevation of hope, motivation, and effort seemingly stimulated by PSTS may not have occurred in CS. Moreover, CS may not have been able to capitalize as much on crisis-induced motivation for change, because of its greater emphasis on long-run objectives.

The structure of CS may not only have failed to produce certain beneficial effects on the client that were induced by various features of PSTS, but it is also possible that some aspects of CS structure had negative consequences for the client. Although service was rarely judged to have made things worse, we still need to account for the higher deterioration rates in the CS caseload. It may have been that CS was unable to reverse certain kinds of deterioration. Or it may have been that in the course of service the CS clients became aware of problems that they might not have recognized earlier. We cannot rule out the possibility, however, that CS may have created certain problems. As various studies have suggested, interpersonal treatment may very well have the capacity for making things worse as well as better.[6]

6. See Allen E. Bergin, "Some Implications of Psychotherapy Research," *International Journal of Psychiatry*, III (March 1967), 139.

For example, termination in CS may have added to the client's difficulties in certain cases. In most CS cases, the point of termination was determined by the client, even though he may have been influenced by the caseworker's opinion about his needs for help. On the surface, it is hard to see how letting the client decide when to stop could add to his trouble. But when we think of the basis he must use for his decision, some of the negative aspects become clearer. If the client could decide to leave because of improvement in his situation, as was the case with about a quarter of the CS clients, perhaps there was no problem. A far more common basis seemed to be that the client decided service was no longer helping sufficiently to warrant his continuing. It is quite easy to see how such a decision may have caused distress. Some clients may have tended to blame themselves for lack of further progress. Others may have interpreted termination as the caseworker's rejection of them, particularly if the caseworker had encouraged the client to quit. The finding that CS clients thought their caseworkers felt less positively toward them than did PSTS clients adds weight to both of these possibilities. Such negative reactions to termination may be temporary or may occur even though real progress has been achieved, and going through the agonies of choice may be good for some clients. Nevertheless, if we grant that the problems of clients such as ours usually do not end with service, a predetermined point of termination, as in PSTS, may lessen feelings of inadequacy and rejection. To return to our educational analogy, it is not hard to imagine the turmoil students might experience at graduation if it occurred at a point when they (or their instructors) felt they were "ready" for it.

The potential or actual length of CS is another aspect of its structure that may have had negative effects. Its *potential* length, its open-endedness really, may have precipitated some of the early withdrawals. The seven CS families that failed to return for a second interview come to mind in particular. Clients may be more willing to see through to the end a service they know will be of short duration than to get started with a service of undetermined length.

The *actual* length of service is quite a different matter. Although no particular length of service is prescribed in CS, service of long duration is generally expected and frequently occurs. It is often assumed that the more service a client receives, the more he is benefited. But any remedy can be taken in excess. We must consider the possibility that some of our CS clients received an "overdose" of casework. For some clients a certain amount of treatment may be helpful but beyond that point may possibly be harmful, whether the point of diminishing returns be the tenth interview or the hundredth.

Treatment extended beyond the client's tolerance level may conceivably stir up dormant problems that would have been better left alone. The tendency for greater use of modifying techniques (as reported by the caseworkers) to be associated with a decline in wives' feelings about themselves in CS (but not in PSTS) may be a case in point.

Extended treatment must also be seen in relation to progress and problems in the caseworker-client relationship. There certainly appeared to be greater evidence of difficulty in these relationships in CS than PSTS. Fewer CS clients expressed liking for their caseworkers, showed an increase in positive feelings toward them during the course of treatment, and saw their caseworkers as feeling positively toward them. It is hard to say what portion of these differences may be attributable to the duration of service, but it is at least clear that the relationships were less positive from the client's point of view in the longer service pattern.

It is expected that a long-term treatment relationship will have its vicissitudes. More specifically the development of a negative reaction on the part of the client toward the caseworker may be a reflection of his interpersonal difficulties in general. According to treatment theory the client is helped to "work through" these "transference" reactions in a way that, it is hoped, will improve his overall functioning.[7] Up to a point the theory of transference offers a reasonable explanation of our findings relating to the client's reaction to the caseworker: PSTS ended during the initial period of positive transference, "the honeymoon period," with which a treatment relationship normally begins. One would expect more negative feelings in CS as transference reactions began to develop. But we would also expect these reactions to be worked through or resolved by the end of treatment. It is at this point that the treatment model and the project data take different turns. In a sizable number of CS cases caseworkers were not able to reverse a downward tendency in the client's feelings toward them. In some of these cases, it may have been negative transference reactions that precipitated termination.

There are other ways of interpreting these findings. The CS client's feelings toward his worker may have cooled off more because he felt he was helped less, or because over time he may have come to perceive the caseworker in more realistic terms, just as a more realistic perception of the spouse is often the essence of loss of affection after the honeymoon. But, however we interpret them, the findings still suggest the possibility that by extending the length of service the caseworker may suffer greater losses than gains in the client's feelings toward him.

Reference has been made to aspects of the structure of CS that may have had negative consequences for *some* clients, at least enough to account for the greater deterioration in CS cases. This structure may well have offered particular advantages for certain clients, although we have no data to support this con-

7. Hollis, *Casework*, pp. 161-62.

tention. We should consider the possibility, however, that certain positive effects of CS were not adequately measured. In other words, our instruments, or our application of them, may have minimized certain kinds of benefits received by CS clients.

Service may have certain transitory effects, or sustaining functions, that are not apparent in measures of change. A continuing relationship with a caseworker may provide the client with certain kinds of benefits that do not entail change: a feeling of having someone to turn to; a chance to get things off his chest once a week; a source of help for day-to-day problems, and so on. As a result, the client may feel better or function better as long as service continues, and some clients no doubt use casework in this way to good advantage. But this kind of benefit may well cease with the end of service. The client may leave service functioning pretty much in the same way as he began, with his major problems in much the same state. Measures of change would indicate that service had no effects. The assessment would be valid in respect to changes between established points of time, but invalid in respect to transient, week-to-week effects, no longer in evidence at the time of evaluation.

Our measurements of change would be relatively insensitive to effects of this kind, and so would obviously operate to the detriment of CS. Almost by definition longer cases would receive more help of this kind, otherwise it would be difficult to explain why clients would continue to keep, and pay for, weekly appointments over long periods of time. This argument raises just one of the many difficulties encountered in attempting to assess the relative effectiveness of two services as different in structure, and possibly in function, as CS and PSTS.

Two points need to be made, however. While the transitory effects have their values, evaluations of service effects are customarily based on the assumption that service should produce changes lasting beyond its duration. This assumption formed the foundation for the assessments of outcomes in this project and these assessments must be seen in that light. Furthermore, some question can be raised about the importance of transitory effects in CS cases in the project. If such benefits constituted a special advantage of CS, one might have expected CS clients to have been more positive in their evaluation of the components and helpfulness of service and of the caseworker, than PSTS clients, and this was clearly not the case.

It can also be argued that our outcome measures, admittedly no less crude than such measures usually are, did not adequately reflect the magnitude of change in some clients receiving extended treatment. For example, the quality of a marriage in a given case might be rated as considerably improved because of an accumulation of modest, positive change, such as fewer quarrels or greater frequency of sexual relations. In another case, both partners might have experienced a total reorientation to their relationship with radical improvement in the quality of the marriage. This case too would have been rated as considerably improved, in this respect. No higher rating was possible. Such a "ceiling effect" could have worked to the disadvantage of CS if, in fact, "considerable" improvement in CS cases was somehow greater than "considerable" improvement in PSTS. It is true, and must not be forgotten, that at this upper level of positive change there was essentially no difference in outcomes between the two patterns. But only a small minority of ratings reached this level in either pattern. It seems unlikely, therefore, that our closing measurements overlooked any appreciable numbers of cases or clients in either pattern achieving a level of improvement beyond "considerable." The comparison of CS interviews did not provide the picture of consistent forward progress one might expect if CS clients had, in fact, achieved a level of improvement not adequately measured by the research observers' and caseworkers' ratings. Finally, if CS clients changed in a more profound way, it could be expected that these changes would prove to be more enduring. The follow-up data provide little support for this contention.

A subtler and more compelling argument would be that greater positive change in CS clients was masked by shifts in their frames of reference or expectations resulting from extended treatment. For example, increased awareness of one's self, problems, or situation may lead to changes in one's very concept of change. Real improvements may be devalued since the client may now be expecting more of himself or of others. Although there is no evidence that increasing the client's awareness was given greater stress in CS interviews, treatment did go on for a longer period, so that it is conceivable that such shifts in the client's awareness were more likely to occur. There is no way to rule out this possibility with available data. This kind of interpretation appears, however, somewhat inconsistent with the caseworkers' impressions that PSTS clients achieved greater changes in self-perception and with the lack of detectable progression in the CS client's understanding of his own behavior. In general, there were no findings to support the notion that the longer exposure to treatment in CS resulted in the client's achieving more awareness, or a different kind of awareness, from what clients achieved in PSTS.

This line of argument has endless forms. One may postulate some special positive effect of CS that might have led to a distortion of measures of change. Or one might argue that longer treatment may have caused CS clients to be more frank and realistic in acknowledging remaining problems. Perhaps enough has been said, however, to make the point that our measures may have underrated certain positive effects of CS.

Given the gross and limited nature of our assessments and the difficulties in comparing two services as diverse as PSTS and CS, one cannot expect a complete accounting for all possibilities. Little evidence could be found, however, to support the arguments that substantial positive effects of CS went unmeasured. These arguments were derived mostly from certain *suppositions* about the effects of extended treatment. While some may disagree, it is our conclusion that more serious question can be raised about the validity of these suppositions than about the validity of our measurements.

AN ALTERNATIVE EXPLANATION

As has been demonstrated, we hope, the major results of the experiment can be plausibly explained under the *assumption* that these differences in outcome between PSTS and CS were largely the *result* of differences in the characteristics of the two services. This assumption, however, is open to question. To confirm causal links between treatment and effects, it is necessary to control for extraneous variables. Although this was the function of the experimental design, at least one extraneous variable was so much a part of the basic difference between the two services, that its control was not possible. We are referring, in general, to the passage of time: more time elapsed between initiation and termination of service in PSTS and CS.

The possible effect of this time variable would be more readily apparent had CS outcomes been the more favorable. Since favorable changes may be associated with the passage of time (the well-known maturation effect) one would have been hard put to know whether to attribute the more favorable outcomes for CS to service effects or to the greater time lapse. Just because the results turned out the other way does not mean we can dismiss this variable as being of no consequence. It is possible that, in some ways, the passage of time may have worked to the disadvantage of CS. Had assessments occurred at comparable points of time for each service (say at the end of four, eight, and twelve months from opening), instead of at closing and six months later, it would have been possible to account in large measure for passage-of-time effects. Unfortunately this plan was not followed, largely because the confounding effects of the passage of time were not fully appreciated.

First we shall consider the possibility that the PSTS-CS outcome differences may have been a function of the combined effects of differences between the services in respect to time span and timing of assessments. Then an attempt will be made to arrive at a final assessment of the outcome differences, taking into account the various possible explanations offered.

For most families receiving PSTS closing asessments were made in the fourth or fifth month following initiation of service; for CS families this period was more variable, but with eight months the median length of time between the beginning of service and the closing assessment. It is possible to explain the differences in outcomes at closing on the basis of this time factor alone, without recourse to service effects. That is, the two services may have been equally effective (or equally ineffective) and still one could have obtained the kind of differences in outcome that were, in fact, obtained.

For example, let us assume that differences in *input* between PSTS and CS really bore *no* relation to differences in service *effectiveness*. It is quite possible that the bulk of improvement in both PSTS and CS cases occurred within the first few months after help was sought. This improvement could have been largely the result of the families' own recuperative powers, of casework intervention, or of a combination of both. But let us suppose that improvement occurred at similar rates in both groups of cases.

With further passage of time most cases might have continued to improve, though at a much slower rate, and some cases may have deteriorated, or at least experienced a slump, after achieving a peak of improvement in the first months. In other words, project cases may have followed a certain kind of improvement curve, marked by a fairly steep rise in the early months after the onset of the presenting problem, followed by a general leveling off, with some cases continuing to improve and others slipping back. The study of client movement over the course of CS lends some support to the validity of this picture. Thus husbands seemed to reach the peak of progress early in treatment. Since wives displayed no marked pattern in this respect it is possible that change in family functioning, particularly marital functioning, followed the husband's improvement curve.

Given this kind of curve, different outcome pictures for PSTS and CS families could have been the result of differences in the timing of the closing assessments. Most PSTS families would have been assessed at a point of peak recovery; CS families, at a point after the rate of improvement had begun to slow down or perhaps after some backsliding had occurred.

Such an explanation is compatible with certain of the data. Thus, a greater number of marital separations had occurred among CS families at the time of the closing assessment. A marital separation is one kind of negative change, negative at least in terms of family functioning, that may be found more frequently after a relatively lengthy time interval than after a relatively brief one. Thus, if one were to begin, as we did, with 120 intact but troubled families, one would expect the cumulative proportion of broken families to increase with the passage of time alone. However, the number of marital separations in PSTS cases up to the time of follow-up (3) was still less than the number in CS cases up to case closing (7).

More generally, on the basis of the curve presented above, one would predict about as many PSTS cases showing some deterioration during the follow-up period as there were CS cases showing deterioration up to the time of case closing. It is true that the proportion of PSTS showing deterioration from closing to follow-up was about the same as the proportion of CS cases evidencing deterioration during the period of service.

It is possible that the time factor had different effects in different areas. Thus marital problems and marital functioning, the area of greatest PSTS superiority, may have been less subject to continued improvement over time, more subject to cycles of improvement and deterioration, than child-related problems and parental functioning, areas in which the outcome differences between the services were less decisive. Our findings indicate that a much higher proportion of project clients experienced a down-turn in marital than parental functioning during the follow-up period. If such vicissitudes are particularly characteristic of marital role performance, then the span of PSTS may possibly have coincided with the span of the presenting marital crisis, from inception to reconciliation. In CS, marital cases may have gone beyond this point, perhaps in some instances to end in the throes of some new cycle of marital conflict.

Finally, it is possible that the "recency effect" observed in the follow-up measures also affected the closing measures. More recent changes may have been given more weight at closing. If so, and if the rate of improvement had in fact begun to slow down after the first few months, the changes reported for PSTS families would have appeared greater than changes reported for CS families. For PSTS families *recent* change would be more likely to coincide with the period of maximum improvement; for CS families recent change would be more likely to reflect the more modest gains that had occurred subsequent to this period.

The fit between our data and this explanation is far from perfect, however. For example, the apparently greater success of PSTS with marital problems is hard to explain completely on the basis of the difference in time span between the two services. The higher proportion of CS families with marital problems who dropped out of treatment prior to the fifth interview cannot be accounted for by the time span differences. As already indicated, the number of marital separations occurring among PSTS cases between the beginning of service and follow-up (3) is still less than the number occurring in CS between the beginning of service and closing (7). While PSTS cases at *follow-up* and CS cases at *closing* showed similar patterns of deterioration, measures of deterioration at follow-up for PSTS cases may not be comparable with such measures for CS cases at closing. Deterioration for a CS case during the service period could be interpreted as a result of treatment. It would be more difficult to make this interpretation for a PSTS case whose deterioration occurred after the service period.

This line of interpretation is also difficult to reconcile with the tendency for family functioning and problems on the whole to improve with the passing of time, as evidenced by the sizable proportions of families who continued to show positive change after the termination of service. Just as one can argue that some families suffered reverses as time passed, one can also argue that time was a friend to other families. In fact it is a general finding in follow-up studies that people with emotional and interpersonal problems tend to get better as time goes on whether they receive help or not.[8] If so, the longer time span in CS may have worked to the advantage of that pattern in some respects just as it may have worked to its disadvantage in others. Certainly one would be more apt to find families who benefited from the healing effects of time in CS than in PSTS. In short, to assume that the

8. Hans J. Eysenck, *The Effects of Psychotherapy*, p. 37.

outcome advantage of PSTS can be explained by its shorter time span is to assume that the passage of time had largely adverse effects. The assumption may have some validity in the case of marital functioning and problems and may be used as one explanation of apparent PSTS superiority in that area. For certain areas, such as parental functioning, the evidence supports the assumption that improvement continued over time. One would then have expected greater and more consistent differences favoring CS in parental functioning and related areas, if time alone were the crucial variable.

Finally, differences in outcome between PSTS and CS were not confined to measures of change. Differences in respect to aspects of service liked and disliked, the client's feeling toward the caseworker, and help-seeking during the follow-up period cannot be so readily explained on the basis of differences in the time spans of the two services.

This analysis has not yielded any definite conclusions about the role the time factor may have played in the differences in outcome between PSTS and CS. Indeed no such conclusions are possible. The differences in the time spans of the two services and in the timing of the closing assessments unfortunately introduce a set of variables whose impact cannot be measured. Accordingly, about the only safe conclusion that can be drawn is that PSTS clients exhibited a more favorable pattern of outcomes than CS clients. Unfortunately we cannot say for sure what caused these outcome differences. Moreover, given the lack of a control group receiving no treatment, we cannot unequivocally attribute outcomes in either pattern to the effects of service. For example, we have no way of knowing if the improvement rates of PSTS families would have been significantly better than the rates of a comparable group of families receiving no service at all.

A FINAL ASSESSMENT OF THE DIFFERENCES IN OUTCOMES

If we assume that casework services in the project had some measure of effectiveness, then the evidence suggests that PSTS was the more effective of the patterns. Taking into account the possibility that certain positive effects of CS were not adequately measured and the possibility that differences in the time spans of the two services may have worked to the disadvantage of the longer pattern, one could make a case for a lack of difference in service effectiveness. However, the data offer *no* basis for arguing that CS was really the more effective of the two patterns and that this greater effectiveness got *reversed* somehow in the measurement process. This point is crucial in view of the greater investments of time, cost, and energy on the part of the client, the caseworker, and the agency in the more extended service. In this particular race PSTS needed only a tie to win.

Even if we discount the seemingly greater effectiveness of PSTS and limit ourselves to the more conservative interpretation of the findings, that CS was no more effective than PSTS, certain conclusions follow. It appears that CS, on the whole, was carried well beyond the point of diminishing returns, even though some cases may have benefited from extended service. CS was not able to better the outcomes achieved by clients in the briefer pattern. If certain families achieved quick improvement in their problems, followed by some deterioration with the passage of time, CS seemed unable to prevent or reverse the deterioration. In short, there is little reason to suppose that the additional investments made by and for CS families were sufficiently compensated by additional benefits.

EIGHT · RESULTS OF OTHER RESEARCH

THE RESULTS of any study must be assessed in relation to the findings of other research. Confidence in one's results and in the validity of generalizing from them increases if similar findings are obtained in similar studies.

Attention will be directed primarily to studies of interpersonal treatment that either compare effects of planned brief treatment and continued treatment given to comparable groups of clients or test the effects of short-term treatment alone. One may logically rule out non-experimental studies in which outcomes of continuers in treatment are compared with discontinuers or which relate number of interviews or length of treatment to outcome. Such studies do not involve a test of short-term treatment as a distinct service plan, with limits set in advance for client and practitioner, and, hence, are not strictly relevant to our purposes. Moreover, clients who choose to continue in open-ended treatment may represent a self-selected group of individuals with special characteristics of motivation and capacity for change. That they may achieve greater improvement than early terminators, as some studies have indicated, may not necessarily be a function of continued treatment.[1]

It should be noted that the majority of studies in the review to follow were reported after the present experiment was begun. Had we had the benefit of the results of these investigations

1. See, for example, Maurice Lorr, "Relation of Treatment Frequency and Duration to Psychotherapeutic Outcome" in *Research in Psychotherapy*, edited by Hans H. Strupp and Lester Luborsky, pp. 134-41.

before launching our own, we perhaps would not have been quite as surprised by our findings.

COMPARATIVE STUDIES

We were able to locate only a handful of studies comparing outcomes of short-term and continued treatment of comparable groups. Our only criteria in searching for such studies were that (1) the comparison involve planned brief treatment and continued or open-ended treatment; (2) there be at least some grounds for assuming comparability of the groups treated.

Phillips and Johnston compared planned short-term and conventional treatment of parent-child problems in two child guidance clinics.[2] The study, although exploratory and lacking in rigor, is of special interest as the only comparative study that we could locate concerned with testing limited and open-ended treatment of the kind of problems dealt with in our experiment, that is, problems in family relations. In one of the clinics short-term treatment was used exclusively during one period of time, conventional treatment during another. The two groups of cases were similar in respect to mean ages of the children; no other data on comparability of the groups were provided. A third group of thirty conventional cases was drawn from the other child guidance clinic.

The short-term treatment followed a theoretical model which emphasized the importance of consistency and limit-setting in dealing with children. The case material provided suggests that direct treatment was largely confined to mother and child. The mean number of interviews per case for the sixteen cases in the short-term program was eleven, reflecting the fact that four cases received substantially more than ten interviews. Conven-

2. E. Lakin Phillips and Margaret S. Johnston, "Theoretical and Clinical Aspects of Short-Term Parent-Child Psychotherapy," *Psychiatry,* XVII (August 1954), 267-75.

tional cases, however, had only a slightly higher number of interviews on the average.

Assessment of outcomes was based on case records, consultations with psychiatrists, psychologists, and social workers treating the cases, and follow-up interviews with the mothers one year following termination of treatment. Three categories of outcome were used: *successful, improved,* and *failure.* They appear to be basically closing measures, even though follow-up interviews were held. Although the authors state that "all cases were treated alike in the judgment process" and that "bias, if any, was more apt to be against short-term treatment," judging procedures are not elucidated.

Two of the 16 short-term cases were judged as successful (the optimum rating) and all the rest as improved. Of the 44 conventional cases, 5 were classified as successful, 27 as improved, and 12 as failures. As can be seen, differences in outcome between short-term and conventional cases in this study were quite similar to what was identified as the basic pattern of outcome differences between PSTS and CS in our study. In the Phillips and Johnston study, as in ours, the major differences in favor of short-term service occurred not in the best but in the other two categories of outcome. There were more unplanned closings (which the authors term "premature withdrawals") in the conventional cases.

In conclusion the authors comment, "The evaluations of the results and the types of endings of the two therapy procedures suggest a reasonably clear advantage for the short-term practice, within the limits specified herein. The suggestion is evident that the short-term structure helps to create a more clear-cut and decisive treatment milieu and to bring about more favorable treatment outcomes."[3]

3. *Ibid.,* p. 275.

Schlien compared outcomes of three forms of treatment: un-limited, voluntarily terminated Rogerian therapy, short-term Rogerian therapy, and short-term Adlerian therapy.[4] The out-come measure used was the self-ideal correlation, a test of self-esteem based on discrepancies between an individual's self-de-scription and his description of his ideal. Clients were tested prior to treatment, periodically during treatment, and about twelve months following treatment.

The investigation was carried out in three stages. In the first stage 30 individuals (whose characteristics are not stated) were given unlimited Rogerian counselling at the University of Chi-cago Counselling Center. The average number of client inter-views was 37. Clients scored significant gains, as measured by the self-ideal correlation and sustained these gains through the follow-up period.

A second group of 20 clients was then given Rogerian treat-ment limited in advance to twenty interviews. The mean number of interviews received was eighteen. The gains for this group proved to be as great and as lasting as gains for clients receiving unlimited treatment, but clients in time-limited treatment im-proved more rapidly in the early phase of treatment (during the first seven interviews) than clients receiving open-ended treat-ment. In other words, the clients in time-limited treatment appeared to get better faster.

Since the authors thought this result might have been a "fluke," they decided to repeat the experiment with a different form of time-limited treatment. Treatment, again limited to twenty sessions, was given to 20 patients applying to the Alfred Adler Institute. The measures in the first two investigations were

4. See John M. Schlien et al., "Effects of Time Limits: A Comparison of Two Psychotherapies," *Journal of Counseling Psychology* (1962), 31-34, and John M. Schlien, "Comparison of Results with Different Forms of Psychotherapy," in *Psychotherapy Research,* pp. 156-62.

applied to analysis of outcome. Findings revealed that patients receiving Adlerian short-term treatment did as well in achieving gains and holding on to them, as the clients receiving either unlimited or limited Rogerian counselling. But again there was the same "sharp increment" in gains during the early phase observed in the outcomes of limited Rogerian counselling. "Early acceleration," to use Schlien's expression, seemed then to be a distinctive feature of the short-term treatments investigated. In appraising the results Schlien comments that, "time-limited therapy, according to this single criterion [the self-ideal correlation] at least, is effective and efficient, since it accomplished in roughly half the time the same outcome achieved by the longer, unlimited therapy."[5]

As a part of a field experiment conducted at the Community Service Society, Blenkner and her co-workers tested the relative effectiveness of a planned short-term service and two open-ended services to clients 60 years of age or older.[6] The short-term service carried out by a specialized unit serving elderly clients only, consisted of not more than four interviews within two months by a caseworker or a public health nurse. The open-ended programs were unrestricted in duration or number of contacts. One was conducted collaboratively by a caseworker and a public health nurse, also in the specialized unit. The other consisted of regular agency casework services to older clients offered in the various Family Service Centers (then called district offices). Older clients applying to Community Service Society for help (primarily for situational problems) were randomly assigned to the three services.

As it turned out, all services were fairly brief, with the conventional service given by the district offices the briefest of all.

5. *Ibid.*, p. 160.
6. Margaret Blenkner, Julius Jahn, and Edna Wasser, *Serving the Aging: An Experiment in Social Work and Public Health Nursing.*

The majority of clients seen at the district offices, which offered largely a referral and steering service, had no more than one interview (although some had a relatively large number). The open-ended collaborative pattern provided more service (mean number of interviews, 5) than the short-term pattern (mean number of interviews, 2.4). The goals of the former pattern were reported as more "ambitious."

Data on outcome were obtained from case records and follow-up interviews. Client change shown in the records was measured by the Community Service Society Movement Scale. The follow-up interviews were conducted by research interviewers six months after application for service. Of all clients receiving two or more interviews (Blenkner's criterion) those receiving short-term service showed greater movement than either clients receiving service from the district offices or open-ended collaborative service. While no service had distinctly superior outcomes at follow-up, short-term service outcomes were superior to those of the open-ended collaborative service on three-fourths of the indices used.

After presenting comparative data on the three services, the authors comment: "The above figures certainly indicate that there was some ingredient in short-term service that produced more movement at less cost (as measured by worker interviews) than either D.O. [District Office] or collaborative service."[7]

Two other comparative investigations, as yet unpublished in complete form, will be discussed briefly on the basis of partial reports. In a study completed by Muench, randomly selected clients in a college counselling center were given a course of treatment limited to ten interviews.[8] Results were compared with

7. *Ibid.*, p. 173.

8. George A. Muench, "An Investigation of Time-Limited Psychotherapy," *American Psychologist*, 19 (1964), 476. The study is discussed in greater detail in Phillips and Weiner, *Psychotherapy and Change*, p. 135.

outcomes of treatment of longer duration. As Muench commented "The results of this study indicate that time limited therapy (ten sessions) is as effective as more traditional therapeutic methods and may suggest a procedure wherein mental-hygiene clinics may increase the number of clients administered psychotherapy without reducing therapeutic efficiency."

Lorr and his associates compared the effects of time-limited and time-unlimited psychotherapy with a group of 60 male outpatients drawn from a number of mental hygiene clinics.[9] The patients were randomly assigned to the different types of treatment. The time-limited treatment was limited to eighteen weeks. Results indicated there was little difference in outcome between the two types of treatment as measured by a variety of tests or by the judgments of the therapists. Patients receiving short-term treatment, however, reported significantly greater gains than patients receiving unlimited psychotherapy.

For our purposes the studies reviewed leave much to be desired. In two studies (Phillips and Schlien) comparability of groups may be questioned because of lack of random assignment or matching procedures. In two others (Muench and Lorr) lack of published reports preclude full analysis. The remaining study (Blenkner) was concerned with a clientele rather dissimilar from our own. Moreover, the definitions of short-term service varied widely, from four interviews (Blenkner) to twenty (Schlien), with corresponding variations among the studies in amounts of actual service. In at least two studies (Phillips and Blenkner) the inputs in the open-ended services were not much greater than in their short-term counterparts, though there were other differences between the two kinds of service in both the studies.

9. Personal communication from Dr. Lorr. Preliminary findings of this study are discussed in Phillips and Weiner, *Psychotherapy and Change,* pp. 136-37.

Despite these and other deficiencies the studies cited provide support for the results of our experiment in two crucial respects: first, recipients of brief, limited treatment quite clearly did at least as well as recipients of open-ended, and usually more extended, treatment; second, whenever differences in outcome appeared, these differences were in favor of the shorter treatment.

SHORT-TERM TREATMENT STUDIES

Studies investigating outcomes of short-term treatment alone are more numerous but, since they lack control or contrast groups, they do not offer a very good basis for inferences about either the absolute or relative effectiveness of short-term treatment. They do offer evidence, however, on the range of outcomes possible from short-term treatment under varied conditions, and, if they contain a follow-up assessment, can provide information on the durability of these outcomes. Three such studies have been selected for review in detail. These studies, rather than others, were chosen because they contained post-service follow-ups, had moderate to large samples, and were fully reported. Moreover, short-term treatment in these studies was not confined, as in some, to carefully chosen clients, with whom any kind of treatment might have a high probability of success.

In a study reported by Avnet, short-term psychotherapy (up to a maximum of fifteen interviews) was provided to 1115 patients by a large number of psychiatrists in private practice, as a part of an experimental insurance program.[10] The patients were similar in certain socio-economic characteristics to the clients in our study: two-thirds were from families with incomes (in 1959) between $4,000 and $8,000. Most were married adults, ages 20 to 45, with less than college educations. They sought treatment for a wide range of social and emotional problems, including

10. Helen H. Avnet, "How Effective Is Short-Term Therapy," in Wolberg, *Short Term Psychotherapy*, pp. 7-22.

emotional distress, marital adjustment, and family conflict. In most cases problems had been present for two years or more. Twenty per cent of the patients were classified by the treating psychiatrists as psychotic.

Treatment consisted primarily of individual outpatient psychotherapy administered by psychiatrists who as a group were "skeptical" about the efficacy of short-term approaches. Sixty per cent of the patients received no other treatment beyond the maximum of fifteen interviews obtained under the insurance program, although the psychiatrists recommended further treatment in almost all cases. The remaining 40 per cent either continued with the project psychiatrist after the limit or sought treatment elsewhere.

Outcome data were derived from reports of the participating psychiatrists and a follow-up questionnaire sent to all patients (77 per cent of whom responded). According to the author, "The interval between project treatment and follow-up study of patients averaged about 2.5 years for the respondents."[11]

At follow-up, patients who had received short-term treatment (fifteen interviews or less) gave, on the whole, positive appraisals of their mental health. Better than three-quarters of these patients reported at least some improvement, more than half thought they were either greatly improved or recovered. Eighty-five per cent of the patients who received more than the fifteen interviews originally planned or received additional treatment elsewhere reported at least some improvement, although as Avnet points out it is not clear whether the somewhat higher improvement rate was due to the additional treatment or whether they had continued in treatment because they were improving. It is of interest that a smaller proportion of these patients regarded themselves as "recovered" than patients who had received brief

11. *Ibid.*, p. 14.

treatment only. The psychiatrists, who judged the patients' status at the close of treatment, reported a better than 75 per cent improvement rate for patients receiving from six to fifteen interviews. For patients receiving less than six interviews, the psychiatrists perceived improvement in only 46 per cent of the cases at closing, though 80 per cent of the patients in this category reported themselves improved at follow-up.

In conclusion Avnet comments on the positive values of the program:

It satisfied the acute needs of a large proportion of patients.

It provided, for many patients, the only alternative to no treatment.

It drew into treatment patients who had been procrastinating because of timidity or misconceptions, for example, the notion that private treatment necessarily involves intensive, extensive analysis.[12]

Shaw et al. reported a follow-up study of 227 families given planned, brief treatment at the Madeleine Borg Child Guidance Institute of the Jewish Board of Guardians (New York City).[13] The families were "descriptively similar to those of the larger JBG population." Socio-economically the families were similar to those in our project, that is, primarily lower-middle and upper-lower class. However, JBG families were largely Jewish, whereas ours were predominantly Protestant. The families had sought help for primarily child-related problems.

Treatment with each family member was limited to a maximum of twelve sessions over a three-month period, with social workers and psychiatrists as therapists. Treatment was "highly goal focused" with use made of joint and family interviews, although the exact amounts of service received were not given.

12. *Ibid.*, p. 22.
13. Robert Shaw et al., "A Short-Term Treatment Program and Its Relevance to Community Mental Health."

Three-quarters of the families completed the course of treatment; less than 10 per cent of the total sample received service beyond the prescribed limits. According to the authors, "Termination caused no special difficulties in the majority of cases; 73 per cent of the mothers, 92 per cent of the fathers, and 75 per cent of the children accepted termination without undue anxiety or symptomatic regression." (As in our study, wives were apparently more likely than husbands to have problems about leaving short-term treatment.)

Follow-up interviews were conducted by the therapist at three-, six-, and twelve-month intervals following the end of service, although only the results of the last follow-up are given. Improvement ratings were also supplied by the therapists or were obtained from analysis of case records. The level of agreement between the two sets of ratings was reported as "satisfactory." At the final follow-up, 56 per cent of the children and 62 per cent of the parents showed moderate or much improvement. Despite initial skepticism, the therapists themselves felt satisfied with the outcomes of 67 per cent of the cases. Children without problems of aggression, with symptoms of less than a year's duration, and in cases where treatment was precipitated by a crisis, did well. Hyper-aggressive children did poorly. According to the authors, the findings suggest that "with proper case selection, short-term treatment is a highly efficacious type of intervention which produces durable benefits."[14] They further concluded that certain kinds of patients, notably the hyper-aggressive child, may not be suited for short-term treatment. This last point may be well taken, although non-comparative studies, like this one, invariably leave such questions hanging, since one cannot be sure that such children would do better in conventional treatment programs.

14. *Ibid.*, p. 20.

The Cincinnati General Hospital conducts a brief psychotherapy clinic to which patients with acute and severe symptoms are referred for treatment consisting of a maximum of six sessions. Gottshalk and his associates reported the results of a careful study of 53 patients treated in this program.[15] The study is of particular interest because of the relative sophistication and rigor of its measurements. The majority of the patients were under 40, female, and with a diagnosis of neurotic reaction. Approximately two-thirds completed the six-interview course of treatment or terminated prior to this limit with the consent of the therapist. Nine of the 36 patients in this group were referred on for long-term treatment. Research interviews were held at the beginning and end of service and at a point three to seven months following termination. Patients were assessed at the three points of time on the basis of data obtained from a standardized questionnaire administered during the interview. The patients' current psychological, behavioral, and psychosomatic symptoms, as well as current interpersonal problems, were rated and the ratings combined into an overall "psychiatric morbidity scale." The measure proved reliable when applied independently by a judge listening to recordings of the interview. (Different interviewers conducted closing and follow-up interviews.)

The great majority of patients, 77 per cent, showed a symptomatic improvement by closing, as measured by differences in psychiatric morbidity ratings before and after service. Of even greater interest, almost as many patients (71 per cent) were less symptomatic at follow-up than they had been when services began. If drop-outs ($n=17$) are excluded the improvement rate at closing rises to 85 per cent and at follow-up to 81 per cent,

15. Louis A. Gottshalk et al., "Prediction and Evaluation of Outcome in an Emergency Brief Psychotherapy Clinic," *The Journal of Nervous and Mental Disease*, Vol. 144 (February 1967), 77-96.

again with improvement measured in relation to initial ratings of psychiatric morbidity. Among the characteristics of good responders to treatment, interestingly enough, was membership in the *lower* social classes (Classes IV and V in the Hollingshead system). The authors conclude that the type of brief psychotherapy investigated "was found to be associated with symptomatic and functional improvement among a high percentage of these psychiatric patients, a change in psychiatric status that was maintained at least for several months.[16]

A number of other quantitative studies have reported similar positive results. Included in this group are outcome assessments of planned short-term treatment of varying or unspecified durations with an unselected group of 119 children from a child guidance clinic;[17] 87 families with child-related problems;[18] 29 families in family therapy;[19] 1,414 psychiatric out-patients;[20] and 1,143 clients and patients from 97 family agencies and child guidance clinics.[21] Closing improvement rates in these studies equalled or exceeded 70 per cent in all but the last which reported 68 per cent improved. Where follow-ups were done (17, 18, 19, 20), treatment gains were reported to have been maintained in the great majority of cases. This list could easily be extended. No study could be found that reported less than a two-thirds improvement rate at *closing* for the recipients of short-term treat-

---

16. *Ibid.,* p. 95.

17. Marjorie K. Hare, "Shortened Treatment in a Child Guidance Clinic: The Results of 119 Cases," *British Journal of Psychiatry,* 112 (1966), 613-16.

18. Edward Murray and Walter Smitson, "Brief Treatment of Parents in a Military Setting," *Social Work,* VIII (April 1963), 55-61.

19. Mordecai Kaffman, "Short-Term Family Therapy," in *Crisis Intervention: Selected Readings,* edited by Howard J. Parad, 202-19.

20. Leopold Bellak and Leonard Small, *Emergency Psychotherapy and Brief Psychotherapy,* p. 163.

21. Parad and Parad, *Social Casework,* XLIX (July 1968), 418-26.

ment or that reported significant deterioration following treatment.

CONVERGENCE OF FINDINGS

The studies reviewed and cited, together with our own experiment, provide an empirical base for some tentative generalizations about brief and continued forms of individualized interpersonal treatment. These generalizations pertain largely to families and individuals voluntarily seeking help for psychological and social problems from family agencies, child guidance and out-patient clinics, and similar facilities. In effect the statements to follow must be limited to the kinds of services and recipients of concern in the various investigations (ours and others) that have been considered up to this point.

Planned, short-term treatment yields results as least as good as, and possibly better than, open-ended treatment of longer duration. The comparative studies (the five reviewed plus the present experiment) are the main source of evidence for this statement. We may also take into account investigations of the outcome of short-term service only. In this way it is possible to compare studies of the outcomes for short-term treatment taken as a whole (whether or not contrast groups were used) with studies of the outcomes of conventional treatment.

Such a comparison may be questionable since different outcome criteria are used and different groups of recipients and practitioners are involved. Also, overall improvement rates are, at best, a crude estimate of changes associated with treatment. Nevertheless, the rates observed in evaluation of short-term treatment do compare favorably with rates generally reported by evaluative investigations of open-ended treatment.

In his review of the effects of psychotherapy Eysenck summarized the results of nineteen investigations of psychoanalyses and psychoanalytically oriented psychotherapy with adults.[22] Of all cases treated (7,293) in these studies 64 per cent had been reported improved to a slight degree or better, at closing. In only two of these studies did the improvement rate exceed 70 per cent. Similarly Levitt found the overall improvement rate at closing reported in evaluative studies of psychotherapy with children to be 68 per cent.[23] Such improvement rates, with roughly two-thirds of treatment recipients showing positive changes, are rather typical of studies of outcome of conventional treatment. By contrast, for the seven assessments of short-term treatment in which such rates were given (2, 15, 17, 18, 19, 20, 21) the median rate was 77 per cent.

While the present experiment did not yield one general measure of improvement, a logical choice, if one had been used, would have been family change in respect to the overall problem situation. It is of interest that the proportion of PSTS families rated as showing at least some positive change (83 per cent) by closing was comparable to the rates of improvement reported by certain other studies of short-term treatment (2, 15, 19, and 20), while the proportion of CS families so rated was 63 per cent, approximately the same as Eysenck's figure.

The argument of Eysenck and others that such rates of improvements are no better than rates of spontaneous remission is not of direct concern here. The point to be made is that the outcomes reported for conventional treatment in general are no better than, in fact tend to be inferior to, the reported results of short-term treatment. Eisenberg and Gruenberg expressed a similar observation in respect to treatment of children following

22. Hans J. Eysenck, *The Effects of Psychotherapy*, p. 30.
23. E.E. Levitt, "The Results of Psychotherapy with Children: A Further Evaluation," *Behavior Research and Therapy*, 1 (1963), 45-51.

their review of research in that area. They concluded that there was a "lack of definitive proof of the effectiveness of intensive psychotherapy" and that there had been a "tentative demonstration that short-term therapy produces equivalent symptomatic results."[24]

Comparisons of outcomes of short-term and continued treatment, whether in the same study or involving different studies, are invariably open to the kinds of questions raised in relation to our own experiment (Chapter Seven). A comparison of outcomes can be decisive only if changes in comparable groups are assessed through a design that can account for possible effects resulting from the differences in time-spans between the two services. To the best of our knowledge no study utilizing such a design has been published.

Improvement associated with short-term treatment appears relatively durable. Short-term studies with post-service follow-ups seem quite consistent on this point. All such studies reviewed in this chapter, in addition to the present experiment, have suggested that whatever improvement has occurred by closing has tended to persist in the great majority of cases to the point of follow-up from several months to a year or more after the end of treament. In studies in which short-term and continued treatment have been compared in this respect the "relapse" rate for short-term cases appears no greater than for cases receiving continued treatment. If it is true that short-term cases are more likely to experience "symptomatic" improvement, it is still notable that such improvement appears to have a persistent quality. One finds little support in these studies for notions that the

24. Leon Eisenberg and Ernest M. Gruenberg, "The Current Status of Secondary Prevention in Child Psychiatry," *The American Journal of Orthopsychiatry*, 31 (1961), 364.

effects of short-term treatment are ephemeral or that these effects will be offset by substitute symptoms. It may well be that the "effects" of any treatment are largely shaped by the recipients' own powers of recuperation, and hence the durability of the short-term service outcomes may represent basically the continued operation of normal recovery mechanisms. Certainly a considerable amount of evidence indicates that untreated psychosocial problems tend to get better with the passage of time. If so, then treatment should attempt to promote as rapid improvement as possible and so would logically be of brief duration.

Short-term treatment can be used successfully under most conditions if its objectives are appropriately limited. Short-term treatment has been used with apparently good results across a wide range of clients and diagnostic categories and in combination with a variety of modalities. As we have seen, successful forms of brief, time-limited treatment have been used with children, adults, the aged, and families; for situational difficulties, interpersonal problems, psychiatric symptoms, and intrapsychic conditions; with supportive and insight-oriented techniques; with individual, joint, and family interviewing; and by analytically-oriented, Rogerian, Adlerian, and eclectic therapists.[25] This kind of catalog serves primarily to demonstrate the potential broad utility of short-term treatment. Perhaps its limitations are less determined by the kind of client or problem than by its objectives. Almost anyone can be treated for a short period of time, and with some success, if standards for success are determined by limited objectives. Although the objectives and attainments of short-term treatment, like any form of treatment, are diffi-

25. It should also be noted that brief, time-limited approaches are being used increasingly in the treatment of groups. For a review of the literature on this subject see Alexander Wolf, "Short-Term Group Psychotherapy," in Wolberg, *Short Term Psychotherapy,* pp. 219-55.

cult to specify, one could not reasonably expect a brief period of help to effect *radical* changes and no evidence has been presented that it can. But it is quite possible that for *most* people seeking help radical changes are neither necessary nor possible. Those for whom such changes are both desirable and attainable may be relatively few, and for these few extended treatment may be the only conceivable route to attain them. But for most, the more limited achievements of short-term treatment may be quite enough.

NINE · PROGRAM IMPLICATIONS

THE FINDINGS of the present experiment, together with the results of related research, provide an empirical base for wide use of briefer, more economical, and better structured approaches. In this chapter we discuss some program innovations and modifications that in our judgment deserve serious consideration in view of the results of research thus far considered. At the same time certain issues in the development and administration of PSTS programs are examined in light of our project experience. The immediate point of reference in proposals presented is the family counseling agency, although they could be considered for any setting which offers interpersonal treatment for family problems.

A PSTS PROGRAM

Evidence from the present experiment and other studies has suggested that planned short-term treatment may be at least as efficacious as open-ended, continued treatment for certain types of problems and a certain type of clientele, namely marital and child-related problems occurring within intact families who voluntarily seek help. Various studies cited, notably those reported by Phillips and Johnston, Shaw, Hare, Murray and Smitson, and the Parads, have yielded results compatible with ours in this respect.

Such families could well be seen as a target clientele for a service program in which brief, time-limited treatment would be the first line service. That is, this kind of family would be offered this service unless there were specific reasons not to do so. A service program built along these lines would reverse the customary position that continued and short-term service currently occupy in treatment of such families. Short-term service would be the main treatment modality, instead of an adjunctive service for special cases; continued service would be moved from a central to an auxiliary position to be used for exceptional cases that could not be adequately accommodated within the standard, or short-term service.

For some agencies this type of program would involve an expansion of already existing PSTS services. For other agencies it would represent a complete innovation. Either the expansion or introduction of PSTS could be carried out gradually with informal or formal testing along the way.

Limiting the program to intact families voluntarily seeking help with marital or child-related problems is based more on empirical than theoretical grounds, on the results of our experiment rather than on formulations of the potential utility of brief treatment. Other types of problems or clients could be included through logical additions to this group, or in light of the agency's prior experience with short-term treatment. The program would not, however, be designed to serve the agency's entire caseload. There would naturally be certain kinds of cases for which PSTS, as such, would not be appropriate. Treatment of certain problems would be limited by the nature of the problem itself. Helping a girl pregnant out-of-wedlock plan for the placement of her future child, or arranging for a plan of care for an elderly couple, or helping a family establish eligibility for public assistance, may be examples of a kind of service that is completed when certain objectives are realized or certain events take place. Certain categories of cases or problems might or might not be excluded from PSTS with the decision depending on such factors as the training and experience of staff, the agency's definition of its responsibilities and its relations with other organizations. For example, the agency may not feel that its staff is sufficiently skilled in direct treatment of children to provide this kind of help on a short-term basis, though it is debatable whether more skill is needed for PSTS than CS. Or an agency may decide that it will take the responsibility in certain cases for child protection and socialization over an indefinite period of time. Exceptions thus far described would be identified early, preferably at application or in the first interview, as non-PSTS, though they would not necessarily all be candidates for long-term treatment.

In addition, there has been relatively little testing of the feasibility and effectiveness of planned short-term service with hard-to-reach "multi-problem" families (impoverished, disorganized, often broken, families), usually distrustful of agencies and resistant to service. Such families were not present in the project caseload and little in evidence in the studies reviewed. The type of PSTS assessed in the present experiment may not be suitable for this type of family. For example, often considerable amounts of professional time and effort must be spent before these families can be even motivated to work on their problems. It is possible that effective models of brief service can be devised to help this type of family and priority should be given to their development.[1] That these families might be considered beyond the limits of the current proposal should offer no grounds for any diminution of efforts to improve means of serving them, whether these means take the form of brief or

1. Some promising efforts in this direction are emerging from use of immediate brief treatment in walk-in clinics serving socio-economically deprived areas. See for example William C. Normand et al., "A Systematic Approach to Brief Therapy for Patients from a Low Socioeconomic Community," *Community Mental Health Journal*, III (Winter 1967), 349-54.

extended treatment. Quite the contrary, the economies resulting from wider use of PSTS with the proposed target clientele could free resources for the development of more effective services for the hard-to-reach.

The proportion of an agency's caseload that would fall within the target clientele, as outlined, would vary, depending on the demographic characteristics of the population it serves, among other factors. For most agencies, the proportion would be substantial. For example, Beck's survey (1960) indicated that over three-fourths of families served in family agencies were intact; in close to half the cases the family's principal problem as seen by the client was either marital or child-related.[2] However, some agencies, particularly those like the Community Service Society that serve inner-city areas, may have a lower proportion of families meeting the suggested criteria. For instance, in a recent survey of that agency's caseload (1964) less than 60 per cent of client families were found to be intact.

Let us suppose that such a program were to be instituted in a family counseling agency. How would it work? What issues would need to be dealt with? What would be its special advantages?

THE PROGRAM IN OPERATION: CRITERIA FOR CS AND SERVICE LIMITS

Families falling within the target group seen at intake and accepted for service, would generally be offered PSTS. The limits would be either fixed or variable, a point to be dealt with later. The offer would normally be made at the end of the first interview, when the treatment "contract" specifying the projected amount and duration of service would be worked out. The case-

2. Beck, *Patterns,* pp. 8, 18.

worker conducting the initial interview would carry the case to completion.

A limited number of cases within this group might require continued service. There would be need to develop criteria by which such cases could be referred to this form of treatment. If PSTS were to be the usual treatment of choice, the question of whether to assign an incoming case to PSTS or CS would be cast in a much different light. Where PSTS is a service used only for special cases, diagnostic criteria are needed for making early decisions about the kind of case that should be referred, since a family given CS "in error" is normally lost to the shorter service. Fortunately the reverse does not hold true. A case assigned in error to PSTS can usually be converted to CS by removing the service limits. Cases could then be assigned to PSTS with the understanding that some of them would need extended treatment. Instead of the question, "Should this case be assigned to PSTS or CS?" we would ask instead, "Should this case be carried beyond the limits of PSTS?" Despite its reformulation, the issue of criteria for brief versus extended treatment would still remain.

While this issue may not arise in most cases (at least, that is what our findings would suggest) it would certainly need to be dealt with in a certain proportion. What these criteria might be is not clear, although our findings give some food for thought. In our project, some PSTS clients, particularly wives, apparently felt a need for more service than they were given. In general, some clients may want a long-term service for its sustaining functions or for the opportunity it may provide for extended exploration of their needs and goals. An agency may wish to offer this kind of extended service simply because there are certain clients who feel a need for it and presumably get some benefit from it. The agency could legitimately ask, however, whether it could afford to see many clients on this basis. Quite possibly the question would not arise if PSTS proved to be as succesful in accommodating the needs of clients as it was in our project.

The occurrence of certain critical situations at the end of the prescribed service period might require that further help be given. A serious flare-up of family problems, an impending mental breakdown, or threatened self-destructive behavior, would be among the possible reasons for extending the limits of PSTS. While such terminal crises did not often occur in our project, they might happen more frequently in a caseload in which there was a higher proportion of disorganized families or seriously disturbed individuals.

Since about as many CS families as PSTS families returned for further help soon after closing, usually with pressing needs that "could not wait," the thought occurred to us that certain crisis-prone families may require, or seem to require, further help at closing or intermittent help over an extended period of time, regardless of the amount of service already given. In other words, such families may be no more of a special problem in a PSTS program than a CS program

Finally, our study would provide some basis for suggesting that extensions of service may be more appropriate with parent-child problems than with marital problems. The lack of a clear-cut advantage for PSTS in respect to child-related problems obviously cannot serve as grounds for suggesting that families with such problems must be taken directly into CS. On the contrary, since CS did not produce better results and since other projects have reported success in brief treatment of parent-child problems, the treatment of choice, even here, might well be the more economical PSTS. Nonetheless, it is possible, as one of our caseworkers suggested, that certain aspects of parental role functioning may lend themselves to a long-term educative approach.

Decisions to convert to an open-ended or extended service would depend then on developments during the course of PSTS. What the criteria for conversion should be is not clear, but the client's motivation for continued help and the criticalness of the client's situation would be among the factors to be considered. Extending treatment would not necessarily mean a shift to an open-ended structure. Clients who wanted "a few more interviews" might be given just that. In general, the PSTS principle of a limited service contract could be applied in extensions of treatment. The client and worker might agree to continue for five more sessions or twenty-five, preferably to work on specific problems or aspects of functioning.

The number of cases that might need service beyond the limits of PSTS would be dependent on the nature of the limits and on the procedures and rules governing their use. The more limited the duration of PSTS, the higher the proportion of cases that might need extensions. But the stronger the agency commitment to the principle of delimited service, the less likely that extensions would be given. Because of its importance in this respect, as well as others, the matter of how limits are defined and implemented merits special examination.

Limits could take various forms. From our own experience, a service limited to eight interviews after intake worked well on the whole, as the study attests. Instead of limiting service to a specific number of interviews, a range of interviews can be used, for example, from six to ten. According to Parad, most family agencies and child guidance clinics that have PSTS programs use a range of interviews.[3] The most frequent upper limit was twelve interviews. Defining the limits of service in terms

3. Howard J. Parad, "Time and Crisis," pp. 121-22.

of a range of interviews permits greater flexibility. For example, interview limits normally apply to the case, but a case in a family agency may vary all the way from a single client to a large and complicated family. In our study each family received a stipulated number of interviews, to be divided, if need be, among individual family members. When permitted to do so, caseworkers made use of joint interviews to provide maximum service to husband and wife. Thus, the fixed service limits may have induced use of a certain kind of interview. This kind of consequence, while helpful in implementing our project design, may have drawbacks in regular practice. One might not want a particular kind of interviewing "forced" by service limits. In any event, it may not be sensible to crowd the treatment of husband and wife or other family members into the same interview allotment given a one-client case. Variable limits might solve this problem.

Use of a range of interviews may sacrifice, however, some of the values of a predetermined point of ending. If the client and worker agree that service may last, say eight to twelve interviews, the mobilizing effects resulting from knowledge that only so many interviews remain may be lost, and planning of the content of treatment may be more difficult. Furthermore if the upper boundary of the range becomes the actual level in the typical case, as may happen, then, in effect, one is back to a limit defined by a fixed number of interviews, whatever the ceiling of the range happens to be. A compromise solution would be to define a range of interviews for the program as a whole. Within this range the practitioner and client could determine the specific number of interviews as part of the initial PSTS contract. The number of interviews per case actually held could be used as a basis for modification of the allowable range or of the practitioners' use of limits within it.

Whether a specific number or a range of interviews is used, the maximum limits of service would need to be decided. In thinking of desirable limits for PSTS there may be a temptation to think in terms of the maximum that would still permit the service to be considered "short." After all, what is there to lose? Service can always be terminated if need be, and with a relatively high maximum there would be fewer cases that would need service beyond the prescribed limits. This is a difficult issue to grapple with since we have little to guide us to the optimum number or range of interviews. But using a maximum figure, say twenty interviews, may have its drawbacks. As suggested, the very brevity of PSTS may have beneficial effects. It may be a factor in retaining clients or stimulating efforts at problem solving, for example. If so, then something would be lost by making service less brief, perhaps more than would be made up by the added cushion of a few interviews. Nor do we know when the point of diminishing returns occurs in most cases. It could well be that most clients would have received maximum benefits from service well before the fifteenth interview. Our own experience in the project suggests that an eight-interview limit, rather rigidly adhered to, may have been too short for some clients, particularly for some of our wives. Although the two to three intake interviews prior to PSTS added to the total service package, they probably did not add to it in a way to make our service equivalent to a PSTS program of ten to eleven interviews, since the intake interviews in our project were oriented to a more extensive diagnostic study than would be necessary in usual practice. If PSTS were to begin with the first client interview, our best guess is that a course of treatment with a range from ten to fifteen interviews would be generally suitable for a family agency clientele.

The other kind of limit used in our project, and generally in

PSTS programs, pertains to the period of time within which service must be conducted. The time span may be constant (three months in our project) or variable, as appears to be the case in most PSTS programs.[4] If interviews are on a regular basis (weekly, as in our project) the time span becomes largely determined by the interview limits. Our experience suggests that both practitioner and client may take the interview limit far more seriously. We found ourselves doing likewise with the result that time lost because of client or worker vacation or illness was not counted as part of the time allotment for a case. In fact there seemed to be no other reasonable solution. Also, some caseworkers found that the last interview could be used to better advantage if it were held two weeks or so after the main course of treatment. Although the time limit may be less important than the service limit, PSTS is a fusion of both kinds of limits. It may really be described as a limited amount of continuous service. Substantial breaks in the flow of service, for example, eight interviews spread over a year's period, would constitute a different kind of treatment.

When and how the projected limits of service are introduced to the client is crucial. Early specification of the duration of service is virtually a *sine qua non* of PSTS. It may also be true that a case really cannot be defined as PSTS unless these limits are presented as definitive. It is common in open-ended treatment, particularly with recalcitrant clients, to suggest a trial period of a few weeks to "see how it goes." No one would think of this stratagem as an introduction to PSTS even though certain limits are being suggested. But this kind of limit-setting may not be much different from telling the client, in a case that is supposed to be PSTS, "Let's plan to have eight interviews and then we can see if there is any need for further sessions," par-

4. *Ibid.*, p. 124.

ticularly if it were said casually or in passing and not elaborated upon. The question is what needs to be said, and how, in order to give the client a real sense that he is being offered a contract to be taken seriously. For example, one caseworker in our project would tell clients that the best way she could help them would be to see them for a series of eight interviews and would follow this by asking them what they wanted most to work on during these interviews. Given such an explanation the client could be expected to regard the offered contract as a serious proposal. Acceptance of it would also be an acceptance of the reality that treatment would be limited.

It is questionable whether the terms of the PSTS contract can be adequately interpreted or adhered to unless the caseworker himself accepts the validity of these terms, at least provisionally. A caseworker who is utterly convinced that PSTS is a form of client deprivation may create a self-fulfilling prophecy each time he carries such a case. It is easy enough to see deep needs for continued help in a particular client if one is convinced such needs exist in all clients. It is also easy to interpret the client's acceptance of an expert's recommendation for continued treatment as an expression of these needs.

It is almost tautological to say that the success of a PSTS program depends on keeping service generally within prescribed limits. If limits are introduced with qualifications and waived with abandon, then the program would become a travesty. The practitioner, more than anyone, seems to hold the key. There is no evidence from our study or from any of the research reviewed to indicate that demands or felt needs by clients for long-term treatment would be a major problem in maintaining limits in a PSTS program. As one family agency executive commented to the authors, "Our short-term service project really never got off the ground. It was too hard for our caseworkers to give up their clients."

C. Knight Aldrich has cited a number of reasons why practitioners tend to prolong treatment in conventional practice:

One reason is the relative lack of emphasis on problems of termination compared with the strong emphasis on diagnosis and early treatment in the training of psychiatrists and caseworkers. Another reason is the security that comes from working with familiar as opposed to unfamiliar patients, as well as the insecurity that comes from unfilled hours or from the absence of a waiting list. Finally, the prestige and the tradition of thoroughness of psychoanalysis and its derivatives—"long-term" psychotherapy or intensive casework— tend to reenforce the therapists option to continued treatment rather than to live with the uncertainty of letting the patient or client take over before all goals are completely attained.[5]

Aldrich's final point merits some elaboration. Since there are few clear indicators by which the clinician can tell when the general goals of extended treatment have been obtained, prospects of termination confront him with doubts about the sufficiency of his treatment. As a result he may interpret the client's desire to quit as a reflection on his professional competence.

Practitioners brought up in the school of extended treatment may have developed then a certain unease about letting clients go after brief periods. A reorientation of program staff, through seminars and similar devices, may be necessary if PSTS is to be effectively implemented. If practitioners can be brought to use PSTS, their attitudes toward it are apt to become more favorable.[6]

5. C. Knight Aldrich, "Community Psychiatry's Impact on Casework and Psychotherapy."
6. For example, Parad found the attitudes of social workers and psychiatrists toward PSTS shifted in a positive direction after it was initiated in their agencies or clinics (Parad, "Time and Crisis," p. 170). Visher reported similar results (Visher, *American Journal of Psychotherapy*, p. 333).

SPECIFIC ADVANTAGES

The cost-effectiveness advantage of PSTS over a conventional service is perhaps the most compelling single argument in favor of the program. If we assume that PSTS is as effective as open-ended service with the clientele in question, a fair assumption in light of the evidence presented, and that it costs less, a fairly obvious conclusion, then it follows that its cost-effectiveness is greater. PSTS would then be judged to represent, in Bell's terms, "the minimum cost at which a specified level of effectiveness is maintained."[7] The present experiment provides one illustration of what this cost-effectiveness difference might amount to. It will be recalled that a total of 422 interviews were given in PSTS as opposed to 1562 in CS. If the intake interviews (on the average of two per family) are added, then PSTS families would receive a total of 542 interviews, CS families, 1682. If we assume a fixed unit cost per interview, then CS was approximately three times as costly as PSTS, with no better results to show for it. If the cost of an interview is figured at $20, a conservative estimate,[8] then the CS program cost approximately $34,000, or approximately $23,000 more than the PSTS program.

The added cost of CS over that of PSTS needs to be taken into account in program planning. If PSTS can accomplish as much for less, the money "saved" can be spent elsewhere in the agency's program. Or if PSTS were expanded, casework services could be extended to more families with no increase in cost. Thus, if the total number of interviews received by the 60 CS families in our project had been allocated to PSTS, it would

7. Chauncey F. Bell, *Cost-Effectiveness Analysis as a Management Tool*, p. 1. For an application of cost effectiveness concepts to social welfare programs see Arthur Schwartz, "The Relationship of PPBS to Evaluation Research in Social Welfare."
8. This figure, the best that could be obtained, is based on the agency's maximum fee.

have been possible (even taking into account the intake interviews) to treat 186 families or about three times as many, with no apparent sacrifice in results.

It is also reasonable to suppose that an expansion of PSTS would alleviate one particular hang-up of conventional programs: the waiting list.[9] While the rate of early termination in open-ended treatment is high, the practitioner normally accumulates a group of regular clients, some of whom may continue for several years. This relatively static portion of the practitioner's caseload is a major factor in the inability of treatment facilities to provide prompt service. The increased use of PSTS with its faster turnover would necessarily result in shorter waiting periods for clients, as long as the rate of applications for service remained constant. However, an agency that manages to reduce its waiting list may be rewarded by a rise in its application rate as word gets around that it is offering service without delay. Although it is doubtful that a PSTS program would eliminate waiting lists, the waiting period would probably be shorter and would certainly be more predictable.

From all indications, a PSTS program would be more successful in retaining clients (one reason for caution in viewing PSTS as a solution to the waiting list problem). Perhaps the crucial point is that in a PSTS program a higher proportion of clients could be expected to complete the planned "course of treatment." There would certainly be fewer cases in which treatment was aborted at an early stage. Although open-end treatment may be concluded successfully after a few interviews, a very high proportion of its early terminators drop out during the preliminary phase of a projected course of extended treatment.

9. For a report of one agency's successful use of brief service to reduce its waiting list, see Rachel A. Levine, "A Short Story on the Long Waiting List," *Social Work*, VIII (January 1963), 20-22.

While the practitioner is completing his diagnostic work-up, or is beginning to "establish a relationship," or is engaging in other forms of anticipatory activity, the client picks up his problem and leaves. What has he gained? Something perhaps, but probably not enough to justify either his or the practitioner's investment in the process. In a PSTS program more clients would be willing to see treatment through to its *conclusion* if only because it *has* a predictable conclusion not too far in the future.

A client completing a planned, brief treatment experience in which limited objectives have been staked out and achieved in some measure has gained more than a client who leaves treatment during the "tooling up process." In the proposed program there should be more of the former clients, fewer of the latter.

Closely related to these considerations is the question of practitioner continuity in the provision of service. A common practice in conventional programs, particularly in large agencies, is to have one practitioner do the initial or intake interviews with a client and a second practitioner assume responsibility for continued treatment if such is offered and accepted. There are a number of problems in this arrangement, such as reluctance of clients to shift to a second practitioner, and duplication of effort and communication problems between the two practitioners. Most would agree that this practice tends to raise, rather than lower, discontinuance rates. Among its justifications are the administrative advantages in having certain practitioners who are intake "specialists" and others who specialize in continued service.

In a PSTS program such an arrangement would have little justification. Because of the compactness of PSTS, the usual distinction between intake and continued service does not obtain. It would make little sense for one worker to hold a series of intake interviews and then transfer the case to a second worker for brief treatment. A special intake phase or worker can be rationalized only as a preliminary to an extended period of treatment. Since there would be no need for specialists for different phases of the client's career with the agency, a PSTS program would not have to contend with problems inherent in a departmentalized service.

There is considerable room for improvement in the effectiveness of interpersonal treatment, whether it be brief or extended. Because of their predictable brevity, short-term service designs are perhaps more susceptible to rapid improvement. PSTS affords greater opportunity for planning and structuring treatment, hence greater opportunity for *systematic* implementation and testing of new treatment strategies. Its shortness enables practitioners and outside observers to achieve a better grasp of what is going on. Thus, in our experiment we are able to obtain a much clearer picture of casework intervention in PSTS than CS. Not only is feedback from PSTS more complete, it is also more rapid. A practitioner or an agency can profit from its mistakes and build upon its success much more expeditiously in a treatment program in which service is of a fixed and limited duration.

The same logic can be applied to the use of formal research as a means of perfecting PSTS designs. Field experiments testing the relative effects of different types of PSTS would require far less time to complete. A sequence of such experiments, each building on its predecessors, could be completed within the time span required for a single experiment, such as the present one, involving study of extended service. Service strategies that appeared effective in the first experiment would be stressed in the second, and so on. In this way research would be an instrument for developing a service model. There is no reason why research and development principles, which have been so effectively used in other fields, cannot be applied to the improvement of designs for interpersonal treatment, if the treatment is brief.

LIMITED INNOVATION

The kind of program that we have proposed is not likely to spring into full-blown existence. Treatment facilities that have initiated or expanded short-term service have generally proceeded with considerable restraint. If we wish to be practical about innovation, we must consider specific means by which PSTS may be given more limited trials. One means is through special projects involving more selective groups of clients. Our findings suggest that couples with marital problems would be a good choice for such a project. PSTS outcomes were distinctly better for families who sought help with this type of problem. The tendency of husbands to fade out of CS cases also raised questions about the suitability of extended treatment for marital problems, since it is particularly difficult to work on such problems with the wife alone.

A PSTS project for couples with marital problems would be just one of many possibilities. Judging from our results, school adjustment problems of children might also be an appropriate focus for a PSTS undertaking. It may be worthwhile in such endeavors to attempt to capitalize on the opportunities PSTS affords for structured treatment of specific problems and for development of service designs through rapid feedback of results. Thus, a certain kind of school adjustment problem could be identified. Cases falling into this classification could be specially recruited through the school system. Common features of this type of problem could be identified and a structured treatment program worked out in advance for the cases as a whole. The treatment program might include a certain sequence of activities, such as initial conference with the parent, an individual session with the child, a family interview, a conference with the parents and teacher, and so on. Further, it may be possible to state the general objectives of the course of treatment, sub-goals for each part of the sequence, areas to be dealt with, and suggested modes of intervention. For example, one common area of concern might be parent-child intervention around the child's homework. One objective of treatment might be to promote more constructive parental involvement in this task. This goal would suggest a certain kind of examination of homework problems with parents, child, and teacher, and certain types of intervention.

Since the cases would be of brief, limited duration, it would be possible, perhaps within several months or at the end of the first cycle of cases, to develop some definite impressions as to which features of the service design for this type of problem were working well, which were not, what needed to be added, and so on. The treatment program could then be modified in the light of this knowledge. This process of feed-back and correction would continue through the life of the project. This means of developing a service design is of course an informal application of the formal research and development approach discussed earlier.

Another way of gradually introducing or expanding PSTS would be to have each practitioner, or a volunteer group of practitioners, take on a certain number of PSTS cases. The group so involved could share experiences through regular conferences. Students in training could well be included; in fact the time-limited nature of student placements affords a natural fit to the time-limited nature of short-term treatment. Although it can be argued that PSTS requires an advanced level of skill, particularly in making rapid diagnostic assessments, that may be beyond the level of the student, just as persuasive an argument can be made that PSTS may be quite appropriate for the novice. The restraints on goals and the faster feed-back would argue in favor of its use by students. Moreover, PSTS lends itself particularly to supervisory assistance in structuring the objectives and content of treatment.

ONE AGENCY'S EXPERIENCE

The Community Service Society affords one example of how the use of PSTS may be expanded within a conventional program of treatment services. Lengthening waiting lists and preliminary findings from the present experiment prompted the agency to establish an evening program in which PSTS was to be offered to clients on the waiting list, most of whom had sought help for problems in family relations and had had one interview. The service was to consist of fifteen interviews to be conducted within a four-month period. The clientele included a somewhat broader range of family problems and types than the sample of our project.

During the first year of operation, approximately fifty families were served in the program. Although no formal research was done, the practitioners in the program and their supervisors seemed generally impressed with what PSTS was able to accomplish with these families. According to their informal reports, holding PSTS to the prescribed limits did not present a special problem, either from their point of view or that of the clients. Very few cases had to be reassigned to continued service. The consensus seemed to be that, for most of the kinds of families and problems treated, the optimum duration of PSTS lay somewhere between eight and fifteen interviews.[10]

Reports of the success of the evening program began to appear at about the same time as final reports of the project were being

10. This program is described in detail in a forthcoming paper by Gertrude Leyendecker, Senior Associate, Department of Family Services.

shared with agency staff. Their combined impact generated a strong push toward greater use of PSTS, at least on an experimental basis, within the regular agency program.

As a result it was decided to require each agency caseworker to carrry at least three PSTS cases (with a fifteen-interview limit) as part of his active caseload. The purposes of this plan were to involve a large number of caseworkers in the practice of PSTS and to test out the usefulness of this service with additional types of clients and problems. The plan is being implemented at this writing (June 1968). Any further comment would be premature. Since the first findings of the project were released to agency staff, the use of PSTS in the agency program as a whole has gradually risen, in part as a result of the evening program and in part because of increased staff interest generally in this type of service. From all indications, use of PSTS at the Community Service Society will continue to increase, a trend that will doubtless be accelerated as each caseworker is encouraged to make greater use of this pattern.

IMPLICATIONS FOR CONTINUED SERVICE PROGRAMS

Finally the results of research examined in this book have implications for the conduct of typical continued service programs. Various hypotheses relating to general, that is, open-ended, casework practice, were derived from the findings of the present experiment and presented in Chapter Seven. Also, certain conclusions concerning the limitations of extended treatment in the experiment were either stated or strongly implied. These hypotheses and conclusions, with support of findings from various other studies, suggest a general direction for the modification of continued service programs.

The evidence presented suggests that continued service programs could be strengthened through incorporation or adaptation of various aspects of the structure, techniques, and rationale of planned short-term service. If this direction were pursued certain changes in customary diagnostic and treatment procedures would follow. The clinician's diagnostic activities would tend to be more focused on immediate problems and more likely to be combined with early efforts to promote change. Treatment objectives would be more limited, confined more to specific problems. There might be more planning in advance with clients as to problems to be dealt with or themes to be discussed, with less improvisation during the course of treatment. More active types of intervention would be stressed.

There would be less expectation that lengthy treatment would be able to substantially modify enduring problems in functioning, hence less need to try to retain clients for extended periods of service. Emphasis would be placed on preparing clients to cope more effectively with underlying problems following treatment by utilizing gains achieved during treatment. There would be experimentation with use of long-range time limits (for example, with "contracts" for treatment of a year's duration) or with time limits introduced at strategic points during the course of treatment (agreements to continue for a certain number of weeks or months longer). An upper limit could be established for the duration of all continued service cases. Special justification could be required before a case would be allowed to exceed this limit.

As open-ended treatment became briefer, as indeed it would if these modifications were incorporated, there would be less need to have intake handled by one practitioner and on-going service by another and less turnover of practitioners within the life of a case. Needless to say, a more compact open-ended service would mean that larger numbers of clients could be served.

THE LONG VIEW

The findings of our research, converging with those of other recent studies, give strong evidence of the potential of a planned brief service to produce significant and desirable benefits for individuals and families. Indications are that such service for certain types of clients is not only *as* effective as an open-ended service of extended duration but may be even more so.

Some practitioners may find the results discouraging, for they suggest that continued service is not able to effect greater change than can be achieved in brief service. On the other hand, it is very encouraging to learn that such gains as are feasible to attain are likely to be achieved rather quickly. It is encouraging to find that alleviation of particular difficulties of a fairly specific nature may lead to or be accompanied by gains in other and broader areas. The practical limits of a planned brief service force the selection of delimited goals and prompt highly focused activity of practitioner and client to attain them, and the results tend to spell satisfaction for both.

Modification of service patterns necessarily occurs slowly, both because of individual and organizational resistance to change and because of the time it takes to develop, learn, and implement new ways of practice. It is hoped that the experience reported here may add momentum to the gradual movement toward more extensive trials of planned short-term service.

Although brief treatment is rapidly losing its status as an experimental and untested mode of intervention, we need to know much more than we do about its capabilities. In particular there is need to expand and refine our knowledge of its usefulness under specified conditions. Given a certain type of individual or family, a certain kind of problem, a certain set of objectives, what then is it able to accomplish? Moreover, there is no single model of short-term treatment. An effort must be made to develop and test a variety of designs for brief service in keeping with the variety of tasks it must perform. An accumulation of knowledge about the characteristics and effects of different forms of short-term treatment under different conditions should permit us to gain a clearer understanding of the place of this modality in the universe of therapeutic and social welfare services.

Appendixes

I · SUPPLEMENTARY TABLES

Table 1. Selected characteristics at intake of families assigned to planned short-term and continued service (Percentage distributions for the 60 families assigned to each service)

Service assignment			Type of problem		
	Marital	Child-related	Marital and child-related	Other	Total %
PSTS	50	32	17	2	100
CS	45	38	15	2	100

			Social position		
	I	II	III	IV	V	
PSTS	8	12	15	43	22	100
CS	3	13	15	43	25	100

		Gross weekly family income			
	Under $100	$100–$149	$150–$199	Over $200	
PSTS	12	43	22	23	100
CS	10	45	27	18	100

			Years married*		
	Under 6	6–10	11–15	16–20	Over 20	
PSTS	35	25	20	15	5	100
CS	28	27	20	18	7	100

		Ethnic characteristics of spouses			
	Both white	Both Negro	Both Puerto Rican	Mixed	
PSTS	53	33	7	7	100
CS	60	38	2	0	100

Table 1 (Continued)

Service assignment	Religion of spouses				
	Both Protestant	Both Catholic	Both Jewish	Mixed, other	Total %
PSTS	45	20	18	17	100
CS	43	28	12	17	100

	Highest educational level, husband				
	College	High school	Grade school	Unknown	
PSTS	43	43	8	5	100
CS	35	55	10	0	100

	Highest educational level, wife				
	College	High school	Grade school	Unknown	
PSTS	35	55	7	3	100
CS	23	67	8	2	100

* Includes three cases in which couples were living together but were not legally married.

Table 2. Change in family problems from opening to closing, PSTS and CS, research observers' and caseworkers' ratings

Type of Problem Present Research observers' ratings	Families						
	Alleviated		No change		Aggravated		
	N	%	N	%	N	%	Total
Marital							
PSTS	(31)	65	(13)	27	(4)	8	48
CS	(28)	55	(11)	22	(12)	24	51
Parent-child							
PSTS	(30)	83	(6)	17	(0)	0	36*
CS	(31)	66	(8)	17	(8)	17	47

Table 2 (Continued)

Type of Problem Present Research observers' ratings	*Families*					
	Alleviated		*No change*		*Aggravated*	
	N	%	N	%	N	% Total
Emotional distress of family member						
PSTS	(43)	74	(14)	24	(1)	2	58
CS	(42)	72	(11)	19	(5)	9	58
School adjustment						
PSTS	(17)	71	(7)	29	(0)	0	24
CS	(11)	50	(7)	32	(4)	18	22
Overall problem situation						
PSTS	(50)	83	(9)	15	(1)	2	60*
CS	(38)	63	(12)	20	(10)	17	60

Caseworkers' ratings

Marital						
PSTS	(34)	64	(14)	26	(5)	9	53
CS	(26)	48	(20)	37	(8)	15	54
Parent-child						
PSTS	(29)	71	(11)	27	(1)	2	41
CS	(32)	67	(12)	25	(4)	8	48
Emotional distress of family member						
PSTS	(33)	75	(8)	18	(3)	7	44*
CS	(19)	48	(17)	42	(4)	10	40
School adjustment						
PSTS	(17)	71	(6)	25	(1)	4	24
CS	(15)	42	(21)	58	(0)	0	36
Overall problem situation						
PSTS	(47)	78	(8)	13	(5)	8	60
CS	(40)	67	(15)	25	(5)	8	60

* $p < .05$ Chi Square 2 d.f.

Table 3. Change in family functioning from opening to closing, PSTS and CS, research observers' and caseworkers' ratings

	Families					
	Improved		No change		Worse	
Research observers' ratings	N	%	N	%	N	% Total
Emotional climate of home						
PSTS	(45)	75	(13)	22	(2)	3	60
CS	(37)	62	(14)	23	(9)	15	60
Quality of marriage						
PSTS	(31)	52	(26)	43	(3)	5	60
CS	(27)	45	(24)	40	(9)	15	60
Functional adequacy of family						
PSTS	(40)	67	(17)	28	(3)	5	60
CS	(35)	58	(17)	28	(8)	13	60
Caseworkers' ratings						
Emotional climate of home						
PSTS	(41)	68	(18)	30	(1)	2	60*
CS	(28)	47	(24)	40	(8)	13	60
Quality of marriage						
PSTS	(31)	53	(26)	44	(2)	3	59
CS	(23)	38	(29)	48	(8)	13	60
Functional adequacy of family						
PSTS	(36)	62	(20)	34	(2)	3	58
CS	(32)	53	(22)	37	(6)	10	60

* $p < .05$ Chi Square 2 d.f.

Table 4. Change in functioning of husbands and wives from opening to closing, PSTS and CS, research observers' and caseworkers' ratings

Research observers' ratings	Improved		No change		Worse		
	N	%	N	%	N	%	Total
			Husbands				
Functioning as spouse							
PSTS	(29)	48	(29)	48	(2)	3	60*
CS	(26)	43	(22)	37	(12)	20	60
Functioning as parent							
PSTS	(22)	42	(30)	57	(1)	2	53*
CS	(27)	48	(21)	38	(8)	14	56
Ego functioning							
PSTS	(33)	55	(24)	40	(3)	5	60
CS	(30)	51	(20)	34	(9)	15	59
Feeling about self							
PSTS	(46)	79	(11)	19	(1)	2	58*
CS	(33)	60	(15)	27	(7)	13	55
			Wives				
Functioning as spouse							
PSTS	(28)	47	(29)	48	(3)	5	60
CS	(25)	42	(25)	42	(10)	17	60
Functioning as parent							
PSTS	(23)	44	(29)	56	(0)	0	52
CS	(26)	46	(28)	50	(2)	4	56
Ego functioning							
PSTS	(39)	65	(18)	30	(3)	5	60
CS	(40)	67	(19)	32	(1)	2	60
Feeling about self							
PSTS	(46)	77	(13)	22	(1)	2	60
CS	(43)	73	(10)	17	(6)	10	59

Table 4 (Continued)

Caseworkers' ratings	Improved		No change		Worse		
	N	%	N	%	N	%	Total
			Husbands				
Functioning as spouse							
PSTS	(31)	52	(28)	47	(1)	2	60*
CS	(22)	37	(30)	50	(8)	13	60
Functioning as parent							
PSTS	(21)	42	(29)	58	(0)	0	50
CS	(21)	38	(30)	55	(4)	7	55
Ego functioning							
PSTS	(27)	47	(28)	49	(2)	4	57
CS	(21)	36	(35)	59	(3)	5	59
Feeling about self							
PSTS	(37)	66	(19)	34	(0)	0	56*
CS	(29)	50	(24)	41	(5)	9	58
			Wives				
Functioning as spouse							
PSTS	(36)	60	(20)	33	(4)	7	60*
CS	(22)	37	(32)	53	(6)	10	60
Functioning as parent							
PSTS	(27)	53	(23)	45	(1)	2	51
CS	(23)	41	(31)	55	(2)	4	56
Ego functioning							
PSTS	(39)	66	(19)	32	(1)	2	59
CS	(30)	50	(28)	47	(2)	3	60
Feeling about self							
PSTS	(47)	78	(12)	20	(1)	2	60
CS	(40)	69	(14)	24	(4)	7	58

* $p < .05$ Chi Square 2 d.f.

Table 5. *Change in family problems and functioning, from closing to follow-up, PSTS and CS, research observers' ratings**

	Families						
	Alleviated or improved		No change		Aggravated or worse		
Family problems	N	%	N	%	N	%	Total
Marital							
PSTS	(22)	48	(13)	28	(11)	24	46
CS	(21)	46	(12)	26	(13)	28	46
Parent-child							
PSTS	(23)	66	(9)	26	(3)	9	35
CS	(24)	59	(14)	34	(3)	7	41
Emotional distress of family member							
PSTS	(31)	60	(17)	33	(4)	8	52
CS	(34)	65	(15)	29	(3)	6	52
School adjustment							
PSTS	(9)	45	(8)	40	(3)	15	20
CS	(8)	44	(7)	39	(3)	17	18
Overall problem situation							
PSTS	(34)	62	(17)	31	(4)	7	55
CS	(36)	67	(13)	24	(5)	9	54
Family functioning							
Emotional climate of home							
PSTS	(30)	56	(18)	33	(6)	11	54
CS	(29)	56	(16)	31	(7)	13	52
Quality of marriage							
PSTS	(18)	33	(27)	50	(9)	17	54
CS	(17)	33	(24)	47	(10)	20	51
Functional adequacy of family							
PSTS	(26)	47	(19)	35	(10)	18	55
CS	(26)	49	(16)	30	(11)	21	53

* No significant differences, Chi Square 2 d.f.

Table 6. Change in functioning of husbands and wives from closing to follow-up, PSTS and CS, research observers' ratings*

	Improved		No change		Worse		
Husbands	N	%	N	%	N	%	Total
Functioning as spouse							
PSTS	(23)	43	(20)	37	(11)	20	54
CS	(16)	31	(23)	44	(13)	25	52
Functioning as parent							
PSTS	(11)	23	(30)	62	(7)	15	48
CS	(19)	39	(27)	55	(3)	6	49
Ego functioning							
PSTS	(22)	41	(27)	50	(5)	9	54
CS	(22)	43	(22)	43	(7)	14	51
Feeling about self							
PSTS	(26)	52	(18)	36	(6)	12	50
CS	(29)	62	(16)	34	(2)	4	47
Wives							
Functioning as spouse							
PSTS	(18)	33	(24)	44	(12)	22	54
CS	(17)	33	(22)	42	(13)	25	52
Functioning as parent							
PSTS	(16)	34	(28)	60	(3)	6	47
CS	(21)	43	(26)	53	(2)	4	49
Ego functioning							
PSTS	(28)	52	(20)	37	(6)	11	54
CS	(28)	53	(22)	42	(3)	6	53
Feeling about self							
PSTS	(33)	61	(18)	33	(3)	6	54
CS	(36)	69	(13)	25	(3)	6	52

* No significant differences, Chi Square 2 d.f.

II · METHODOLOGICAL CONSIDERATIONS

MISSING DATA

Exclusions from reported totals, closing and follow-up data.
Totals reported in the tables and text presenting these data do not include families or individuals in "unknown" and "not relevant" categories. With the exception of certain ratings, to be specified below, the margin of difference between reported totals and maximum possible totals is made up largely of unknowns, usually the result of failure to secure research interviews.

Totals for family ratings are reasonably complete since research interviews were obtained with at least one spouse in 90 per cent of the cases at closing and follow-up, and at closing the 4 cases not receiving a research interview were rated by research observers on the basis of casework interview tapes and the caseworkers' summaries. Since in most cases ratings of individual functioning of the non-interviewed client could be made on the basis of the information provided by the interviewed partner, totals for these ratings also approach the maximum. However, items which required ratings to be made from the client's point of view or which required the client to give his opinion could not be completed unless the client received a research interview. Thus, text tables presenting such items (5.2, 5.3, 5.4, 6.2) generally report lower totals. Such totals are usually less for husbands than for wives since a relatively larger number of husbands were not interviewed. Twenty-three husbands, as compared with 13 wives, were not interviewed at closing. Similarly at follow-up, we were unable to secure interviews with 37 husbands, whereas the comparable figure for wives was 22. In some cases and for some items the client's attitude and opinions were obtained through brief telephone "interviews" conducted after the client had refused a full in-person or telephone interview. These brief interviews are not counted in the interview totals cited above.

Lack of relevance lowered reported totals for two kinds of items. Child-related items (functioning as a parent, and so forth) exclude the twelve childless couples in the project caseload. For items pertaining to changes in specific family problems, reported totals include only cases in which observers judged the problem to be present during the service period.

Scattered ratings of unknown or not relevant occurred in both the research observers' and caseworkers' data for reasons other than those given, including lack of evidence, client unwillingness or inability to give an opinion, and, in general, the special circumstances of particular cases.

Possible effects of missing data on PSTS-CS differences. More CS than PSTS cases involved clients not interviewed at closing by the research interviewers. Thus 19 of the 32 cases in which one or both spouses were not interviewed were CS cases. Fifteen of the 23 husbands and 8 of the 13 wives not interviewed were from this service pattern.

It is difficult to assess the effects of this uneven break on closing ratings of PSTS and CS cases. Some clues may be gained, however, from the fact that the main reason for not obtaining interviews was the client's refusal to be interviewed (31 of the 36 clients). Some clients refused explicitly; others refused implicitly through repeated cancellations of appointments and the

the like. The persistence of our interviewers left little doubt that clients located but not interviewed were clients that did not wish an interview. When it was possible to obtain reasons for refusal, these turned out more often than not to be related to the client's dissatisfaction with service or to his current distress. It does not seem likely that interviews with these clients would have increased the proportion of favorable outcomes for the service to which they had been assigned; in fact the opposite would probably have occurred. Since the majority of these clients were from CS, whatever bias resulted from their refusals to be interviewed may well have worked against PSTS, particularly in respect to items concerning client attitudes and opinions toward service.

At follow-up, no interviews at all were secured from 6 CS and 5 PSTS families. In all, 33 CS clients and 25 PSTS clients were not interviewed. Thus, as in the closing interviews, a somewhat higher proportion of missing respondents were found in CS cases. Again the principal reason seemed to be refusal to be interviewed. Again it was assumed that whatever bias resulted from the missing respondents would not work to the advantage of PSTS.

FACTOR ANALYSIS OF CLOSING MEASURES

A factor analysis served as a guide in the selection of the key measures of change and of other measures used in the analysis of outcomes. It also brought to light certain patterns of relationship among the closing data.

The factor analysis comprised 73 closing items, including all overall measures of family and individual change. Only the research interviewers' data were used, since the analysis was carried out prior to the decision to combine the ratings of research interviewers and review judges. It was assumed that a factor analysis based on the review judges' data or the combined data of interviewers and judges would yield similar results since the same individuals served as both interviewers and judges.

Husbands' and wives' data were analyzed separately producing, in effect, two factor analyses. In each analysis the spouse's data were pooled with measures of family change. Since the replications yielded comparable results, discussion is confined to the analysis based on data for wives and families.

The principal components method with varimax rotation was used. In all, 17 factors were extracted. Most of the significant loadings (.30 or greater) fell within two factors. In one of these factors variables with the higher loadings ($\geq$ .70) pertained to various aspects of change in family functioning and in marital functioning and problems. The central role of marital functioning in this factor emerges when one observes that the two variables with the highest loadings were change in *overall functioning as a spouse* (.87) and in *quality of the marriage* (.85). (Both were selected as key measures of change.) Within this factor fell *functional adequacy of the family* (.73) and the *overall problem situation* (.59). Thus change in the marriage seemed closely tied, in our measures, to changes in general family functioning and problems.

In the other factor, variables with the highest loadings pertained largely to evaluations of service by clients and interviewers, such as their assessment of the helpfulness of service. Moderate loadings appeared for change in *ego functioning* (.52) and *feeling about self* (.56) and the *overall problem situation* (.45). In general, evaluation of service appeared to have a degree of independence from other measures, although it seemed related to the more psychological aspects of change and to change in the overall problem situation.

The remaining factors consisted of small clusters of variables with significant loadings. Most of these factors are of secondary interest, since they pertain to variables not directly relevant to the major service goals of the project. These variables either showed little change during the course of service or no differences among service patterns. In this group we have factors relating to physical health, housing conditions, occupational functioning, economic circumstances, and the like.

Four of these remaining factors, however, proved to be of some importance in the selection of key ratings and of help in understanding the relations among these ratings. One of these factors concerned the client's functioning as a parent. (The client's *overall functioning as a parent* and its sub-ratings were the only variables with significant loadings.) In a second, all the high loadings consisted of ratings pertaining to family problems involving parent-child relationships. It was of interest that changes in various aspects of parenting seemed relatively independent from changes in marital performance and general family functioning. It was also of interest that some degree of independence was achieved between measures of change in *functioning* as a parent and in *problems* relating to this aspect of functioning. These observations are consistent with findings that suggested that PSTS-CS differences in outcome varied between marital and parental role functioning and between parental role functioning and child-related problems. These findings had pointed to the kind of independence among these dimensions that we observe in the factor analysis.

The third of these four factors was made up of a small group of items with generally low loadings (between .30 and .40) except one, *emotional climate of the home* (.68). This was the only factor in which this variable had a significant loading. Thus *emotional climate of the home* for reasons suggested in the text (Chapter Five, p. 97) appeared to tap a dimension of family change not measured by other variables. For this reason primarily it was chosen as one of the key measures.

The final factor to be considered consisted of two items: the *client's feeling toward the caseworker* and the *client's perception of the caseworker's feeling toward him* (with loadings of .74 and .90, respectively). These items seemed relatively uncorrelated with other measures, although there appeared to be some association between the first of these items and evaluations of service. (This item had a loading of .41 on the "evaluation-of-service" factor, the only other factor in which either had significant loadings.) It was somewhat surprising to find independence between the client's reaction to the caseworker and measures of client change, since these two dimensions are commonly thought to be highly interrelated. The statistical independence of this factor provided added grounds for the special attention given to it in the analysis of outcomes.

The decision to focus analysis of data on the *overall* ratings of client role functioning was influenced by the relative loadings of sub-ratings and overall ratings on the various factors. For example, research observers rated change in the *affectional, sexual,* and *decision-making* aspects of *functioning as spouse* separately in addition to making a summary rating of *overall functioning as spouse.* That the overall rating served as a summary was indicated by the fact that the loading for this rating (.87) was greater than that for any of the three sub-ratings (.84, .76, and .71). (All appeared in the first factor discussed.) Similarly on the "parental functioning factor" the overall rating for *functioning as parent* (.75) was greater than those for any of the sub-ratings for this dimension, *physical care* (.53), *emotional nurture* (.66), and *socialization* (.68).

In summary, the factor analysis yielded a number of separate dimensions relevant to the assessment of outcomes at case closing. With some over-simplification these comprised changes in family and marital functioning; in parental functioning; in parent-child problems; in emotional climate of the home; and in the client's reaction to the caseworker. In the key measures selected for detailed analysis and presentation, each of these dimensions was represented by a specific item or items that, on statistical grounds, could be considered to be good indexes of the dimension as a whole.

THE RATING SCALES

The various observers used essentially two 5-point scales to rate change, one for family problems, the other for individual and family functioning.

Original scales

For family problems	For individual and family functioning
5. Problem no longer present	5. Considerably improved
4. Substantially alleviated	4. Slightly improved
3. Slightly alleviated	3. No perceptible change
2. Unchanged	2. Slightly worse
1. Aggravated or new problem developed	1. Considerably worse

When the ratings of the research interviewers and review judges were averaged, the resulting means could fall at any whole number on the 5-point scale or midway between any two scale points.[1] It seemed desirable to collapse the resulting 9 positions into a smaller number of categories approximating the original scales.

Definitions of change in the composite scales were based on the same whole number values found in the original scales.

1. If the rating of one observer was missing, the rating of the other observer was used in place of the mean.

Composite scales based on mean ratings of research observers

For family problems		For individual and family functioning	
Mean ratings	Change categories	Mean ratings	Change categories
4-5	Substantially alleviated*	5.	Considerably improved
3-3.5	Slightly alleviated	4-4.5	Slightly improved
2-2.5	Unchanged	3-3.5	No perceptible change
1-1.5	Aggravated or new problem developed	1-2.5	Worse

* As point 5 of the original scale, "problem no longer present," was very rarely used, occasional mean ratings of 5 or 4.5 were interpreted as substantially alleviated.

Thus, a mean rating of 3 or 3.5 in the composite functioning scale signified "no change," as did 3 in the original scale. Although straightforward, this transformation, in effect, made the composite scales somewhat more "pessimistic" than the original scales since half-steps of upward change in the composite scales were disregarded. Any decision about categories of change in the composite scales would be necessarily arbitrary. The decision made seemed the best of several arbitrary possibilities.

Its justification may be briefly stated. The definitions of positive change in the original scales were rather permissive and somewhat loose. As a result positive ratings predominated in most items and there were a sizable number of one-step differences between interviewers and judges in respect to ratings of no change versus slightly improved. The more stringent definition of positive change in the composite scales served to correct these tendencies to some degree.

The nature of this correction can be illustrated with the composite functioning scale. Since ratings of 4 or greater were required for improvement, the original ratings of interviewer and judge had to consist of one of the following combinations: 5-5, 5-4, 4-4, or 5-3. Combinations of 4-3, in which one observer reported slight improvement and the other reported no change, led to mean ratings of 3.5 or no change in the composite scale. The 5-3 combination was relatively rare, less than 5 per cent of the composite ratings defined as improved resulted from this combination. Therefore it can be said, with little chance of error, that a composite rating in the improved category signifies that *both* research interviewer and review judge reported improvement in the original ratings. A mean rating of 5 (considerably improved) could only have occurred if the original ratings of *both* interviewer and judge were 5, a strict but clear criterion.

There is no reason to suppose that the composite scales, as constituted gave "unfair" advantage to PSTS, the pattern with the more favorable outcomes. In fact, had results been reported in terms of the original scales used by the research interviewers and review judges, there would have been about the same proportion of significant differences in favor of PSTS. Separate analyses of the research interviewers' and review judges' ratings for the 16 key closing ratings of change (combined into categories of improved or alleviated, no change, and worse or aggravated) produced 9 significant differences in favor of PSTS and none in favor of CS. Three of these differences were contributed by the research interviewers and six by the review judges. Thus slightly over a quarter of the comparisons (9 out of 32) were significantly in favor of PSTS when the ratings of the research observers were analyzed separately, using the original scales, whereas exactly a quarter (4 out of 16) were found to be so when analysis was based on the mean ratings (Chapter Five, p. 102). The separate analyses produced significant differences on all the items found to be significant in analysis of the mean ratings; in addition, significant differences in favor of PSTS occurred in respect to review judges' ratings of wives' *functioning as spouse, problems of marital relations,* the *emotional climate of the home,* and the *functional adequacy of the family.*

The scale to assess the *overall helpfulness of service* (Chapter Five, p. 116) was treated similarly, that is, half points were disregarded in defining categories of helpfulness of service in the composite scale based on the mean ratings of research interviewers and judges. The caseworkers' ratings of individual and family change, which were based on scales identical with those used by the research interviewers and review judges, were analyzed in their original form.

INTER-OBSERVER RELIABILITY

Summary of principal studies. Reliability investigations carried out in the project consisted for the most part of tests of agreement between pairs of observers presumably viewing the same phenomena. The tabular summary presented below is confined to those measures upon which the major findings of the experiment rest.

The total number of items tested in each investigation is given (in parentheses) following a description of the items. In questions permitting multiple responses (the majority in A and D) each possible response was counted as an item. For example, *the client's perception of service* (D) involved ten possible responses on ten separate items (five each for husband and wife). The median and the range of values for each set of items tested are given in the last two columns. Thus, for the 16 correlations for key ratings of individual and family change from opening to closing (B), the median correlation was .68, the highest was .87, and the lowest .30. Comparisons between judgments of research interviewers and review judges obtained at closing were

Summary of reliability studies

Text references	Observers and observations compared	Coefficient	Median	Range
	Research interview with review judge			
A Ch. 3 pp. 44-52	Major problem types; recency of origin of problem; client perception of cause of problem; client reaction to problem (13 items)	Per cent of agreement	71	89-52
B Ch. 5 pp. 96-99	Key ratings of family and individual change, opening to closing. (16 items)		.68	.87-.30
C Ch. 5 pp. 116-17; 122-23	Closing ratings of helpfulness of service; client's feeling toward caseworker; client's perceptions of caseworker's feeling toward him. (7 items)	r	.77	.88-.64
D Ch. 5 pp. 118-21	Client's perception of service; aspects of service liked, disliked at closing. (20 items)	Per cent of agreement	84	95-66
E Ch. 6 pp. 136-38	Key ratings of family and individual change, closing to follow-up. (16 items)	r	.66	.87-.29
F Ch. 6 pp. 144-50	Presence or absence of help during follow-up period; client's evaluation of help received; perception of need for help at follow-up; future need for help. (7 items)	Per cent of agreement	85	92-71

Summary of reliability studies

Text references	Observers and observations compared	Coefficient	Median	Range
	Research observers with caseworkers			
G Ch. 5 pp. 96-99	Key ratings of family and individual change, opening to closing (mean ratings of research observers and ratings of caseworkers). (16 items)	r	.53	.69-.23
	Pairs of interview analysts			
H Ch. 4 pp. 69-73	Profiles of casework technique. (121 taped interviews)	rho	.75	.93-.27
	Interview analyst with caseworker			
I Ch. 4 pp. 79-80; 86-88	The use of selected techniques in 121 interviews as judged by the interview analysts and as reported by the caseworker. (6 techniques compared)	Contingency coefficient 2 d.f.	.28	.48-.17
	Principal judge with reliability judge			
J Ch. 5 pp. 124-29	Seventy-four paired comparisons of continued service interviews. (9 items)	Per cent of agreement	55	67-45

based on 115 cases; comparisons of judgments obtained at follow-up, on 104. The missing data are accounted for by cases in which closing or follow-up interviews were not taped and by the cases not interviewed at follow-up.

The correlations of research interviewers' and review judges' ratings on the 16 key measures of change from opening to closing (B) are of particular interest because the most important findings of the experiment emerged from these ratings. As reliability coefficients in this type of research, the correlations on the whole can be considered to be satisfactory. Eleven of the 16 equaled or exceeded .65, as did all correlations involving the four ratings that yielded significant outcome differences in favor of PSTS: *overall problem situation,* .72; *problems of parent-child relations,* .66; husband's *functioning as spouse,* .65; husband's *feeling about self,* .70.

The remaining five correlations were rather low, less than .50, although all were statistically significant ($P<.01$). Four of these comprised change in husbands' and wives' *ego functioning* and *functioning as parent.* These correlations fell within a .45 to .49 range. The fifth, change in *problems of emotional distress of family members,* was only .30. The low correlations for *ego functioning* and *problems of emotional distress* could be attributed to the vagueness of the underlying constructs and to the complexity of the ratings. The low correlations for *functioning as parent* are more puzzling. *Functioning as spouse,* a rating with comparable ambiguities, yielded much higher correlations (wives, .80; husbands, .65). Also a higher correlation (.66) was found for changes in *problems of parent-child relations.* In any event the five ratings that yielded low correlations become somewhat questionable as measures of change. Findings based on these ratings must be assessed with added caution.

Correlations of research observers' ratings of change between closing and follow-up (E) show a quite similar pattern. As in the closing data, all correlations were .65 or higher with the exception of the five involving ratings of *functioning as parent, ego functioning,* and *problems of emotional distress of family members.* Three correlations (*ego functioning* of husband and wife and *problems of emotional distress*) were particularly low (.29 to .30). *Functioning as parent* yielded correlations of .41 for husbands and .54 for wives.

Correlations between research observers were generally highest for closing ratings of the *helpfulness of service, client's feeling toward the caseworker,* and the like (C). The reason seemed to be that the observers were usually able to base such ratings on fairly explicit responses from the clients. Thus the observers were in close agreement on the assessment of the helpfulness of service from the point of view of husbands ($r = .88$) and wives ($r = .87$). Apparently in making their ratings both observers stuck close to what the clients actually said (as they were supposed to); otherwise it is hard to account for the magnitude of the correlations. As would be expected, the observers agreed less well ($r = .68$) in assessment of the helpfulness of service from their own point of view, a more complex judgment in which possible differences between the husband's and wife's ratings would need to be taken into consideration.

Tests of agreement between research observers on nominal items (A,D,F) involved comparisons of judgments of research interviewers and review judges on items consisting of two or more discrete categories. All of the items in D consisted of two categories, whether a particular client response was judged to be present or absent. All of the items in A involved three or more categories, for example, a client could perceive a cause of his problem as major, minor, or not present. F contained a mixture of both kinds of items.

The level of agreement between research observers on nominal items was generally acceptable. Only 6 of 40 percentages of agreement fell below 70 per cent. All but one of the low percentages involved items consisting of more than two categories, in which case a lower rate of agreement would be expected.

Moreover, all the percentages of agreement covered by the summary exceeded levels that might be expected through chance alone. This was determined through use of a coefficient of agreement developed by Jacob Cohen (Cohen's k).[2] Employed as a coefficient of interjudge agreement for nominal scales, it is directly interpretable as the proportion of joint judgments in which there is agreement after chance agreement is excluded. Its upper limit is +1.00 and its lower limit falls between zero and —1.00, depending on the distribution of judgments by the two judges. When obtained agreement equals chance agreement, k equals zero. The k's ranged from .29 to .79 for the 40 items, with a median of .55. All were significant at the .05 level, all but a few at the .01 level.

We have already seen that the ratings of the caseworkers and research observers (G) were grossly consistent in respect to the overall direction of PSTS-CS outcome differences. That is, both sets of ratings produced a number of significant differences in favor of PSTS and none in favor of CS. At the same time, significant differences in the caseworkers' ratings usually did not prove to be significant in the research observers' ratings, and vice versa. These inconsistencies were not dealt with in any detail for a number of reasons. By design, the caseworkers' ratings were treated as subordinate to the ratings of the research observers. It was the latter set of ratings that determined which differences would be given the greatest weight in the presentation

2. Jacob Cohen, "A Coefficient of Agreement for Nominal Scales," *Educational and Psychological Measurement*, XX (1960), 37-46.

and interpretation of the findings. Moreover, a high level of agreement between research observers and caseworkers was not expected on the application of specific measures to particular cases. (The caseworkers received far less training in use of the scales than did the research observers and the caseworkers rated families and individuals from a rather different vantage point.) Finally, minor variations in ratings could cause a difference to be statistically significant in one set of ratings but not quite significant in the other.

Nevertheless, since caseworkers and research observers were presumably judging the same phenomena, some measure of correlation between their ratings would be expected. If little were found, the overall congruence between the two sets of observations in respect to outcome differences would assume less significance.

As noted in the summary, the correlations for the 16 key ratings of change ranged from .69 to .23 with a median of .53. All correlations exceeded .40 with the exception of wives' *ego-functioning* (.38) and *problems of school adjustment* (.23). Most of the correlations then were in the moderate range, indicating a certain degree of covariation between the two sets of ratings. As expected, the correlations were generally lower than correlations between research observers for the same items (median = .68), although certain of the caseworker-research observer correlations were higher, notably husbands' *functioning as parent* (caseworkers-research observers .58, research interviewers-review judges .45) and *problems of emotional distress* (.46 as opposed to .30).

It is of some interest that the high correlations between research observers, on the one hand, and between mean research observers' ratings and caseworkers' ratings on the other, generally related to aspects of marital functioning. All correlations in this area exceeded .60 in both sets of comparisons. The three highest research observer-caseworker correlations all involved marital items: changes in *marital problems* (.69), wives' and husbands' *functioning as spouse* (.68 and .66, respectively). It appears then that our measures of change in respect to marital functioning and problems proved generally the most reliable of the various key measures of change employed by the caseworkers and research observers.

Agreement between interview analysts (H) was determined by rank order correlations (Spearman's rho) between pairs of interview profiles.[3] Each profile consisted of frequencies of responses falling into 10 categories of technique. All but 10 of the 121 correlations exceeded .50, the value needed for significance at the .05 level. Most of the low correlations involved one analyst who differed noticeably from the rest in her interpretation of certain definitions of technique. On the whole the correlations suggest that the analysts were able to achieve a reasonable level of agreement in respect to the ordering of frequencies of responses in the various categories. Thus if one analyst classified 15 responses as confrontation and this number ranked third in her set of ten frequencies, it is likely that it would be ranked relatively high in the frequency distribution obtained from the judgments of a second analyst listening to the same interview. This measure of agreement has certain obvious limitations. It does not require agreement on particular responses. It also does not take into account the magnitude of interjudge differences in frequencies reported for particular categories. Its limitations seemed reasonably well suited, however, to the limitations of the instrument, which, like most of its type, represented

3. A rationale for the use of the rank-order correlation with this type of data may be found in Hollis, *Development of a Casework Treatment Typology*, pp. 35-36.

a fairly primitive effort to measure an extraordinarily complex set of operations.

Comparisons between the interview analysts' and caseworkers' judgments of the use of techniques (I) posed special difficulties since the two sets of judgments involved different instruments and different scales. It was finally decided to trichotomize the proportion of the analysts' responses for a given technique (based on the average frequencies of the profiles obtained from each) into "no use" (less than .01), "some use" (.01 to .049) and "substantial use" (.05 and above). The caseworker's estimates were dichotomized into "used" and "not used" categories. Contingency coefficients based on the resulting 2 x 3 tables were computed for six techniques across the 121 interviews judged by both analysts and caseworkers. Four techniques in the system used by the analysts (*exploration concerning the client's milieu, exploration concerning the client's own behavior, structuring the treatment relationship,* and *identifying specific reactions*) could not be compared since there was a lack of comparable categories on the instrument used by the caseworkers. All coefficients were significant at the .01 level, except *clarifying intrapsychic causation* ($p < .05$) and *logical discussion* ($p < .20$). The degree of association was greatest in respect to *advice* ($C = .48$) and *confrontation* ($C = .41$). In general, it may be said that the level of agreement between analysts and caseworkers was statistically significant but low. Within the variation unexplained by the contingency coefficients there was ample room for the sort of divergence between analysts and caseworkers observed in the caseworkers' tendency to over- and under-report use of modifying techniques.

As reported in the text, agreement between judges in the comparison of interviews (J) was regarded as adequate in three of nine items. For the three items, percentages of agreement between the judges were 61, 65, and 67. (It should be noted that the judges could check "can't decide" in the event they could not make up their minds as to which interview of the pair best fitted the statement; thus the percentages are based on the possibility of three, rather than two choices.) For these three items, interjudge agreements was significantly better than chance, as determined by Cohen's k (the k's were .30, .36, and .32, respectively). For the remaining items, k values were not statistically significant.

The general low level of agreement is consistent with the hypothesis that the interviews compared did not differ essentially in respect to the items under consideration. If they did not, then the judges would have little basis for choosing one instead of another; hence one would expect generally poor interjudge agreement. While other explanations of the low level of agreement are possible, there is evidence to suggest that lack of agreement was not simply a function of the type of judging task, that is, listening to segments of two interviews and selecting the one best fitting a given description of the interview. The interview comparison instrument contained fourteen items concerning various aspects of caseworker-client communication (for example, "In which interview was caseworker more assertive?"). Interjudge agreement on this set of items was generally higher (median percentage of agreement = 64); most of the k values were statistically significant.[4]

Ratings of individual and family status. Although no findings were based on ratings of individual and family status at opening, closing, and follow-up, a brief discussion of our experience with these ratings may be of interest to researchers concerned

4. Substantive findings based on these items will be reported at a future date.

with problems of measuring behavioral change. We had originally planned to make major use of change derived from *differences* in ratings of the status or level of individual and family functioning made at different points of time, particularly at opening and closing. As previously mentioned (Chapter Three, p. 52) research interviewers rated various aspects of the functioning of families and individuals prior to service. These ratings were repeated at closing. The ratings consisted of assigning a numerical value (from 1 to 11) to the quality of functioning for a given dimension—the better the functioning, the higher the rating. Anchoring definitions describing various levels of functioning were developed for each major aspect rated. It was thought that changes in functioning associated with service could then be assessed by determining the difference between the opening and closing ratings of the research interviewer. To illustrate, if a husband were given a rating of 2 (or poor) in respect to his *functioning as a spouse* at opening and a rating of 5 (or fair) on this variable at closing, a change or difference score of +3 would result. In theory, difference scores derived in this fashion have two advantages over the kind of retrospective measures of change that were ultimately used: first, difference scores permit a more precise description of the degree and quality of change since change can be measured in terms of movement from one defined level to another; second, they avoid the problem of memory loss and distortion that invariably occur in retrospective assessments.

If these theoretical advantages are to be realized, however, the measures of change must have an adequate degree of reliability. Unfortunately the difference scores derived from the interviewers' opening and closing ratings did not appear to meet this criterion. The details of our misfortune may be instructive to others.

Assessment of the reliability of a change measure based on differences between two sets of scores involves a number of considerations. These considerations have been succinctly summarized in a recent report by the Group for the Advancement of Psychiatry.[5]

The reliability of the measure of change will be a function of the reliability of the initial and final score. . . . Moreover, if the initial and final scores are highly intercorrelated (that is, if they presumably measure the same thing or if the members of a group keep their same relative functions in the two distributions) the reliability of the measure of change will be much less than the reliability of either the initial or final scores. This is because the change measure, in addition to its own reliability, contains within it the unreliability of both the initial and final measures used to determine it.

In our data the reliability of the research interviewers' initial ratings of individual and family functioning was not high to begin with. The median correlation was only .48 for research interviewers' and review judges' ratings of nine aspects of individual and family functioning selected for analysis.[6] The low level of correlation seemed related to the lack of variation in the sample on the one hand and to the grossness of the scale on the other. Most ratings fell in the middle of the scale (5-7), the "fair" range. There were no guidelines for discrimination within this range. Our criteria for what constituted poor and excellent functioning turned out to be of little use. At closing the inter-

5. *Clinical Psychiatry,* reports by the Group for the Advancement of Psychiatry, pp. 310-11.
6. This set of items comprised husbands' and wives' *functioning as spouse* and *parent* and *ego-functioning* and *the emotional climate of the home, the quality of the marriage,* and *the functional adequacy of the family.* These were among the key dimensions used in analysis of retrospective ratings of change at closing (Chapter Five). The remaining dimensions, involving the client's *feeling about self* and the various problems of the family, received only closing ratings of change.

viewer-review judge correlations for these ratings of functioning were somewhat higher (median = .68), possibly the result of added experience on the part of the observers in use of the scales. However, the median correlation between research interviewers' opening and closing ratings for these variables was .58, indicating a limited amount of variation in ratings of individual and family functioning between the two points of time.

Following the logic of the G.A.P. report and statistical procedures suggested by Gulliksen, the reliability of the interviewers' difference scores was determined.[7] As Gulliksen observed "if the average reliability of the two tests is about the same as their intercorrelation, the reliability of the difference is approximately zero."[8] Using the median values cited to represent the reliabilities of the interviewers' ratings at opening and at closing and the intercorrelation of these ratings between opening and closing, one observes that the average reliability of the ratings is .58 (.48+.68/2) which is equal to their correlation between opening and closing (.58). Hence the reliability of the difference scores, based on these median values, would be equal to zero. A computation of the reliability coefficients of the difference scores for each variable yield a median that was, in fact, in the neighborhood of zero (.06).

Webster and Bereiter point out, however, that Gulliksen's formulation is based on the assumption that pre- and post-tests are unmatched.[9] According to these writers, if identical forms of an instrument are used at time one and time two (as in our case) the reliability of the difference scores may be higher. Moreover, they go on to say, one cannot "rule out the use of scores

7. Harold Gulliksen, *Theory of Mental Tests*, pp. 351-55.
8. *Ibid.*, p. 353.
9. Harold Webster and Carl Bereiter, "The Reliability of Changes Measured by Mental Test Scores" in *Problems in Measuring Change,* edited by Chester W. Harris, p. 51.

from tests of low reliability for testing hypotheses concerning mean changes in groups of persons."[10] In view of these considerations, we conducted an exploratory analysis of the difference scores for the nine items selected. The mean difference scores for individuals and families ranged from +.14 to +.73 with a median of +.23. On the average, then, these scores recorded relatively little forward progress, less than a quarter of a point on an 11-point scale. While scores were almost uniformly higher (more positive) for PSTS than CS cases and clients, none of the differences was statistically significant. We concluded that the relative lack of discrimination in these scores was a function of the poor reliability of the measure: that the relative lack of reliability of the scales at opening, in combination with an additional amount of unreliability at closing, produced a measure not sufficiently sensitive to the apparently modest change in ratings between the two points of time. It was decided therefore to base assessments of outcome on the more reliable retrospective evaluations of change made at case closing.

TESTS OF SIGNIFICANCE

Tests of significance were used in this study to furnish a guideline by which to decide whether a given difference should be attributed to chance variation or accepted as reliable. It was decided in advance of analysis of data to use the .05 level of significance. That is, if a difference could have occurred by chance more often than once in twenty, as determined by standard statistical tests, the null hypothesis (the hypothesis of "no difference") was accepted; if less than once in twenty, the null hypothesis was rejected and the difference accepted as reliable, that is, as likely to occur again with samples drawn from the same hypothetical populations from which the samples in the

10. *Ibid.,* p. 56.

experiment were taken. By and large only statistically significant differences as defined were regarded as "true," as findings to be taken seriously. Some weight was given, however, to close-to-significant differences ($p < .10$) if they occurred within a set of variables yielding a pattern of differences generally significant at the .05 level.

Two-tailed tests were used throughout, with the exception of tests involving comparisons of the characteristics of modifying and supportive treatments. In this instance a prior directional hypothesis permitted the use of a one-tailed test.

ANALYSIS OF VARIANCE

According to our original plan, differences in outcome among the service patterns were to be tested through a 2 x 2 x 2 analysis of variance, the theoretically "correct" test for the kind of factorial design utilized in the experiment. This type of analysis was applied to research observers' and caseworkers' ratings of change at closing for the 16 key variables, resulting in 32 separate tests. The findings will be summarized briefly.

The only significant differences ($p < .05$) occurred in overall comparisons between PSTS and CS; in each instance the differences in mean ratings favored PSTS. The research observers' data yielded only one significant difference (the *overall problem situation*) whereas the caseworkers' data yielded four (the *emotional climate of the home,* the *quality of the marriage,* and *functioning as spouse,* both husband and wife). Mean change ratings for PSTS individuals and families exceeded comparable CS ratings in 24 of the remaining 27 tests, although to a nonsignificant degree. While PSTS-CS differences are less marked when tested in this fashion than when tested through Chi Square, the pattern of difference still clearly favors PSTS.

It was decided, however, not to use the results of the analysis of variance as major project findings. The reason for this decision was two-fold. First, use of this method of analysis in the present experiment makes sense only if we assume that we are comparing *several* groups of cases, with each group receiving a different pattern of service. Data on service inputs have suggested that this assumption does not obtain in this experiment. It was impossible to detect significant input differences in respect to the modifying and supportive classifications. The individual versus joint interview division held under conditions of PSTS, but not under conditions of CS. Although on paper the design was a 2 x 2 x 2 factorial experiment, in reality it was much closer to a two-group experiment in which half the cases were assigned to PSTS and half to CS. Second, on inspection, the differences in outcome between PSTS and CS (the only comparison that yielded meaningful outcome differences) seemed to lie more in the distribution of ratings rather than in the mean ratings. The analysis of variance is of course essentially a test of differences among means rather than a test of differences between total distributions.

The Chi Square test seemed to be better suited to the data, since it is designed to test differences in distributions. Accordingly it was used as the major statistical test of PSTS-CS outcome differences.

In sum, analysis of variance of outcome differences among service patterns, the test originally planned, yielded results consistent with findings that emerged from use of Chi Square, a test that seemed better suited for the data at hand. One cannot say, therefore, that the major outcome findings of the experiment are the product of post-hoc analysis, the peculiarities of the Chi Square test or an arbitrary reduction of a factorial experiment into a two-group comparison. Furthermore, the higher mean ratings for PSTS suggest that outcomes for this pattern also appear more favorable when numerical weights are given to various amounts of change, that is, when greater weight is given to considerable improvement than slight improvement, and so on.

TREATMENT OF NON-LINEAR DIFFERENCES

A few of the significant PSTS-CS outcome differences based on Chi Square were somewhat anomalous since higher proportions of CS than PSTS ratings fell in *both* the most positive and negative categories of the rating scales. Three such non-linear differences were observed in the major outcome findings. These differences occurred in respect to closing ratings of change in husbands' *functioning as parent* (Appendix I, Table 4, p. 223) and the overall assessments of the *helpfulness of service* from the point of view of research observers and husbands (Table 5.2, p. 42). Since in each instance deviations from expected frequencies in both the most positive and negative categories contribute to the value of Chi Square, it becomes difficult to interpret the meaning of the statistical significance of the differences. From inspection of Table 5.2 we could say the very slight edge for CS in the "helped considerably" column contributes only minimally to the Chi Square values. In respect to change in husbands' parental functioning, on the other hand, it appears as if the significant Chi Square is a product of differences in both the "improved" and "worse" columns.

Since we wished to avoid arbitrary conclusions based on inspection of the data, we made use of additional tests as a basis for evaluating the differences. First, in order to determine the contribution of the CS edge in the most positive categories ("improved or considerably helped") we compared them with remaining categories combined in tests of PSTS-CS differences for each of the three variables. None of the Chi Squares derived from these fourfold comparisons (1 d.f.) was significant. To determine the contribution of the remaining categories to the overall difference, we excluded the most positive categories and compared the two remaining, again in a series of tests of PSTS-CS differences. The resulting Chi Squares (1 d.f.) proved to be significant ($p < .01$) for the two assessments of *helpfulness of service* ("helped slightly" versus "no positive effect") but not for husbands' functioning as parent ("no change" versus "worse").

On the basis of these partitions of Chi Square, it could be said that the significant PSTS-CS differences in respect to assessments of the *helpfulness of service* were a function of the PSTS-CS differences between proportions rated as "slightly helped" as opposed to proportions given ratings of "no positive effect."[11] One could also say that the significant difference in respect to husbands' *functioning as parent* was a function of PSTS-CS differences in both "improved" and "worse" categories since neither partition of Chi Square could itself produce a significant difference. These results provide then statistical grounds for asserting that differences on balance favored PSTS in respect to the first set of variables but favored neither pattern in respect to the last variable. The same or similar partitioning procedures were applied as well to significant non-linear PSTS-CS differences in secondary measures, in separate analyses of interviewers' and judges' ratings, and the like. In general, significant differences reported as favoring one service pattern over another are either linear differences (the great majority) or are non-linear differences in which partition of Chi Square yielded significant differences in favor of one pattern and none in favor of the other.

11. For a general discussion of partition of degrees of freedom in contingency tables see A. E. Maxwell, *Analysing Qualitative Data*, pp. 52-62.

BIBLIOGRAPHY

Aldrich, C. Knight. "Community Psychiatry's Impact on Casework and Psychotherapy." Paper presented at the Monday Night Lecture Series, Smith College School for Social Work, July 24, 1967.

Avnet, Helen H. "How Effective is Short-Term Therapy" in *Short Term Psychotherapy*, Lewis R. Wolberg. New York, Grune and Stratton, 1965.

Beck, Dorothy Fahs. *Patterns in Use of Family Agency Service*. New York, Family Service Association of America, 1962.

Bell, Chauncey F. *Cost-Effectiveness Analysis as a Management Tool*. Santa Monica, California, The RAND Corporation, 1964.

Bellak, Leopold, and Leonard Small. *Emergency Psychotherapy and Brief Psychotherapy*. New York, Grune and Stratton, 1965.

Bergin, Allen E. "Some Implications of Psychotherapy Research for Therapeutic Practice," *International Journal of Psychiatry*, III (March 1967), 136-50.

Blenkner, Margaret, Julius Jahn, and Edna Wasser. *Serving the Aging: An Experiment in Social Work and Public Health Nursing*. New York, Community Service Society, 1964.

Casework Treatment of the Family Unit. New York, Family Service Association of America, 1965.

Clinical Psychiatry. Reports by the Group for the Advancement of Psychiatry. New York, Science House, 1967.

Cohen, Jacob. "A Coefficient of Agreement for Nominal Scales," *Educational and Psychological Measurement*, XX (1960), 37-46.

Coursey, Patricia, Gertrude Leyendecker, and Else Siegle. "A Socio-Economic Study of Agency Clients," *Social Casework*, XLVI (June 1965), 331-38.

Edwards, Allan L. *Experimental Design in Psychological Research.* New York, Holt, Rinehart and Winston, 1950.

Eisenberg, Leon, and Ernest M. Gruenberg. "The Current Status of Secondary Prevention in Child Psychiatry," *The American Journal of Orthropsychiatry,* 31 (1961), 355-67 .

Eysenck, Hans J. *The Effects of Psychotherapy.* New York, International Science Press, 1966.

Family Service Statistics, Part III. New York, Family Service Association of America, 1961.

Frank, Jerome. "The Dynamics of the Psychotherapeutic Relationship," *Psychiatry,* XXII (February 1959), 17-39.

Gottshalk, Louis A., Peter Mayerson, and Anthony A. Gottlieb. "Prediction and Evaluation of Outcome in an Emergency Brief Psychotherapy Clinic," *The Journal of Nervous and Mental Disease,* 144 (February 1967), 77-95.

Gulliksen, Harold. *Theory of Mental Tests.* New York, John Wiley and Sons, 1950.

Hare, Marjorie K. "Shortened Treatment in a Child Guidance Clinic: The Results of 119 Cases," *British Journal of Psychiatry,* 112 (1966), 613-16.

Hollingshead, August B. *Two Factor Index of Social Position,* 1965, Yale Station. New Haven, Connecticut, 1957. (Mimeographed, copyright by author.)

Hollis, Florence. *Casework, a Psychosocial Therapy.* New York, Random House, Inc., 1964.

────── "Continuance and Discontinuance in Marital Counseling and Some Observations on Joint Interviews," *Social Casework,* XLIX (March 1968), 167-74.

────── *Development of a Casework Treatment Typology.* Final Report to the National Institute of Mental Health. New York, Columbia University School of Social Work, 1966, mimeographed.

────── "Explorations in the Development of a Typology of Casework Treatment," *Social Casework,* XLVIII (June 1967), 335-41.

Kaffman, Mordecai. "Short-Term Family Therapy" in Howard J. Parad, ed., *Crisis Intervention: Selected Readings.* New York, Family Service Association of America, 1965.

Kogan, Leonard S. "The Short-Term Case in a Family Agency, Part I. The Study Plan," *Social Casework,* XXXVIII (May, 1957), 231-37.

—— "The Short-Term Case in a Family Agency, Part II. Results of Study," *Social Casework,* XXXVIII (June, 1957), 296-302.

—— "The Short-Term Case in a Family Agency, Part III. Further Results and Conclusion," *Social Casework,* XXXVIII (July, 1957), 366-74.

Levine, Rachel A. "A Short Story on the Long Waiting List," *Social Work,* VIII (January 1963), 20-22.

Levitt, E. E. "The Results of Psychotherapy with Children: A Further Evaluation," *Behavior Research and Therapy,* 1 (1963), 45-51.

Lorr, Maurice. "Relation of Treatment Frequency and Duration to Psychotherapeutic Outcome" in Hans H. Strupp and Lester Luborsky, eds., *Research in Psychotherapy.* Washington, D.C., American Psychological Association, 1962.

Malan, D. H. *A Study of Brief Psychotherapy.* Springfield, Illinois, Charles C Thomas, 1963.

Maxwell, A. E. *Analysing Qualitative Data.* New York, John Wiley and Sons, 1961.

Method and Process in Social Casework, Report of a Staff Committee of the Community Service Society of New York. New York, Family Service Association of America, 1958.

Muench, George A. "An Investigation of Time-Limited Psychotherapy," *American Psychologist,* 19 (1964), 476. (Abstract of paper given at 1964 annual convention of the American Psychological Association.)

Mullen, Edward J. "Casework Treatment Procedures as a Function of Client-Diagnostic Variables." Unpublished doctoral dissertation, Columbia University School of Social Work, 1968.

Murray, Edward, and Walter Smitson. "Brief Treatment of Parents in a Military Setting," *Social Work*, VIII (April 1963), 55-61.

Normand, William C., Herbert Fensterheim, and Susan Schrenzel. "A Systematic Approach to Brief Therapy for Patients from a Low Socioeconomic Community," *Community Mental Health Journal*, III (Winter 1967), 349-54.

Parad, Howard J. "Time and Crisis: A Survey of 98 Planned Short-Term Treatment Programs." Unpublished doctoral dissertation, Columbia University School of Social Work, 1967.

Parad, Howard J., and Libbie G. Parad. "A Study of Crisis-Oriented Planned Short-Term Treatment, Part I," *Social Casework*, XLIX (June 1968), 346-55.

Parad, Libbie G., and Howard J. Parad. "A Study of Crisis-Oriented Planned Short-Term Treatment, Part II," *Social Casework*, XLIX (July 1968), 418-26.

Perlman, Helen H. "Some Notes on the Waiting List," *Social Casework*, XLIV (April, 1963), 200-05.

Phillips, E. Lakin, and Margaret S. H. Johnston. "Theoretical and Clinical Aspects of Short-Term Parent-Child Psychotherapy," *Psychiatry*, XVII (August 1954), 267-75.

Phillips, E. Lakin, and Daniel N. Wiener. *Short-Term Psychotherapy and Structured Behavior Change.* New York, McGraw-Hill Book Company, 1966.

Pinkus, Helen. "A Study of the Use of Casework Treatment as Related to Selected Client and Worker Characteristics." Unpublished doctoral dissertation, Columbia University School of Social Work, 1968.

Population Characteristics 1964. Report No. 1, Population Health Survey. New York City Department of Health, April 1966.

Rapoport, Lydia. "The State of Crisis: Some Theoretical Considerations," *Social Service Review*, XXXVI (June 1962), 211-17.

Reid, William J. "The Center for Social Casework Research: Its Potential for Social Work Education," *Social Work Education Reporter*, 15 (December 1967), 20-21 and 60-62.

———— "Characteristics of Casework Intervention," *Welfare in Review,* V (October 1967), 11-19.

Ripple, Lilian. *Motivation, Capacity, and Opportunity: Studies in Casework Theory and Practice.* Chicago, School of Social Service Administration, University of Chicago, 1964.

Schlien, John M. "Comparison of Results with Different Forms of Psychotherapy" in Gary E. Stollak, Bernard C. Guerney, Jr., and Meyer Rothberg, eds., *Psychotherapy Research.* Chicago, Rand McNally, 1966.

Schlien, John M., Harold M. Mosak, and Rudolph Dreikurs. "Effects of Time Limits: A Comparison of Two Psychotherapies," *Journal of Consulting Psychology* (1962), 31-34.

Schwartz, Arthur. "The Relationship of PPBS to Evaluation Research in Social Welfare." Paper presented at the NASW Symposium, San Francisco, California, May 25, 1968.

Shaw, Robert, Harry Blumefeld, and Rita Senf. "A Short-Term Treatment Program and Its Relevance to Community Mental Health." Paper presented at annual meeting of the American Orthopsychiatric Association, March 20, 1965, mimeographed. Used with permission of author.

Shyne, Ann W. "An Experimental Study of Casework Methods," *Social Casework,* XLVI (November 1965), 535-41.

Shyne, Ann W., and Patricia Coursey. *A Search for Criteria for Planned Short-Term Service.* New York, Community Service Society, 1965, mimeographed.

Sifneos, Peter E. "Two Different Kinds of Psychotherapy of Short Duration," *American Journal of Psychiatry,* 123 (1967), 1069-74.

Statistical Guide for New York City 1964. New York City Department of Commerce and Industrial Development.

Stone, Anthony R., Jerome D. Frank, Earle H. Nash, and Stanley D. Imber. "An Intensive Five-Year Follow-Up Study of Treated Psychiatric Outpatients" in Gary E. Stollak, Bernard C. Guerney, Jr., and Meyer Rothberg, eds., *Psychotherapy Research.* Chicago, Rand McNally, 1966.

Taft, Jessie. *The Dynamics of Therapy in a Controlled Relationship.* New York, The Macmillan Company, 1933.

Visher, John S. "Brief Psychotherapy in a Mental Hygiene Clinic," *American Journal of Psychotherapy,* XIII (1959), 331-42.

Webster, Harold and Carl Bereiter. "The Reliability of Changes Measured by Mental Test Scores," in Chester W. Harris, ed., *Problems in Measuring Change.* Madison, Wisconsin, University of Wisconsin Press, 1967.

Wolberg, Lewis R. *Short Term Psychotherapy.* New York, Grune and Stratton, 1965.

——— *The Technique of Psychotherapy.* New York, Grune and Stratton, 1954.

Yamner, Ruth, and Judith Jafee. "The Relations between Characteristics of the Casework Interview and Changes in the Client's Functioning." Unpublished master's thesis, New York University School of Social Work, 1967.

INDEX